History of Kent

Classic County Histories of England and Wales

General Editor:
Dr Jackie Eales,
Reader in History,
Canterbury Christ Church University College,
Canterbury CT1 1QU.

HISTORY
OF
KENT

Henry Francis Abell

*With original Sketches and Maps
by the Author*

**Glasgow
The Grimsay Press
2004**

The Grimsay Press
an imprint of
Zeticula
57 St Vincent Crescent
Glasgow
G3 8NQ

http://www.thegrimsaypress.co.uk
admin@thegrimsaypress.co.uk

Transferred to digital printing in 2004

First published in Great Britain in 1898 by
Kentish Express (Igglesden & Co.) Ltd.

ISBN 0 902664 92 1 Hardback
ISBN 0 902664 82 4 Paperback

Contents

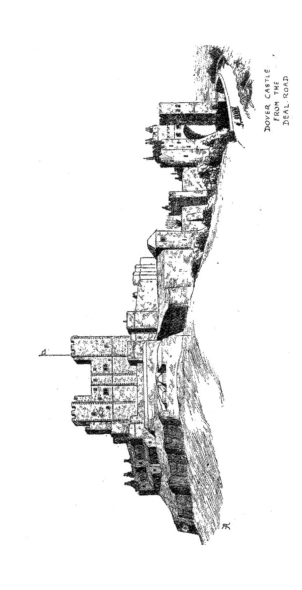

DOVER CASTLE
FROM THE
DEAL ROAD

List of Sketches

MONKTON
STOCKS.

SO presumptive a step as the publication of a new History of Kent when the ground has already been exploited by masterly hands demands an explanation.

Until within quite recent years the orthodox County History consisted of a detailed account of the various parishes, abounding with such details as pedigrees, monumental epitaphs, biographies of local celebrities and others, and various statistics of very little interest to the general reader. In the following pages I have endeavoured to paint the picture of by-gone Kent with a larger and a fuller brush, and I have carefully avoided all details which, however valuable *per se*, and however interesting to a few readers, do not appeal very strongly to the lover of Kent who is desirous of getting some idea of Kent's place in our national history—perhaps a more distinguished place than is occupied by any other county.

To many sins of omission I may, therefore, in the eyes of some people have to plead guilty. Such sins of commission as may be exposed will not at any rate have been caused by any want of thoroughness in my attempts to get at the truth, for I have personally visited almost every place in the county in the smallest degree associated with its history.

The illustrations are from my own sketches made upon the spots represented, with four exceptions—the views of Cobham Hall and of the roof of Eltham Palace, which are copied from engravings, and the portraits of Alfred Mynn and Fuller Pilch, which are copied from lithographs at the Gate Inn, Leeds Castle.

The Map of Kent is the result of a careful examination of the opinions of acknowledged authorities on the subject, and of a personal investigation of the country. The Map of the Armada Beacons is copied, with a few alterations, from a Map in the British Museum, re-produced for the information of the War Office at the time of the Invasion scares at the beginning of the present century.

My best thanks are due to Mr. Payne, Honorary Secretary of our Archæological Society, for help in the Chapter on Roman Kent; to Mr. Knocker of Dover, Mr. Hughes of Sandwich, Mr. Bagshawe of Hastings, Messrs. Stringer and Stokes of Romney, for assistance in the Cinque Ports Appendix; to Mr. Philip Martin for permission to make extracts from his book on the West Kent Cricket Club; and to various anonymous helpers in other matters.

HENRY FRANCIS ABELL.

Kennington Hall, Ashford,
September, 1898.

HISTORY OF KENT.

I.—EARLY KENT.

THE first real knowledge we get of our county is from the pen of Julius Cæsar. Previous to him it is quite impossible to distinguish myth from history, and we may at once dismiss, as unworthy of serious consideration, the many fables associated with the so-called earliest mentions of Kent. Certain established facts, however, cannot be overlooked— that for several centuries before the Christian era there was a commercial relationship between Britain and the civilized nations of the South, and that for probably a considerable time before Cæsar's invasion in B.C. 55 there had been established a large trade in slaves and grain between Kent and Roman Gaul. That the island of Thanet may be identified with the great tin shipping port of Mictis or Ictis we cannot believe, if only because it prompts the question: Why should the Phenicians trouble to carry the tin they got in Cornwall along three hundred miles of coast to Thanet because of the short sea passage thence to Gaul when their ships were stout enough to traverse the seas of all the then known world?

Without, therefore, wasting time and space upon conjectures and guesses about matters the real truth of which can never be established, let us at once deal with certainties, and endeavour to picture the County of Kent as from various incontrovertible evidence it seems to have been presented to the eyes of its first invaders.

The three chief features of physical change in Kent during the nineteen centuries and a half which have elapsed since Julius Cæsar made his first prospecting expedition are :

1.—In the face of the county generally.
2.—In the configuration of its North East Corner.
3.—In the aspect of its South East Marsh Land.

(I)—The General Aspect of Kent.

There is abundant evidence to show that Kent at the period of the first Roman expedition was essentially a wooded county, broken only by lines of open down such as that which stretches in a semi-circle from Dover to Chartham, by the valleys of the greater rivers, and by the tracks of marshland. One third of the county was genuine forest—trackless, uninhabited, dense forest, the haunt of many animals and birds which have long since disappeared from our national *fauna*. This was a portion of the great Sylva Anderida which extended over and beyond the neighbouring County of Sussex, and which was known as the Weald. Roughly speaking the Northern Kentish limit of this forest is marked by the line of the South-Eastern Railway from Westenhanger to Sevenoaks, although the valley of the Medway cuts deeply through it at one point, whilst on the other hand between Tonbridge and Sevenoaks the forest makes a bold Northerly trend. Place names are a pretty sure guide in our delimitation of the natural Wealden boundary, which, we need not remark, is a very different affair from the political or social Wealden boundary, and when we get away from the "hursts" and "dens" and "charts" and "hatches," we get away from the Weald.

Between this Northern Wealden Boundary—or, for the sake of clearness, let us adopt the artificial line of the South-Eastern Railway, and another artificial line, the

Roman Watling Street, the country consisted almost entirely, as it does to this day, of woodland, sufficiently scattered and thin to allow of the residence of a large population, and of the course of roads and trackways.

North of the Watling Street from where Sandwich now stands as far as Woolwich, was marshland, broken West and North of Canterbury by the Forest of the Blean, and all along its western course by innumerable inlets and arms of sea and river.

(II)—THE CHANGE IN THE NORTH EAST CORNER OF KENT.

This is highly interesting, and although to some degree conjecture must enter into a modern consideration of this change, and opinions are necessarily divided as to details, certain main facts seem to have become established.

Thanet was an island in the real sense, inasmuch as between it and the mainland stretched mud-flats covered at high tide by water through the midst of which wound the "river" Wantsum. In 597, says Bede, the River Wantsum was about three furlongs wide, so that we may estimate the space between Thanet and the mainland to have been at the widest points about a couple of miles, although between the site of Regulbium and where Brook End marks the end of a deep inlet the distance is nearer four miles.

This Estuary was a much used line of communication between London and the Channel, and so existed until about the year 1460, and perhaps from this trade connection with London, the ancient name of Stonar— *Lundenwic* may be traced.

The land on which the few houses constituting Stonar stand was in Roman times a narrow spit of beach coming straight down to opposite Sandwich from Cliffsend on the one side and Ebbsfleet on the other. Beach stones have been found at more than one place along this stretch of land twelve feet below the surface. That the Wantsum river ran to a considerable depth owing to the contributions it received from the " fleets " on either side, would seem to be proved by the fact that during its entire length of eight miles there were but two fords, at Sarre and at Sandwich.

After the year 1460 the process of obstruction, which had at a much earlier date gained for the river its name (so say some etymologists) became very marked, although fifty years later there were men living who remembered having seen laden barges pass along it, and even in 1590 one John Twine says that there were eight men living who had seen large ships go through. Leland says that in the time of Henry VIII. salt water ran in at the North mouth more than a mile towards Sarre.

Stourmouth, now four miles inland, marks where the Great and Little Stour rivers united to flow into the estuary, the Stour being navigable as far as Fordwich, which was the port of Canterbury, down to the days of Elizabeth, and, as a " limb " of Sandwich, enjoyed Cinque Port privileges. Fordwich was until comparatively recently, a corporate town, but when the north mouth of the estuary began to be blocked, and Sandwich Haven became silted up, it lost its importance.

At Sarre there had been a ford at a very early date, and so late as 1485 it could be used for an hour at very high spring tides.

Ebbsfleet was a port in the 12th century, but in Roman times it was probably what its name signifies, a tidal channel. Minster was a busy port in the 13th century, Minster Fleet being its haven. The imposing ruin of Richborough stands upon what was evidently an island, and the fortress commanded the Southern entrance of the Wantsum Estuary, just as Regulbium commanded the Northern. Indeed one may trace to-day almost exactly the dimensions of Richborough island despite the fact that the land stood higher—or rather that the level of the water was very much lower—than the level of the Marsh which now represents it.

Whether Ebbsfleet or Stonar is to be distinguished as

the landing place of the first Jutes and of Augustine, is still a much disputed point. At any rate Stonar was for centuries an important town and port. That the Romans occupied it is evident from the remains which have been from time to time discovered; possibly it was the second Rutupia, thus accounting for the plural form of the Latin name of Richborough. It was for some time a rival of Sandwich, and until the French burned it in 1385 was a chief port of this part of Kent.

It has yet to be settled at what exact point the fortress of Richborough was connected with the two roads coming from Canterbury and from Dover which should seemingly unite at Each End, although the latter stops short at Woodnesborough. This point must have been an important place, and interesting results might reward examination.

To trace the coast of the mainland at the time of Cæsar's first invasion we may follow this route; from Sandwich by the Polders to Each End, by Brook Street to Cooper Street, thence to the farmhouse which marks where may have been the port of Fleet, then by Goldstone and West Marsh to Lower Stourmouth. Thence to Upper Stourmouth, across the Little Stour to Grove, across the Great Stour at Grove Ferry to Up Street, Wall End, and by Chislet—the " beach eyot " to the site of Regulbium.

It can hardly be described as an encursion brimming with rollicking excitement, for the Marsh World is very dead, the poor villages contain very few objects of interest, and the scenery is unlovely. But it gives a far clearer idea of the ancient geographical " lie " of the country than any map or descriptive letter press, and the line between upland and marsh is still so clearly defined, that here perhaps more completely than in other places over which waves of change have passed we can fill in the picture of the Past.

(III)—The Aspect of the South Eastern Marsh Land.

The changes wrought here have a different sort of interest from those just treated of, inasmuch as they have been to a great extent the work of man. When Cæsar first arrived in Kent the great marshes of Romney, Denge, Guldeford, and Walling formed a tidal morass, a vast mud-flat alternately covered and uncovered as the tide rose and fell, and, probably at no remotely previous period had been a regular bay of the sea.

The River Limen or Rother, coming from Sussex through Newenden, flowed to Appledore where it ran into an estuary of the sea which followed the base of the cliffs pretty closely along the line of the modern Military Canal, to Lympne where, no doubt, was a bay of the sea.

It was perhaps during the Roman occupation that accumulations of shingle at Hythe and Lympne began so much to reduce the volume of tidal water to Appledore, that the idea became feasible of partially shutting it off. We say partially, instead of entirely, because it is evident that unless the operation was carried out at a very much later date than is generally supposed, there was water communication between Lympne and Appledore in the year 893, when the Danes sailed from the former port to burn the latter.

This was carried into effect by the construction of that great engineering work, the Rhee Wall. This was a channel of from eighty to a hundred feet in width, with high banks, cut from Appledore to where New Romney now is, into which the waters of the Rother were turned at Appledore, and forming at Romney a safe and capacious harbour.

By the making of this Rhee Wall, along the course of which the present high road from Appledore to Romney runs almost exactly, the whole of what we call Romney Marsh proper became capable of reclamation and culti-vation, as with the Rhee Wall on the South West and the encroaching shingle bank on the South East it was protected from the sea. It is probably just to credit the Romans with this fine work by which 24,000 acres of land were made available for human use, as the whole area of Romney Marsh proper is scattered with remains of a character not met with in the other Marshes. At any rate it seems to be established that Romney Marsh was utilised and inhabited long before the other Marshes were even reclaimed. Not until late in the thirteenth century was Walland Marsh reclaimed, and by that time Nature had wrought great changes in Romney Marsh.

Between 1236 and 1287 a series of violent storms swept away the towns of Oswardestone, Dengemarsh, Old Winchelsea and Broomhill, and Dungeness was formed, Lydd thereby being saved.

These inundations threatened Appledore, forced the river Rother from its old bed at Appledore, and opened a new course for it which made Rye its outlet, and took the water from the Rhee Wall. In vain the Romney men struggled gallantly against the fate which threatened their town. A new channel was cut, and all through the fourteenth and fifteenth centuries cutting, and digging, and devising went on, but Leland, writing in the reign of Henry VIII., can only speak of Romney Haven as something which "hath been," and records that the sea was two miles away.

It is a question if Old Romney ever had a separate existence, much less an importance of its own at all. At any rate that which we call New Romney was a famous place before the Conquest and so remained for more than two hundred years after. As a distinctive name New Romney is never used in documents before the fifteenth century, Romney alone being spoken of, so that perhaps the view of Mr. Furley, an acknowledged authority on the Weald and the Marshes, that Old and New Romney merely represent two communities South and North of the Rhee Wall is plausible. Dymchurch Wall as we know it is of comparatively modern origin. It was not until the reign of Henry VIII. that by the rapid accumulation of shingle at Dungeness the safety of the lands lying behind the line of the present wall was threatened, and even down to 1825 the only means of protection was a system of brushwood piles. From that year dates the modern stone wall, and it is only by the most constant watching and at a heavy expense that even this barrier is kept effective.

In conclusion of this very interesting portion of our brief survey of Old Kent it may be noted that up to the present day the wide region generally known as Romney Marsh has retained a character and even a dialect of its own ; and until Lydd became an important military centre, and golf gave a new lease of life to Romney, it remained a *terra incognita* to the majority even of Kentish people.

The phrase in old documents "according to the laws and customs of Romney Marsh" points to a separate political and judicial existence ; as does the record that when in 796 Cenulph King of Mercia invaded Kent, he laid it waste, and *also* the province which is called Merscwari ; and Kemble suggests that the Merscware or Marshmen had a kingdom or duchy of their own.

At any rate, until well within the memory of living men the true Marshman rarely intermarried with or owned any community of interests with folk "from the shires" or "from beyond the hills ;" he was born and married, he lived and died amongst his own ; he had his own dialect, his own customs and traditional observances, and neither knew nor cared much about what went on in the world beyond his own limits except so far as it affected the mutton and wool markets.

A few general changes may be noted.

The Channel at the Straits of Dover was probably very much shallower in Cæsar's time than it is now, and the encroachments of the sea on the North East Coast and at the South West corner of Romney Marsh, at the Isle of Sheppey and along the Ramsgate and Reculver Coast are still going on. Broomhill, which suffered in the great storms of the thirteenth century is said by Harris to have had fifty inns and taverns, and the ruins of its church were visible in the middle of the 17th century.

The River Stour down to the reign of Elizabeth was a navigable river of some size ; there was traffic on it as far inland as Chilham, at which there was a "port"—which may mean a market as well as a place of call for vessels, and when Fordwich was the port of Canterbury, the Stour must, of course, have been very much wider and deeper than it is now.

Kent is especially rich in human remains of the Paleolithic Age; and in specimens of human workmanship, but not of human beings belonging to the Neolithic and the Celtic or Bronze Age.

II.—ROMAN KENT.

IT should be premised that almost all the history of Roman Kent is based upon conjecture—scientific conjecture it is true; the conjecture of men who have devoted and are devoting their efforts to the dispersal or brightening of the cloud which hangs over a period separated from that which we are enabled at any rate to get a glimpse of by the light of documentary and monumental evidence, by absolute night; of men who, though following a profession notorious for its proneness to jump at conclusions and to work upon flimsy hypotheses, assert nothing and guess at very little; of men, best fitted in fact by nature and attainments to succeed as far as possible; but still conjecture.

A singular poverty of monumental inscriptions in Kent prevents the would be historian from arriving at such exactitude as marks the conclusions of antiquaries in the world let us say of Hadrian's Wall. Not a dozen inscribed altars have been discovered in the whole of Kent: in Northumberland and Cumberland hardly a month passes without some such discovery being made, and through the medium of such discoveries antiquaries have been enabled to put piece and piece of evidence together, and to arrive at tolerably exact conclusions of which the result is history. Moreover Kent being the earliest county to be civilised, that is to say washed over and over again by waves of change, being for a long time the most populous part of our island, has naturally suffered most from the

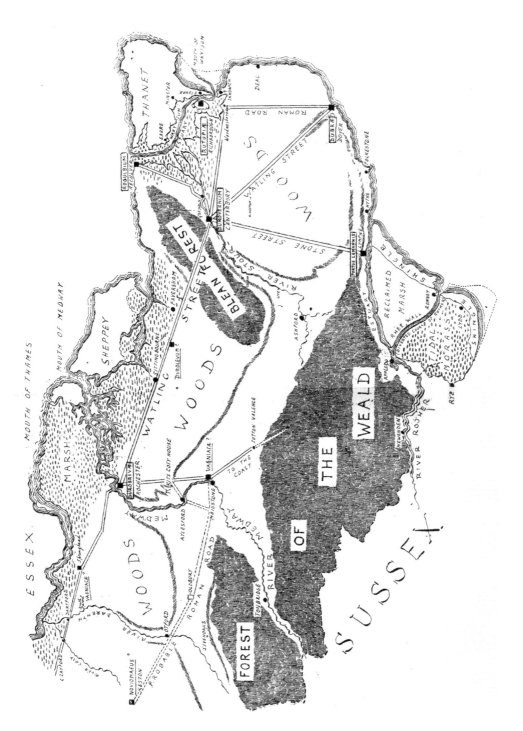

Kent during the Roman Occupation

obliteration both by destruction and by burial, of such monuments and records as would be of the most value in the compilation of a rational history.

In short the Kentish antiquary is handicapped to an extent with which his Northern brother is entirely unfamiliar. Hence the uncertainty with which every assertion about the history of Roman Kent must be made. One instance will suffice. There were three Roman towns of importance in Kent—in that small tract of country which Roman Kent comprised—to wit, Noviomagus, Vagniacœ, and Durolevum, the very sites of which are sturdily combated problems to this day. Along the entire course of Hadrian's Wall there is not a mile castle or a supporting camp, much less a fortified town, of which the position is not merely exactly known, but of which some remains cannot be seen.

In B.C. 55 Julius Cæsar prepared for an expedition of reconnaissance to Britain, a land which promised to be a valuable addition to the Roman Empire, not only for its commerce in metals and grain, but as a recruiting ground for the Roman legions. Of the British tin trade, of course, he had long been aware; his intercourse with Gaulish merchants taught him the magnitude of the British grain trade, and without doubt during his Gaulish campaigns he had discovered the prowess of the stalwart, fearless British warriors.

The Britons, who had probably received hints of Cæsar's intended interference from their business friends over the water, and who no doubt had heard of his renown, sent an embassy. This was civilly received and was accompanied home by an officer, Comius, who had instructions to keep his eyes open, and, if possible, to induce the Britons to become allies of his master—a very convenient arrangement for Cæsar, as he could then pursue the policy of the Jutes of a later age and carry out his scheme of colonisation under the plea of friendship without the worry and expense of fighting.

At the same time Cæsar had sent Volusenus to examine the British Coast and report upon the best place for

landing, for from the Gaulish traders, whom he specially
interviewed, he had learned nothing. Comius returned
with the report that the Britons, no doubt warned that
their fate would be the usual one of tribes who had been
induced to "ally" with Cæsar, were by no means enthusiastic
over the prospect of a Romano-British alliance.

Volusenus returned after five days' absence, but without
having been ashore, so that it may be surmised he brought
no valuable information.

At any rate on August 27th Cæsar started from Portus
Itius, which may be located at Wissant, between Calais
and Boulogne, or at Boulogne itself according to French
archæologists, with two legions, numbering with auxiliaries
about 14,000 men, and in nine hours was off the Kentish
Coast.

Here he found the cliffs crowded with natives assembled
to oppose his landing, and, after calling a council of war,
he sailed seven or eight miles to an "*apertum et planum
littus.*"

Here comes in the question—and for Kent people it is
an intensely interesting question : In which direction did
he sail these seven or eight miles ?

According to modern calculations based upon the
hypothesis that the Channel tides have not changed in
force and direction since Cæsar's day, the seven or eight
miles sail from Folkestone—for Folkestone answers to
Cæsar's description of the shore off which he first anchored
as well as does Dover—would have brought him opposite
almost exactly where now the ruins of Portus Lemannis
stretch down the hill side from Lympne church.

But with a south-westerly wind he might here as reason-
ably been carried to where Deal Strand now is, in the
opposite direction, and, with all deference to the ably
argued view which places Cæsar's landing-spot between
Bulverhithe and St. Leonards in Sussex, our opinion goes
with the concensus, that about Deal is to be located the
arrival point of the Roman legions.

Wherever it was, the Britons were ready, and lost no

time in impeding the process of landing as effectively as possible. Severe fighting ensued which confirmed Cæsar's advices that the Britons were skilful as well as fearless warriors, but the tried discipline and superior armament of the Romans prevailed, and it was only their lack of cavalry which prevented them from utterly routing the Britons.

Cæsar formed a camp and awaited a reinforcement of cavalry without which he could not hope to checkmate the guerrilla-like movements of his adversaries. The ships came in sight, but were driven back to Gaul by contrary winds. Nor was this all. It was harvest time, and men of the Seventh Legion were engaged at some distance from the camp in getting in the grain : they fell into an ambuscade, and but for the timely arrival of reinforcements would have been cut to pieces. Again, the Roman ignorance of the great rise and fall of the tides on the British shores led to the insecure mooring of the ships, so that when bad weather came on, the fleet was severely damaged.

The prevalence of bad weather put an end to active operations for some days, but at length Cæsar saw his opportunity, sallied forth, completely rolled up the Britons, and, being now reinforced by some cavalry, pursued them and returned.

The Britons now sued for peace, which was granted, and Cæsar, taking hostages with him, made sail for Gaul after a campaign of twenty-five days.

Next year, B.C. 54, Cæsar carried out a thoroughly prepared plan of invasion. On July 20th he left Gaul with 600 ships carrying five legions, and 2,000 cavalry, the latter principally Batavians famous at swimming rivers, probably a force of 35,000 men, and landed, it is supposed, at the same spot as before.

He marched inland at once and at a distance of about twelve miles—"*millia passuum circiter duodecim*"—came in sight of the enemy on the banks of a river. It is impossible to say with any degree of probability what river it was.

From as minute a personal examination of the country as its difficult character will permit, we are inclined to agree very closely with Mr. Jenkins in the supposition that Chilham was the scene of Cæsar's first battle in his second expedition.

Nor are we by any means inclined to sneer as unworthy of acceptation the derivation of the modern name of the ancient barrow on the invaders' side of the river, Jula-berry's Grave, from Laberius, the Roman tribune who fell in the battle here. True, his name was Quintus Durus, but there is a good deal in the last three syllables of the popular name which is at any rate suggestive. It does not seem to us at all improbable that, in a sequestered, thinly inhabited country such as this around Chilham was, the name of a famous foeman killed in battle should have been handed down from century to century until at this long distance of two thousand years it should still exist in a scarcely altered form.

The rustic in general, and the Kentish rustic in particular, has never given play to much fancy in the christening of places, and has been quite content to call anything he knows nothing about in the way of ruin, or crom-lech, or mound, or earthwork, after Cæsar or the Devil, both being the same sort of toiler without rhyme or reason in his estimation. Wherever a peculiar name is given to such objects as we have enumerated, the science of historical or antiquarian research is pretty sure to get at some probable fact in support of its etymology, and had we space at our command we could give many instances in support of our statement.

Here we have a name the nearest approach to which may be found in the Julian's Bowers scattered about our country, and which is not to be explained away unquestioned as having anything to do with Selebert or the origin of the name Chilham itself.

At any rate, Cæsar fought a battle and stormed a strong-hold which may have been according to divers opinionists Burg Wood by Hurst Green in Sussex, or the *oppidum* at

Kingston, or that on Patrixbourne Hill, or Grove Ferry, or Bursted near Lower Hardres, or Iffin's Wood near Canterbury, but which we prefer to think was Chilham.

We know, as surely one can know about such antiquities, that Chilham was an important British stronghold; that when Sir Dudley Digges excavated in building his house here in 1610 he found many Roman relics; and, as Mr. Jenkins points out, the polygonal shape of Chilham Keep is distinctly Roman.

Cæsar fortified himself in the captured *oppidum* after he had driven its defenders out. Whilst thus engaged the news was brought him that a violent storm had almost completely wrecked the fleet off Deal, so he returned and with characteristic energy at once started the work of refitting.

The Britons, hearing of the straits in which was their enemy, assembled under their prince Caswallon, better known as Cassivelaunus, and fortified themselves in the *oppidum* which we place at Shottenden, but which Mr. Vine considers to have been at Key Coll Hill near Canterbury. Here the Romans did not gain a great victory even if they did not suffer actual repulse, but evidently they regained their lost laurels, and the Britons retreated.

Cæsar's next movements are topographically indistinct. What we know is that he pursued the retreating Britons, crossed a river, and attacked and took the town of Cassivelaunus. If he proceeded northwards—be it from Chilham or from near Canterbury, he must have got into Sheppey. If, as we dare to think, he followed the Britons along their trackway, he would have crossed the Thames, and would have come to London, which certainly best answers to the description of the capital of Cassivelaunus to which Cæsar did not even condescend to give a name— protected on the North by a vast forest full of wild beasts, and on the south by marshes.

Where he crossed is one of these questions about this period which will always remain unsolved. All we know is that the ford was eighty miles from the sea. If it was

at the Coway Stakes—which, by the way, are evidently the
remains of a bridge—he must either have for strategical or
other reasons have gone a great deal out of a direct line, or
our notions of the topography of this campaign are entirely
at fault.

Cassivelaunus finding that his ill-disciplined, ill-armed
troops were no match for the Romans at close fighting, had
recourse to guerrilla tactics, but finally Cæsar got him at
bay, perhaps in the Wimbledon Camp, and the failure of
the attack by the four "Kings" of Kent on the Coast
Camp, coupled with the submission of the Trinobantes to
Cæsar, compelled him to surrender.

Cæsar gladly came to terms, for domestic sorrow and
cares of state were calling him back to Rome, whilst his
success in this campaign, which we thoroughly believe was
conducted in Kent, was very poorly balanced by the cost,
and, after imposing an annual tribute and receiving
hostages, he sailed for Gaul. No part of Britain was
really conquered. Both Horace and Tibullus speak of the
"unsubdued Britons," and Tacitus remarks that Cæsar
merely showed the way to those who came after him.

For nearly a century the state of affairs in Europe
distracted the attention of the Romans from Britain, for
the puerilities of Caligula are unworthy of notice. In
A.D. 43 some difficulty about a British fugitive from
justice at Rome brought about an expedition under Aulus
Plautius.

He landed, it is thought at Porchester, with 50,000 men,
and met with no opposition, either because the Britons
were divided amongst themselves, or because the memory
of previous contests with the Romans had taught them to
avoid fights in the open.

The history of the campaign is very dim, but it would
seem that the Romans pursued the Britons into their
woods and marshes, and round by the Cotswolds to a part
of the Thames where " it empties itself into the ocean and
becomes an estuary at high water." Aulus Plautius is
supposed to have crossed into Essex from Kent by the

DINNER
IS SOLVED

← (KEEP ME) →

HelloFRESH

£40 OFF

£20 OFF 1ST & 2ND BOXES

HelloFresh.co.uk/GiftCard
Claim within 30 days

DELICIOUSNESS
IN 3 SIMPLE STEPS:

Choose your favourites from our weekly menu.

We'll source and deliver all the pre-measured ingredients you'll need.

You cook amazing meals each week.

£20 OFF 1st and 2nd boxes

1 Go to hellofresh.co.uk

2 Choose the perfect box.

3 Enter the code WMA5X at checkout.

7/00017606

Causeway at Higham, still existing, and known to be Roman, on the way defeating the two sons of Cunobelin, Caractacus and Togidumnus, and scattering the tribe of Dobuni or Boduni.

The want of knowledge about this campaign is much to be regretted, for it was evidently, from the extent of new country embraced, a very big affair, and really was the foundation of the Roman Colony of Britain. All we know is that at length the Roman general found himself in an awkward position in a country of forest and marsh, and, in obedience to instructions, after intrenching himself, perhaps in the great *oppidum* at Holwood, he sent to Claudius for help. Claudius came, took Camalodunum, the modern Colchester or Chesterford, the capital of the late King Cunobelin, and conducted a successful campaign which earned him a triumph.

The subsequent history of Roman rule in England in no way affects Kent, which seems to have settled down to peaceful, prosperous, industrial life, and to have become a favourite residential district for Roman officials.

We started with the statement that Cæsar's main object in conquering Britain had been to make money out of her.

The southern part had been long linked to the civilised world by commercial ties. It is believed that many hundred years before Christ the Phenicians carried on a tin trade with her, it is known that the Greeks succeeded them, and that the Romans succeeded the Greeks. The Kentish folk were no barbarians of the kind "pleased with a rattle, tickled with a straw;" they knew the value of money; Sir John Evans says that they minted in the second century before Christ gold coins modelled on Greek coins of the age of Pythias, and that in 30 B.C. they had gold coins stamped with letters. Besides tin, Britain exported slaves, hunting dogs, lead, coin and skins, and Mr. Boyd Dawkins thinks, possibly worked the iron ore of the Weald. In return they received brass, pottery, glass and ivory. Britain was also a valuable recruiting ground, not merely for the legions, but for the

c

amphitheatre, and our forefathers were always remarkable for stature, strength and agility.

Corn growing, pottery making, and possibly iron smelting, were the chief Kentish industries during the Roman period. The North Kentish shore from Faversham to Rochester was under the Roman dominion one vast potter's field, and at the present day the marshes of the Medway below Upchurch and extending from Otterham Creek nearly to Chitney, are full of Roman remains in the shapes of pottery banks, and traces of the life of the workers.

The peculiar bluish black Upchurch ware, although not so fine in quality nor so elaborately ornamented as that manufactured along the banks of the Nen in Northampton-shire and known as Caister ware, was evidently much esteemed, as specimens of it have been found, not only at some of the remotest stations in Britain, but on the con-tinent. A pottery for ware of a finer kind has been discovered at Dymchurch. The immense quantity of pseudo-Samian ware unearthed in different parts of our island has suggested the existence of manufactories in Britain, but it is now considered to have been made in Gaul. A large amount has been dredged up from time to time at the Pan Sands between Margate and Reculver, a fact which points to the wreck here of a vessel laden with pottery.

The whole of this country of marshes and creeks, which by the way is believed in Roman times to have been dry land protected by embankments, must have been the seat of a very large industrial population, for the demand for pottery was enormous, as is proved by excavations all over the country which show that the Romans employed pots for many uses to which we are unaccustomed, notably in connection with their funeral ceremonies, and as receptacles for money and treasure. Associated with this industrial class was another of proprietors and employers, and the private dwellings of these extended along the banks of the Medway and Darenth, as well as being in the neighbourhoods of the large towns on the line of Watling

Street. Of the Roman iron industry in Kent there are but few traces, for it never could compare with that in the Sylva Anderida across the Sussex border, but remains of furnaces and ash heaps have been found near Cowden and Frittenden, and there was perhaps a furnace at Lyminge. Chalk was dug at Dartford and Crayford and exported, and Hasted states that in Zealand have been found altars dedicated to the goddess of the Kentish chalk workers.

Sheppey, Thanet, the river valleys, and the cleared uplands, were the Kentish grain districts : Solinus speaks of Thanet as *Frumentariis campis felix et gleba uberi :* Gibbon writing of the reign of Julian, about A.D. 350, says that six hundred large barks made several voyages to the coast of Britain and returned from thence laden with corn. " If " says he, " we compute the 600 cornships of Julian at only 70 tons each, they were capable of exporting 120,000 quarters of grain."

It is some small consolation for us who grumble at our modern climate, and who sigh for "good old-fashioned weather," to hear that Pythias the Greek merchant from Marseilles, who landed in Britain during the fourth century before Christ, remarked that the British farmers were obliged to thresh their grain under cover because of the uncertainty of the weather.

We may now briefly examine the principal Roman remains in Kent, and for convenience may thus classify them ; (1) Fortresses. (2) Earthworks. (3) Roads. (4) Various.

(I)—Fortresses.

There were three *Castra*—Rutupiœ,—Richborough, Regulbium—Reculver, and Portus Lemannis—Lympne.

There were three *walled towns*—Dubris, Dover ; Durovernum, Canterbury ; and Durobrivœ, Rochester.

About the sites of three other important stations controversy still rages. These were Vagniacœ, claimed by Maidstone, Southfleet, and with the greatest show of reason, Springhead near Northfleet ; Noviomagus—ten miles from London according to the itineraries—claimed by Keston, by Crayford, by Woodcote in Surrey, but probably on the Watling Street; and Durolevum, claimed by Syndale, near Faversham, by Lenham and by the neighbourhood of Ospringe.

Of only two of these are remains at all considerable— of Rutupiœ and of Portus Lemannis : of Regulbium only part of the South and East walls remain, whilst the remains of Durovernum and Durobrivœ consist entirely of pavements, foundations and so forth which are unearthed from beneath the streets of the modern cities, and those of Roman Dubris of the work in the Pharos and the church in the Castle.

(II)—Earthworks.

What we call Roman earthworks are almost in every case Roman adaptations of British *oppida* of fortifications. There is probably not in the county a single camp of Roman *origin* in the sense that the camps North and South of Hadrian's Wall and others are Roman. The best known because best preserved are the camps at Holwood, Oldbury, Shottenden, Ewell, Judds Hill near Faversham, Fossberry, Lingfield Mark, Castle Hill near Ton- bridge, Postling, the Camp Hill behind Folkestone, the works on Barham Downs and on the hills round about ; others such as the works in Bigberry and Iffin's Woods near Canterbury, Penny Pot Wood near Chilham, Syndale near Faversham, and Blackheath, were probably merely temporarily occupied by the Romans unless we accept Syndale to be Durolevum.   It is by excavation alone that we can arrive at any probable conclusions concerning earthworks.

(III) Roads.

There are so many undoubted Roman Roads, or British trackways adapted by the Romans in Kent, that we can only deal with the principal. These were the Watling Street from London to Dover, still with a few deviations the main road of Kent ; the Stone Street from

Lympne to Canterbury,—a perfectly straight line still except where Monks Horton Park causes a bend; a straight road Northwards from Dover to Woodnesborough, whence originally it ran to East End, in Roman times on the shore opposite Richborough island; a road from Richborough viâ Fleet to Canterbury, and a road from Canterbury to Reculver.

There was also without doubt a great main road from the Camp in Holwood Park, viâ Oldbury and Maidstone into the Sylva Anderida, perhaps to Anderida itself; a road from Rochester to Maidstone, and perhaps one from Maidstone to Lympne. Possibly the great main road first mentioned in its length between Holwood and Maidstone acted as a winter relief-road to Watling Street, as the latter for many miles runs through a country which in those times must have been almost under water during rainy seasons, the line joining Watling Street by Key Street west of Sittingbourne.

From the frequent discovery of Roman remains along the line of what is now known as the Pilgrims' Way to Canterbury from Surrey and South West England, it is conjectured that this too was used by the Romans, but it cannot be classed amongst Roman roads proper. The "Pilgrims' Way" was the British Road right through the country. As for the subordinate roads—*viæ vicinales*, branch roads; *agrariæ*, country roads; and *deviæ*, by-roads, their name is legion, and it is a remarkable instance of the tenacious longevity of tradition that to this day many of them are known to the country folk as Roman roads.

(IV)—Various Remains.

Notwithstanding our knowledge that Kent under Roman rule was on the whole the centre of greater wealth and refinement than any other county, we are faced by the fact that the evidences of this are comparatively small. No such luxurious country palaces as the villas at Woodchester, at Bignor, and at Brading have been unearthed in Kent. We have no wealth of tesselated pavements,

sculpture, architectural decoration, and personal adorn-
ment, such as have been disinterred from London and a
score of places in the country. Altars and inscribed
stones are almost unknown. And yet we must believe
that Roman Canterbury and Rochester and Maidstone
and Richborough were as much the homes of wealthy,
refined and leisured people as were York and Colchester,
and Leicester and Silchester, and Wroxeter and Cirencester,
and the cities along the Wall.

A glance through the index of the Roman Collection
of the Kent Archæological Society in the Maidstone
Museum will reveal the fact that at one place alone, Richborough, have a few pieces of sculpture and architectural
ornament been found. Kent, however, abounded with
villas. Of those the best known are those at Hartlip, at
Wingham, at and round about Maidstone, at Westbere,
and last but by no means least, the fine house unearthed
at Darenth in 1894 by Mr. Payne.

At all these villas interesting relics have been found;
and, to use Mr. Payne's words, "all things conducive to
comfort, health, and enjoyment" seem to have abounded,
but they seem to have been the residences of successful
officials and men of business, rather than of virtuosos and
gentlemen of leisure. Mr. Payne has recorded the sites of
50 villas in his survey, of which only some half-dozen have
been touched.

Of temples and religious edifices we can only call to
mind the Mithraic temples at Burham, and near Mottenden,
and the small fragment at the top of the War Bank at
Keston, but in Roman funerary remains Kent is rich.
Cemeteries line the roads leading from all the sites of
Roman towns, are hidden away in what are now woods and
coppices, abound in the brick-fields near the Sittingbourne
and Faversham marshes, and are sometimes mingled with
the Saxon grave-sites.

We may presume to account for the comparative meagre-
ness of our Kentish Roman general relics by the fact that
the flood of civilisation rolled and settled over Kent at an

earlier period than over other English counties. There are no isolated Roman towns in Kent such as Cilurnum and Borcovicus in Northumberland, or Silchester in Hampshire, or Wroxeter in Shropshire, for without doubt Noviomagus, Durolevum and Vagniacœ lie buried beneath modern hives of life, just as Roman Rochester and Canterbury lie beneath modern Rochester and Canterbury, and could we burrow under Rochester and Canterbury as men have burrowed under Torre del Greco and exposed Herculaneum, we cannot doubt but that we should light upon remains as magnificent as have been unearthed anywhere in Britain.

With permission I may conclude with some remarks by Mr. Payne upon the subject of Roman Kent. He says : " The archæologists of the present day, who are worthy of the name, do not jump at conclusions, but deal only with facts, such facts being brought before the highest authorities ere they become matters of history.

" The statements of the older historians, so far as Pre-Norman remains are concerned, must be respected, but received with caution. They had not the great advantages we have ; and they did not see the gigantic importance of excavating to prove or disprove their theories. We do this so far as we can ; brickmakers and quarrymen do the rest. Roman Kent can only be written *as illustrated by the discoveries already made.*"

NOTE.—THE LANDING PLACE OF CÆSAR.

The late Astronomer Royal argued upon scientific grounds for Pevensey, twelve miles from which would have brought Cæsar to Robertsbridge on the Rother, if he followed, as he probably would, especially as it was a night march, a native trackway.

If as Mr. Hussey argues, likewise upon scientific grounds, that Cæsar landed between Bulverhithe and St. Leonards, twelve miles would have taken him near no river at all.

If as Mr. Lewin argues, he landed at Lympne, a twelve mile march along the trackway, afterwards made into the Roman Stone Street, would certainly *not*, as Mr. Lewin says it would, have brought Cæsar to Wye or anywhere near it.

The concensus of modern opinion seems to be that Cæsar landed
in quite an opposite direction—at or about Deal, and this is based
upon the very rational supposition that he might just as well have
been carried eight miles by the wind in one direction as by the tide
in another.

From Deal no satisfactory site for the battle which followed can
be found which corresponds with Cæsar's express statement that it
was fought on the banks of a river, if we accept literally the
measurement of twelve miles.

Twelve miles due west from Deal would bring us to Barham
Downs, and here, at Kingston, the Emperor Napoleon, who is
followed by Mr. Vine, places the site of the battle, Cæsar's route
having been by the British trackway through Upper Deal, Knowlton, Goodnestone and Adisham, whence he saw the Britons lining
the crest of Barham Downs.

But why are we to conclude that because Cæsar sighted the
Britons after a twelve mile march, they were posted at a spot
twelve miles from the sea?

A twelve mile march at night through a difficult and dense
country would not have been finished before daylight, and Cæsar
might perfectly well in this country of hills have first sighted the
enemy at five, six or seven miles distance.

Again, we read that the enemy retreated as far as the river, which
means to a defensive position, and here the Napoleon-Vine theory
falls to pieces.

There is no evidence that the diminutive stream which runs
through Bourne and Charlton Parks was ever bigger than it is now,
and even if we grant that it was we must remember that it was
midsummer, and that it could not have been of a width and depth
to be considered a strategic obstacle.

But if we assume—and we are all bound to assume in a case like
this ; even the scientific theorists have to assume that the Channel
tides were two thousand years ago exactly the same as they are
now—if we assume that the Britons were sighted by Cæsar about
twenty miles from the coast, we seem to be able to imagine the
campaign which followed with very tolerable reasonableness.

The river we then get is the Stour, which we *know* was many
hundred years after Cæsar's day navigable as far as the " port " of
Chilham ; Cæsar's position is on the hills about Penny Pot and
Kettle Benden ; and the Britons are under the shadow of the
oppidum upon which was to rise Chilham Castle.

THE KINGDOM OF KENT.

PREFATORY.

It will be observed that we speak of Hengist and
Horsa, of Vortigern, Catigern, Vortimer, and of their
contemporaries as historical personages. This we do, not
in a settled belief in their existence as makers of history,
but for convenience. It is impossible with the scanty
materials at hand to ascertain when, in the history of
these dim, early days of our country, fiction ends and truth
begins. At any rate no more harm is done by assuming
for the sake of clearness and convenience that Hengist and
his contemporaries were real beings of flesh and blood than
there is in firmly believing that Cinderella's slipper was of
glass and not of "vair," that King Arthur, and Whittington,
and Robin Hood were real beings and not mere types, and
that Wellington really said " Up Guards and at 'em ! " at
Waterloo.

Moreover there is no reason for doubting the existence
of these our early conquerors and patriots, other than the
absolute lack of reliable records of their times. They were
not giants or magicians : they did nothing improbable :
their arrival and their subsequent proceedings fit in
admirably with what we know must have been their
surroundings : above all, tradition, general and local, gives

them places in history, and tradition, as every historical student, every antiquary, and every archæologist knows, is not merely not to be despised, but is often of great aid.

At the same time, we repeat, our treatment of Hengist and his contemporaries as historical beings is not to be interpreted as unqualified belief in them as such.

A writer in the *Archæologia* in support of a theory that Vortigern and not Hengist was the real subduer of the Britons quotes the Historia Miscella of Paulus Diaconus, the Lombard historian who wrote almost as early as Bede, and attributes the substitution of Hengist for Vortigern to the pride of the Jutes in a later day when they had attained position and power, which induced them to glorify one of their own race at the expense of truth.

I have been called to task for speaking of peoples who called themselves English as Anglo-Saxons. Again the plea of convenience must be urged and accepted. If through all the early fightings and operations between the natives and their invaders strict adherence was held to the term " Britons " for the one, and " English " for the other, in what an irremediable, hopeless muddle the student's mind would be ! Besides, they may have called themselves what they liked, but the fact remains that they came from Saxony and Angle-land, and that Anglo-Saxon describes them very sufficiently.

III.—THE KINGDOM OF KENT.

IN Appendix A will be found sufficient evidence to sustain the claim of our County above all others, with the exception, of course, of London, to be considered as *par excellence* the Royal County. This name is now generally given to Berkshire simply because Windsor Castle happens to be in Berkshire, but, apart from the reasons given in the Appendix, Kent was once a Royal County in the truest sense of the phrase inasmuch as it was a Kingdom.

With the end of the Roman rule the real history of Kent may be said to begin. We are on comparatively firm ground, and can sometimes say with some degree of certainty that such an event happened, and that such a person did this or that thing, whereas, about the Roman period, as we have before remarked, there is a great deal that can only be guessed at, a great deal of which we can only speak as *probable*, and a great deal more about which we know nothing at all. Not that there would have been much to record in history about a colony under military despotism, but the land of our birth and residence has always a claim upon our affection strong enough to make us curious about the life of those whose home it was, even if they were but slaves.

The last Roman soldier was withdrawn from Britain about A.D. 413, but for more than a century later Rome regarded Britain as part of her empire, and it was even granted by Belisarius to the Goths as a sop. Practically

the land was left to itself, and in as helpless and miserable
a condition as can be imagined.

If it be asked what impress did the Mistress of the
Ancient World leave upon her Northernmost Colony, the
answer is practically Nothing.

As Mr. Norman remarks in a paper in our Archæologia,
" It is somewhat remarkable that while Spain and Gaul
were thoroughly Romanised, generally adopted the
language of their conquerors; were studded with splendid
cities, and produced many men distinguished in the career
of literature, nothing similar seems to have happened in
Britain."

It is impossible to say if any racial traces wrought by the
intermarriage of Roman and Briton were observable when
Hengist and Horsa landed in Kent, as, after so long an
acquaintance as four hundred years, one might expect,
although some modern ethnologists have imagined that
here and there to this day, notably in one corner of Sussex
and in the country about King's Lynn in Norfolk, Roman
blood is discernible in the appearance of the inhabitants.

Assuredly however Hengist and Horsa found Kent in a
more civilised, if not more prosperous, condition than she
was destined to enjoy for many years after.   At the same
time it appears that this civilisation was very partial.   It
was confined to the towns and centres where the Roman
tongue alone prevailed, and the bulk of the population,
although completely under Roman rule, lived their own
life, and even enjoyed their own forms of social
government.   It must be emphasised too that the Roman
system of colonisation, which was a purely military
despotism, had knocked out of the natives all capacity for
independent, sturdy action, if not their physical pluck.
Britons fought in the Roman legions, but never were
permitted to rise from the ranks; and we may be quite
sure that there was none of the respect and enthusiasm
amongst them for the eagle, which, existing so strongly as
they do amongst soldiers of all creeds and colours for the
British flag, is so marvellous and striking a testimony in

favour of our colonial system. So in civil life. British merchants perhaps prospered and made money, but they do not seem ever to have been permitted to share civil dignities with their Roman companions.

It was this want of cohesion, this division of the abandoned island into two communities so distinct as almost to be regarded as foreigners to each other—the Romanised Britons of the towns, and the native rural population—which laid the land open and defenceless to the Northern invader who had only been kept in check by the Roman arms. Directly the protecting hand was withdrawn the vultures came down on their prey, and the period between the departure of the Romans and the arrival of the Jutes is the darkest in our history because it is absolutely without annals. All we know is that the Picts, who had been kept within bounds by the garrisons of Hadrian's Wall, just as the Scandinavians had been kept in check by the Count of the Saxon shore, swooped down upon the land and carried fire and sword to its very heart. With these came the Scots from Ireland, and so when Aetius, the Roman Governor of Gaul, found it impossible to answer the pathetic appeal embodied in the " Groans of the Britons," help had to be looked for elsewhere.

This was in 443, Vortigern being King of Kent. In despair Vortigern turned for help to foemen, promising them lands and pay in return for services rendered, making use of one race of pests to rid himself of others, and in so doing strictly following the Roman custom of employing "fœderati."

Three tribes of the Cimbrian people occupied the North West Coast of what is now Germany, from the mouths of the Rhine to the Peninsula of Denmark. These were the Jutes, the Saxons, and the Angles, known to the Romans as Saxons, and by themselves called English. The Saxons lived on the narrow neck of the Denmark Peninsula and about the mouth of the Elbe, and with them were the Frisians. Their land is now Schleswig-Holstein. North of the Saxons lived the Angles, and beyond them, in what is still Jutland, the Jutes. To this last people, no strangers to the land which called to them for aid, Vortigern appealed, and in 445 Hengist and Horsa landed in "three long ships" at Stonar, so say the latest examiners of the question; at Ebbsfleet, so say nine people out of ten who will not easily give up the creed of their fathers, erroneous as it may be.

From 445 to 452 Jutes and Britons fought side by side against Picts and Scots and with success. All the time however Hengist was quietly turning Thanet into a Jutish colony and recruiting his forces from the mother country, intimate enough with Vortigern to give him his daughter Rowena as wife, and craftily lulling him into the most unsuspecting security, until he saw the time ripe for the development of his long-cherished plan.

In 452 Hengist threw off the mask, and made some trivial dispute about the payment of his ever increasing bands of warriors, an excuse to burst out of Thanet, seize the fortresses at Richborough and Reculver before Vortigern could make any resistance, march on to Canterbury, which he burned, and continue towards London.

Whether his further progress was barred by the Roman walls of Rochester, or whether he was tempted aside by the riches of the Medway Valley, but he suddenly marched southwards, along the line of the hills, past what was probably then the mound covering the stones of Kits Coty House, and so down to the river at Aylesford.

Here in 455 he met the Britons under Vortigern. A terrible fight ensued—terrible as may be imagined between two leaders one of whom was fighting for a kingdom and the other for self-preservation—which ended in the utter rout of the Britons. Horsa and Catigern the son of Vortigern met in single combat, so says tradition in this land full of tradition, much of which may be accepted as history, and both fell. Catigern, it is said, was laid beneath Kits Coty House, whilst the village of Horsted on the road to Chatham is said to mark the

KITS COTY
HOUSE .

burial place of his rival. Mr. Payne says that a stone structure of the Cromlech type stood here in former times, and that when Fort Horsted was built it was destroyed. This traditionally marked Horsa's tomb.

After this victory Hengist declared himself King of Kent, but that his dominion was as easily kept as it was won must not be imagined; his was but the commencement of a subjugation which was to occupy sixty years, and every hour of his reign was employed in attacking and being attacked, in burnings, slayings, and destroyings. In 457 there was another bloody battle, at Crayford, resulting as did Aylesford in the defeat of the Britons.

Through the cloud which hangs over this miserable period we can only discern that there seems to have been a great revolt of the Britons under Vortimer, son of Vortigern, acting as general under Aurelius Ambrosianus, a Romanised Briton, Count of the Saxon shore, and that after three great battles fought at Derwent in West Kent, at Stonar—the Stone of the Title—and at Wippedsfleet, the Jutes were driven into Thanet in 456. The locality of the last battle is by no means certain. Tradition says that it was fought between Hythe and Folkestone, and that the bones now in the crypt of the former church, and those formerly in the latter church are the remains of the Britons and Jutes who fell in the fight. (See Note A at end of Chapter).

Until 465 we know nothing of what happened, and we may suppose that Hengist and his Jutes remained shut up in Thanet; but in this year Hengist won a great victory over the Britons at Wippedsfleet, in which "twelve Welsh aldermen were slain," and recaptured Richborough and Reculver. In 473 another victory firmly established him on the Kentish throne with his son Esc as partner.

It is necessary here for the sake of continuity to follow briefly the history of the Saxons who, hearing of the successful issue of Hengist's enterprise in Kent, thought that a kingdom in Britain might be theirs also. Accordingly, in 477, came Cymen to Selsea Bill in Sussex, and landed

at Cymen's Ora, still perhaps recognisable in the name
Keynor, just as Lancing, Cissbury, and perhaps Chichester
reflect the names of his sons Wlencing and Cissa.   But
the Andredswald—the Black country of Britain, was
" up," and its sturdy miners offered such a resistance that
it was not until Anderida—known to us as Pevensey, had
been after a terrible struggle captured and utterly destroyed that the Saxon conquest could be called complete
and not until 495 was the kingdom of the South Saxons
established.   Between 495 and 508 other bands of Saxons
landed, it is supposed at Porchester, and these, who are
known as the West Saxons, were constantly engaged for
ten years in conflict with the Britons who seemed to have
formed an alliance with the Jutes of the Isle of Wight.
In 521 the West Saxon kingdom was established under
Cerdic and Cynric, and without detailing matters which
have no immediate, although an important general, relation
to the Kingdom of Kent, it may be said that the West
Saxons pushed their way Westward and Northward
until Hampshire and Wiltshire were conquered, and with
the fall of Calleva, the modern Silchester, the valley of the
Thames lay open, the flank of the great Wealden forest
was, so to speak, turned, and there was nothing between
the invaders and London.   This was accomplished by 556.
Of Kent and its Jutish conquerors we hear nothing until
the time of Ethelbert, the great-grandson of Hengist, who
ascended the throne in 564, and we may surmise that,
protected by the almost impassable character of its
natural boundaries, the little kingdom gradually recovered
from the utter desolation which accompanied the Jutish
conquest, that commercial intercourse was resumed with
the Continent, and that people slowly began to re-inhabit
the Roman towns which had remained deserted, ruined
objects of superstitous awe.   How absolutely cities like
Canterbury and Rochester had been destroyed is evident
if we compare plans of those cities as we know them with
the plans of them under Roman rule as evinced by the
traces of walls and buildings, and note how even the lines

of the Roman streets were obliterated by the time the first bold men forsook the habit of building outside the heaps of Roman ruins and commenced to build over and amongst the ruins themselves. But so slowly did this work of re-population progress that it was not for another three hundred years that the entire area was covered with buildings.

Ethelbert, partly alarmed at the progress of Cynric and his West Saxons towards the Northern boundary of his kingdom, and partly perhaps ambitious to extend his domains, marched to meet them. He found them en-trenched on Wimbledon Common, no doubt in the old British *oppidum* known as Cæsar's Camp, fought them and was most thoroughly thrashed. This was in 568, and the battle of Wimbledon is notable as being the first fight on English ground between Englishmen.

In 583 or 584 Ethelbert married Bertha, daughter of Charibert, King of Paris, a Christian, and with her she brought a chaplain, Liudhard, bishop of Senlis, for whose use the ruined church of Saint Martin at Canterbury, which had been, it is now almost universally agreed, a Roman Christian temple, was repaired and set apart.

This event, the most important in the history of Kent, and one of the most important in the history of England, leads us to consider briefly what Christianity there had been in Britain.

Tradition attributes the first introduction of Christianity into England to a King Lucius of Kent, about A.D. 160, but as the very existence of this King Lucius is questioned, until more is discovered it is safe to relegate him to the world of myths along with the traditions about St. Paul, St. Bran the Blessed, father of Caractacus, Joseph of Arimathea at Glastonbury, and so forth. Christian Missionaries from Gaul are however known to have landed in Britain during the Second Century, and to have made some progress amongst the town-dwellers, but very little amongst the rude bulk of rustics.

We may also believe that when the Roman Christian

Emperor Constantine was crowned at York in 309, Christianity became not merely the tolerated but the recognised religion of the land, and it is from now that we may perhaps date the relics bearing Christian inscriptions and monograms which have been unearthed from time to time at widely different parts of the country, such as Dorsetshire, the Thames, Gloucestershire, Northumberland, Silchester, and also the building of or the adaptation of the churches of St. Martin and St. Pancras at Canterbury, and perhaps those at Reculver and at Brixworth in Hampshire. Under Diocletian St. Alban is said to have been martyred near the town which bears his name, although Diocletian's Governor in Britain was the tolerant Constantius. In 314 three British bishops are said to have been present at the Council of Arles, and Athanasius speaks of three British bishops being present at his trial at the Council of Sardis in 353. When the first invaders landed from the Schleswig shores they found Britain Christian, but between that date and the year of Ethelbert's marriage the religion was utterly swept from the land. Gibbon says : "After the destruction of the principal churches the bishops, who had declined the crown of martyrdom, retired with the holy relics into Wales and Armorica; the remains of their flocks were left destitute of any spiritual food ; the practice, and even the remembrance of Christianity were abolished ; and the British clergy might obtain some comfort from the damnation of the idolatrous strangers."

Devon, Cornwall and West Wales became the refuges of British Christianity, and although the real conversion of Cornwall by missionaries from Ireland only dates from the fifth century, the Christian religion has prevailed there for fourteen hundred years uninterruptedly. It was this toleration by Ethelbert of Christianity which instigated the great Pope Gregory to send Augustine as a missionary to Britain.

In 597 he landed in Kent, whether at Ebbsfleet, or at Richborough, or at Stonar is immaterial. The King,

ST MARTIN'S
CANTERBURY.

ST. AUGUSTINE'S
CANTERBURY.

after some hesitation, was converted, thousands of his countrymen followed his example and were baptised. *(See Note B at end of Chapter).* The ancient Roman Christian Church of St. Pancras, "the idol house where King Ethelbert according to the rites of his tribe was wont to pray, and with his nobles to sacrifice to his demons," as the fourteenth century Benedictine Thorn writes, was cleansed and purged and dedicated by Augustine to St. Pancras; and later on the King, with all a proselyte's zeal, gave Augustine a building eastward of the Roman City limits which he had used as his own palace, and which was the precursor of the present magnificent Cathedral. This was followed by the building of the Monastery of SS. Peter and Paul, designed as a burial place for Kings and Abbots, which gradually became known by the name of its founder, and later on as St. Augustine's Abbey, actually rivalled the Cathedral in magnificence, and of which the Gateway, put to sadly base uses at the beginning of this century, still exists.

The establishment of Christianity in Kent brought that Kingdom into active intercourse with the Continent, and raised it to an equality with the powers thereof, and, to quote Mr. Green, "the civilisation, the arts, the letters which had fled before the sword of the English Conqueror, returned with the Christian faith."

In 604 the bishopric of Rochester was established, subordinate to Canterbury it is true, but indicating that even under Ethelbert the division between East and West Kent, between the Men of Kent and the Kentishmen, was a real one almost amounting to the division between two separate States *(See Note C at end of Chapter);* and, moreover, illustrating that so intimate was the connection between Church and State in these early days of our Christianity that the bounds of States came to be defined by the bounds of episcopal dioceses. Hence, the armoured ecclesiastic was now, and continued to be for another seven hundred years, a familiar figure on the battlefield, and the war story of our country, more especially that of the Northern Counties and the Border, rings with the deeds of clerical strategists and fighters.

In the meanwhile Ethelbert, quieted down after his reverse at Wimbledon to the development of his own little Kingdom, saw in the disunion and dis-organisation of his great rival Wessex the long looked for opportunity of extending the boundaries of Kent beyond the Andredswald and the Thames. Such success attended his arms that by the year of his conversion, 597, the Kingdom of Kent extended from the Humber in the North, across the Midlands to Sherwood, down to Huntingdon, by the Western Borders of Bedfordshire and Hertfordshire to the Thames, thence by the East Border of Surrey and the West Border of Sussex to the sea. Ethelbert was lord therefore over the West, Middle and South Angles, the East Angles, the East, Middle and South Saxons, and Kent formed one of the three great divisions of the land, the other two being Wessex and Northumbria. The severing of this large domain commenced in East Anglia, Redwald, the titular King, who had married Ethelbert's sister Ricca, had consented to become, or probably was commanded to become, a Christian. His people, however, refused to follow his example, and so by way of compromise he placed the altars of Christian worship amongst the idols of popular worship. This sort of half-and-half action of course did not suit Ethelbert ; a series of conflicts between over-lord and vassal ensued, which ended in the open revolt of the latter. The flame of disaffection spread with such fierceness and rapidity that by the year 616, when Ethelbert died, all that remained were Essex, Middlesex and Kent itself, and in the same year Sibert, the titular King of the East Saxons, who had married Ethelbert's daughter and become Christian, threw off both authority and religion, and Kent shrunk again to the dimensions she originally possessed. Ethelbert was succeeded by his son Edbald, who at once threw off Christianity, an example which was followed by his people. St. Lawrence, however, re-converted him, and by way of penance ordered him to re-build Christian churches which had been allowed to fall into ruin, amongst others that within Dover Castle.

It was probably during this period of repentance that he allowed Ethelburga, daughter of Ethelbert, to marry Edwin, the King of Northumbria. At first he refused, saying that a Christian maiden was not allowed to be given in marriage to a heathen, lest the faith and sacraments of the Heavenly King should be profaned by commerce with a King who was wholly unacquainted with the worship of the true God. But upon Edwin's promise that she and her attendants should be allowed to practice their religion unmolested, she was sent, and with her went Paulinus, one of the original companions of Augustine, ordained bishop by Archbishop Justus.

This was in 625. In the following year Edwin allowed his own daughter to be baptised, together with eleven of her household. Thenceforth Paulinus worked incessantly at the conversion of Northumbria, and in 627 King Edwin himself was christened at York, his example being followed by thousands of his people.

Thus, as Dean Stanley says, from Canterbury the first Christian City, from Kent the first English Christian Kingdom, has by degrees arisen the whole constitution of Church and State in England which now binds together the whole British Empire.

But in 633, Penda of Mercia, and Cadwalla of North Wales, both heathens, revolted against Edwin, and defeated and slew him at the battle of Hatfield—either near Doncaster or on the Severn. This ruined Christianity in Northumbria ; Paulinus and Ethelburga fled back to Kent. Here, says the Comte de Montalembert, " She obtained from her brother the gift of an ancient Roman villa situated between Canterbury and the sea, on the side which looks towards France (at Lyminge). There she founded a monastery, herself took the veil * * * * The ancient church of her monastery still exists where is shown the site of the tomb of her who passed here the last fourteen years of her life, and who as the daughter of the founder of Canterbury, and widow of the founder of York, constitutes the first link between the two great homes of Catholic life among the Anglo-Saxons." We may supplement Dean Stanley's remarks with an extract from the little book edited by Canon Mason for the occasion of the thirteenth centenary of the landing of St. Augustine.

" The history of the Church of England begins with Augustine and centres round his See of Canterbury. Probably much more was effected by the Church of Canterbury during the first seventy years than is evident upon the face of the records. Its influence must have been felt even where its claims were not recognised. People passed through Canterbury on their way to and from the Continent. Princes of other English Kingdoms, like Redwald, visited the Kentish Court, and carried away with them more or less of its Christianity As Ethelburga had taken Christianity into the heathen realm of Northumbria, so her daughter Eanfled took the Kentish form of it back to Northumbria when she went to be married to Aidan's disciple Oswy, attended by her Kentish presbyter Romanus. * * * * Christians from Kent kept coming into the North, and Christians from the North went to learn in those schools of Canterbury which were the model schools of England."

The history of Britain from this time for more than a century is made up of a series of supremacies during which hitherto independent Kingdoms were swallowed up in the dominion of a supreme power. Kent was, on the whole, less affected by these convulsions than any other part of England, but this immunity, it must be admitted, was owing far more to her inaccessible position behind forests and marshes than to the greatness of her Princes or the martial prowess of her sons.

For instance, when in 625 Edwin of Northumbria united the whole of England under his sway, Kent alone remained independent, but there was a marriage tie between the Royal houses of Kent and Northumbria which may account for this. Again, there were the supremacies of Oswald of Northumbria, of Penda of Mercia, and of Oswin of Bernicia (the East of North Britain from the Tyne to the Firth of Forth), and during these Governments Kent seems to have been alternately in a state of independence and submission, but generally retaining her own sovereigns.

Thus in 688 Cadwalla of Wessex, ambitious of spreading his dominion along the entire Southern Coast, attacked Kent, but was repulsed, whilst his successor Ine in 694 overran Kent, and thus extended the West Saxon supremacy from Dorsetshire to Essex, including London.

It was just at this time of turmoil, in 690, that Archbishop Theodore, who in 669 had come from Rome to organise the Northumbrian, Wessex and Mercian bishoprics—the first Archbishop, says Bede, whom the whole church consented to obey—founded the famous school at Canterbury for the teaching of religion, classics, sciences and arts, whence radiated the first written English literature, and of which Aldhelm was the most distinguished *alumnus*.

To follow the fortunes of the Kingdom of Kent in detail during the last century of its existence would be a monotonous and profitless task.

Shuttlecock-wise it seems to have been tossed from Wessex to Mercia, and from Mercia back to Wessex; we hear of a fierce three years revolt of the Kent men against Offa which in 775 ended in their defeat at the battle of Otford ; of another revolt in 823 which proved the end of things, for Egbert of Wessex and his son Ethelwulf finally put an end to the Kingdom of Kent by the dethronement of its King Baldred, after an existence of three hundred and sixty-eight years.

So now the three peoples which through all these long years had been flying at each others' throats—the Jutes, the Angles, and the Saxons, became, when Egbert conquered Northumberland, one nation, for, although Northumbria, Mercia, and East Anglia continued to elect their own rulers, all paid tribute to Egbert and acknowledged his supremacy.

The last years of Egbert's reign were marked by the appearance in Kent of a fiercer foe than had yet come from over the seas. The so-called Danes, really Scandinavians from Norway and Sweden, first landed in Sheppey and committed terrible depredations in 832.

In 837 Egbert died, and Kent with the other South Saxon counties came under the rule of Athelstan, his son, who fought the Danes at Sandwich in 851, but without success, as they burned Canterbury and London, and wintered in Thanet—an ominous proceeding which seemed to indicate an intended residence in England.

In 854 Canterbury was again burned, and the story of invasion and slaughter continues without a break until in the year 871 when Alfred, grandson of Athelstan, ascended the throne of all England, which—an important saving clause—was not subject to the Danes. He at once set himself to his life's task of combating the Danes, who were certainly masters of East Anglia, and almost as certainly had firm footings in the South and West, and it is pleasing to be able to record with tolerable certainty the fact that in Kent some of the deeds which have established him as one of the historic darlings of the English people were performed.

In 885 the Danes besieged Rochester, which is believed to have been relieved by Alfred.

In 893 the Danish chieftain Hasting sailed from Boulogne with 250 ships, came to the mouth of the Limen at New Romney, sailed up to Appledore by the Rhee Wall (see Note D at end of Chapter), burned it, and carried fire and sword through all the country round as far as Great Chart. At the same time another fleet had landed an army at Milton near Sittingbourne, and the two held our hapless county entirely at their mercy.

At a battle in 903 near Bury St. Edmunds between Edward the Elder, Alfred's son, and a son of Alfred's elder brother Ethelbert, Ethelward by name, who had made an alliance with the Danes, a critical moment arose in the fortunes of the King when a retreat was ordered.

All obeyed but the Kent men. These stood their ground, and as both Ethelward and the Danish King were slain we may suppose that victory rested with our county men.

From now until the end of the century the story of Kent is the same sad relation of a harried, ravaged county. Sandwich " *Omnium Anglorum portuum famosissimus,*" was the usual landing place ; East and West Kent suffered alike, and opposite policies such as that which ordained the wholesale massacre of the Danes on St. Brice's Day 1002, and that of buying off the foemen, resulted in the same way—the vengeance or the faithlessness of the pirates, and the gradual extension of the Danish rule throughout England.

In 1011 Canterbury stoutly held out against the foe, but treachery was at work within. Elfmer, Abbot of St. Augustine's, admitted the besiegers, the cathedral and a great part of the city were burned, and the Archbishop, afterwards canonised as St. Alphege, murdered at a brutal feast held within the precincts of the royal palace, or, as other accounts have it, dragged on board the Danish ships, kept in captivity for seven months, and murdered at Greenwich.

The end was not far off. The terror of the Danish name was such that a single Danish warrior sufficed to put to flight half-a-dozen Saxons ; Sweyn, King of Denmark landed, Ethelred the Unready, with his family fled to Normandy, and England passed under the Danish dominion. This was in 1013.

Sweyn, however, died soon after his accession to the sovereignty of England ; the Danes in England appointed Canute his son to be his successor, but the Saxon Witan resolved to recall Ethelred from Normandy.

In 1015 Canute endeavoured to land at Sandwich, but appears to have been driven off, and took his fleet westward. Ethelred also came over from Normandy, but desertion and dissension raged amongst those to whom he looked most for support, and he died in 1016.

Edmund Ironside, Ethelred's eldest son, was the successor chosen by the bulk of the people, but the nobles and the clergy were in favour of Canute. Each was crowned king—Canute at Southampton, Edmund in London, and the civil strife broke out anew.

Canute besieged London but was forced to withdraw; at Otford in 1016 Edmund defeated the Danes. *(See Note E at end of Chapter,)* but treachery withheld from him a chance of sweeping Canute and his army out of existence, and a defeat near Saffron Walden in Essex at what is variously called Assandun, Ashlingdon, and Assingdon, proved fatal to his cause, and shortly afterwards he was assassinated, and Canute became King of England. Under Canute there was a lull in the wearisome work of war and pillage, but in Kent a figure was rising who was destined to leave a deep mark on the county history. This was Godwin Earl of Kent and Sussex. It was he who assisted Edward the Confessor to the crown of England in 1042, probably having had a hand in clearing the other Atheling Alfred out of the way, and three years later married his daughter to the King.

In 1048 a fleet of Norwegian pirates appeared off Sandwich, and the town was plundered and burned, but they were repulsed in an attack on Thanet chiefly by the ecclesiastics of Minster Abbey.

In 1051 an incident occurred at Dover which, although unimportant in itself, was fraught with serious consequences, and moreover exemplified the deep hatred of foreigners which had been burnt and hacked into the bosoms of the men of Kent. Eustace Count of Boulogne, who had married the sister of Edward the Confessor, the Countess Godgifa, had been paying a visit at the English court, accompanied by a large armed retinue. That his visit had been purely one of international courtesy may be very much questioned when we see how William of Normandy was at this time strengthening himself at home, when we note how Norman influence was slowly but surely asserting itself in England, how the three chief bishoprics and many minor posts were held by Normans, and how in particular the Archbishop of Canterbury had selected Earl Godwin, the recognised representative of at any rate the national feeling of South England, as an object of hatred.

At any rate the men of Dover, who shared with their fellows of the other Kent Ports the distinction of being able to value any foreigner at his real worth, resented practically the overbearing behaviour of Eustace's Normans with the result that the Normans were chased out of the town with the loss of many men. Eustace complained to the King; the King instructed Earl Godwin to punish the town ; the Earl refused to obey, and in lieu presented a list of grievances borne by his countrymen at the hands of the insolent foreigners who were beginning to monopolise the chief offices of Church and State.

The King would pay no attention to the complaints, and at the instigation of the Archbishop of Canterbury the charge of having murdered Alfred Atheling was again brought up against Godwin, and his offer to clear himself on oath was refused. At the General National Assembly held at Gloucester Godwin appeared with his sons and men all armed, and demanded that Eustace and his men should be surrendered to him. The request was of course refused, and Godwin was ordered to quit the kingdom within five days, whilst, to accentuate his wrath, the King actually sent away his own wife, Godwin's daughter. This was in 1052. In 1053 Godwin returned from banishment with his sons, was enthusiatically received by the men of Kent and Sussex, secured the fleet of what were afterwards known as the Cinque Ports, went to London and simply terrified the poor weak King into receiving him actually with distinction, upon which his chief Norman enemies made off as best they could He was restored to his honours and possessions, his daughter the Queen, was recalled from the nunnery of Wherwell, the Archbishop of Canterbury was outlawed, and Frenchmen in high positions made room for Englishmen.

It was during Earl Godwin's banishment that William,

Duke of Normandy, made his first visit to England
and possibly it was whilst on this visit that he won
from Edward that strange promise that he should
succeed to the English throne, which he extorted from him,
or cajoled out of Harold at a later date. Godwin died
soon after his restoration to honour, and his son Harold
succeeded to the Earldom, whilst another son Tostig
became Earl of Northumberland by the death of the
Siward who had fought with the Macbeth of Shakespeare.

It was probably in 1064 that Harold was the hero of
that mysterious incident of the oath taken to William
of Normandy, which was to mark the future course
of our national history.. What the oath was, and under
what circumstances it was taken, authorities are not
agreed, but that Harold did place himself under some
tremendous obligation to William, the non-fulfilment of
which led to the Norman Conquest of England, is very
certain. Edward the Confessor died in 1066, and on the
next day Harold, son of Godwin, was crowned King
of England, not, be it noted, by the Archbishop of
Canterbury.

REMARKS ON SAXON KENT.

Before we survey the relics of the Saxon dominion in
Kent which have come down to us, we will concisely
examine the form of Government.

The office of *King* was partly hereditary and partly
elective :—Hereditary so far as there was always a Royal
Family—a family from which the sovereigns were chosen ;
elective in that the Witenagemot selected the individual.

Next in rank came the *Ealdormen,* probably appointed
by the King. When the Kingdom of Kent as an
independency came to an end its sovereigns retained their
positions as viceroys under the conquering monarch
under the name of Ealdormen or Earls. In the inde-

pendent Kingdom of Kent the Ealdorman was merely a dignity. There were three—East Kent, West Kent and Romney Marsh.

Below the Ealdormen came the *Gerefas* who may be described as the fiscal and administrative officers of the Crown. These were :—

1.—The *High Reeve:* An official who went from place to place on special duties.

2.—The *Shire Reeve :* Head of the Shire ; formerly head of the County Court, but as the King gained power his was diminished, and he became the principal political officer, chief of the freemen, had charge of the county defences, held the folk-mote, and controlled the mints.

3.—The *King's Reeve :* Who attended to the King's personal affairs.

4.—The *Burgh Reeve :* A royal officer in charge of the burghs.

5.—The *Port Reeve:* Controller of commercial affairs. "Port" formerly meant much the same as market.

6.—The *Wic Reeve:* The village officer.

7.—The *Tung Reeve :* An estate officer, a steward.

8.—The *Swan Reeve :* Controlled herdsmen, foresters and pastures.

After the Reeves ranked the *Thanes*, of whom there were two, or perhaps three, classes; *tenants in Francalmoigne*, who held lands bestowed on people devoted to religious service; *soldiers*; *soc men*, described by Morgan as "commended men of great lords," chiefly in Romney Marsh and the Weald border; *labourers* and *villeins* who were personally free men, but unable to alienate lands without their lords' permission, and paying rent by services as well as in money ; and, lastly, the *Bordarii*, free men, but poorer than villeins.

These comprised the freemen of the county.

Slavery in Kent existed as generally and as strongly as in any other county, but the lot of the slave in Kent was probably better than elsewhere on account of the free character of Kentish tenures. Slaves were of various kinds—by conquest, by marriage, as in the case of a free man marrying a slave-born woman he descended to her estate, by parental decision, and by birth,

There was a large slave trade in Saxon England of which London was the principal mart. Under Alfred the condition of the slave was much ameliorated, one of his laws being that a Christian could only be sold for six years, after which time he or she was free.

The proportion of slaves in Kent has been calculated at about one-tenth of the population, which at the time of Domesday Book was about 13,000, but it is difficult to make an exact estimate on account of the ambiguity of the word *servus*.

The position of men was measured by the amount of *weregild* to be paid for them in cases of murder or injury by the offenders. Thus the *weregild* of an Ealdorman exceeded that of a *ceorl* or yeoman three times. We may here note that a Kentish shilling was worth more than five times as much as a shilling in Wessex or Mercia.

The General Council of the Realm was the *Witenagemot*, a non-elective body, summoned by royal writ and con sisting of the King, the princes of the blood, the great ecclesiastics, ealdormen, thanes, and soldiers. It met usually at Easter and Christmas ; it considered all public acts before they received the Royal sanction, considered new laws, made peace, war, and alliances, elected and de- posed the King, appointed, with the King, prelates, and generally controlled ecclesiastical matters, levied taxes, raised forces, and was the Supreme Court of Justice both in civil and criminal cases.

Kentish *Witans* were held at Faversham, Bapchild, Bearsted, Canterbury and Aylesford.

Shire or *Folk Motes* were held three times a year, always in the open air. Penenden Heath near Maidstone has been from time immemorial the great Kentish gathering place, but all over the county place-names such as The

THE ANCIENT BOROUGH OF
SAND PETT. CHARING

Mote, the Shire Oak, the Shire Stone commemorate the sites of these ancient assembly spots, just as the "Gathering Stones" of the North Country mark the ancient clan and tribal meeting places of that district.

Court Leets were held once in every three weeks in each Hundred in the open air for criminal matters, and at these all residents were bound to attend. *Court Barons* were manorial assemblies at which the free tenants were obliged to be present. As for the ancient *Court of Dens*, peculiar to the Weald of Kent, we can best refer readers to Mr. Furley's exhaustive remarks upon it, and his confutation of Mr. Kemble's theory that it was an outcome of the old *Mark* system, in the volumes on the Weald of Kent to which we owe so much in this present work.

The County of Kent was divided as follows :—

1.—Into East and West Kent, and possibly into a third part—Romney Marsh. Although this was nominally an ecclesiastical division, for some centuries it remained practically a political division.

2.—*Laths :* as peculiar to Kent as were Rapes or Ropes to Sussex, Ridings to Yorkshire, and Parts or Trithings to Lincolnshire. The word is said to be derived from *gelathean*, to gather together. There were seven Laths in Kent :—Canterbury, Eastry, Limen (afterwards Shepway), Wye, Milton, Sutton-at-Hone and Aylesford. (*See Note F at end of Chapter*).

3.—The Laths were divided into *Hundreds*, it is conjectured, in the time of Alfred. In Domesday there are 63 Kentish Hundreds ; at present there are 73. What a Hundred consisted of is not known, whether families, or persons, or hides of land, or villages.

4.—The Hundreds were divided into *Boroughs* or *Townships*, consisting each of ten freemen or heads of families who were sureties for each other's good behaviour. The Borough head men were known as *Borsholders*. (*See Note G at end of Chapter*).

Parishes, it is not generally known, were originally distinctly ecclesiastical divisions, and were not, as has been often asserted, co-extensive with manors.

"In Kent," says Mr. Furley, "the sites of our Anglo-Saxon churches formed the nucleus of our present parochial system," and, says another writer, "were circuits of ground committed to the charge of those who had the cure of souls therein."

To show how extremely conservative Kent has always remained in the matter of ancient rights and customs, it may be cited with regard to tenures that whilst on the Surrey Border the tenure of Borough English by which real property descends to the youngest son is general, Westerham is the only parish in Kent where it prevails. Again, in the manors of Bayham and Frant, each of which is situated half in Kent and half in Sussex) Gavelkind (inheritance equally to all sons) prevails in the Kentish half, and primogeniture in the Sussex.

As briefly as is permissible let us review the remains of the old life in our county during the period between the departure of the Romans and the Norman Conquest, which are still visible.

(I)—THE CHURCHES.

If it was only because the Anglo-Saxons built their churches generally of wood it is not surprising that so few specimens of their ecclesiastical architecture have been spared until our times. Indeed, the only specimens extant are mere fragments scattered here and there, such as the clerestory arches in the church of Minster in Sheppey, bits in walls such as those in the crypt of Canterbury Cathedral, in the churches of St. Pancras and St. Martin, Canterbury, in the latter of which the font and a door are also Saxon, windows at Lyminge, and perhaps the nave of Orpington.

The chief religious foundations of this period, generally Benedictine, were Christ Church and St. Augustine's, Canterbury, between 598 and 605 A.D.; St. Martin's,

Dover, by Eadbald, son of Ethelbert, in 620; Folkestone Nunnery, also by Eadbald, in 630: Lyminge in 633 by Ethelburga, the daughter of Ethelbert; Reculver in 669; Minster in Sheppey, 670; Minster in Thanet by Sexburga, Queen of Ercombert, King of Kent, in 675.

The clergy occupied a high position during this period. A high *weregild* was paid for them; the oath of a priest or deacon was worth more than that of a free man; they acted as lawyers in property transfers, but were bound like seculars by the services of tenures.

(II)—CASTLES.

Although under King Widred Dover Castle was much strengthened, no traces of Saxon work are extant, except perhaps the outline of the defences of the ancient *burgh*. Of Saxon Rochester there are few (if any) traces. Allington, Canterbury and Chilham are on Saxon sites.

(III)—CEMETERIES.

The Anglo-Saxon relics unearthed from the cemeteries of Kent are unequalled elsewhere in England both for quality as well as quantity. Almost every year brings us news of a fresh discovery, and, although the finest collection has left the county, enough remains to confirm the words of Mr. Wright:

"The Kentish graves, abounding in ornaments of gold and silver and other jewellery, and containing many articles indicating social refinement, show a people who were rich and powerful, far more so than the other Anglo-Saxon States where the precious metals are rarely found, and the gold ornaments are replaced by gilt bronze; and this explains to us the high position held by Kent towards the other States at the dawn of our Anglo-Saxon history."

The great superiority of the workmanship and of the designs of these Kentish relics over relics of the same character discovered elsewhere is thought to have been due to Roman influence, but we decline to assent to this. The chief Saxon and Romano-Saxon Cemeteries—for Roman skeletons are often found alongside Saxon—are at Bifrons near Patrixbourne, Ozengall in Thanet, Bourne Park, Sarre, Sittingbourne, Gilton Town and Ash near Sandwich, Wingham, Breachdown, Eynesford, Lullingstone, Kingstone, Sibertswold, Milton, Cliff, King's Mead, Faversham, along the hills on each side of the Medway Valley, and perhaps along the Wye Downs. This is by no means a comprehensive list, but is sufficient to show how widely distributed is this antiquarian wealth.

The most interesting articles are weapons, the metal parts of shields, armour, and horse furniture, knives, a few axes, *fibulæ* or brooches of extraordinary variety—circular (characteristic of Kent) or cross-shaped, of gold, of filigree work, set with stones or enamelled, of bronze and brass and bronze gilt—rings of silver, bronze, bronze gilt and brass, ear-rings, arm-rings of gold, bead necklaces, spoons, crystal balls, vases, cups, urns, draughtsmen, keys, bead bracelets, chatelaines, hairpins, combs, scales and weights, and iron instruments of many kinds, glass drinking cups, gilt-bronze bowls, buckets, and, of course, Roman and Saxon coins. In Kent cremation does not seem to have been frequent. The bodies were buried in full dress, surrounded by the articles most associated with the lives of the dead, and these articles are so invariably placed according to rule that experienced excavators can tell exactly from the discovery of one how the others will lie. Occasionally the discovery of bones in the mound above the grave shows that the very general custom of killing slaves or prisoners at funerals was practised by the Anglo-Saxons. As a rule Anglo-Saxon barrows are on hill tops, and in Kent at any rate are rarely solitary.

(IV.)—SUNDRIES.

Our Kentish place names are naturally strongly Saxon. Most of the names into which the syllable *ing* enters commemorate the settlement of tribes, families, or, as Mr. Kemble calls divisions of land held in common by several households or several men, of marks, and in Kent these are very numerous. But they are hardly interesting etymologies when compared with some others around us. For instance, our sense of the ancient individuality, so to speak, or even importance of some present-day obscure village is not heightened much by the knowledge that it was the settling place of the Syllingas, or the Bilsingas, or the Semesingas ; but when we connect it with mythology and the worship of deities of whom nothing else is left but the names of the days of the week, when we associate Eastry with Eostre, the Saxon Aurora, and Woodnes-borough with Woden, or Welling with the Scandinavian Vulcan, Wayland, or Thurnham with Thor, or Godmersham with Godmer, the British giant slain by Canutus, one of the companions of Brutus—as we have as much right to do as to associate them with other things just as misty and uncertain—they become invested with a special interest. At any rate, invaluable aid has been afforded to our Kentish diggers and delvers in the mine of the Past by names which at first sight suggest nothing.

Of Kentish industries during the Saxon period that of corn growing was the first, despite the constant inter-ruptions from invasion and war. Indeed it has been computed that as great an acreage was under cultivation in Kent in Saxon times as there was at the commencement of George III.'s reign.

There were extensive salt works near the coast—at Rochester, Canterbury, Lympne, Milton, and Faversham. There were vineyards at Leeds, Halling, Chart Sutton, Teynham, and other places. Wool was already a staple commodity, and Canterbury was its chief market.

NOTES ON THE KINGDOM OF KENT.

A.

The mystery of the bones in Hythe crypt will probably never be satisfactorily cleared up. This is a summary of expert opinion :—

   (1) Only 10 out of 723 skulls examined show signs of injuries inflicted before death.

E 2

(2) The greater part of the skulls belong to Celtic and English races ; two seem to be Roman ; two to be Lap or Danish.

(3) Skulls and bones belong chiefly to men in the prime of life ; three belong to children, and one to a person who had not cut his wisdom teeth.

(4) Previously to being buried, if they have been buried at all, the remains had evidently lain a long time in the open air.

(5) No record exists of the placing of the remains here, but it is almost certain they must have been stacked here since the Reformation.

(From the Vicar of Hythe's Pamphlet, and from notes by Dr. Randall Davis, of Hythe).

B.

Augustine and his followers, according to Bede, landed at Richborough, and waited there until it pleased the King to see them. He says :—

"Which thing the King hearing came shortly after into the isle of Thanet unto his pallace or castle of Rupichester, situate nigh the old city of Stonehore, and the King sitting under the cliff or rock whereon the Castle is built commanded Augustine and his followers to be brought before him."

Ethelbert was baptised, after some hesitation, on the Feast of Pentecost, 597, perhaps in the church of St. Martin or St. Pancras. Bede says :

"St. Augustine and his followers in this church (Saint Pancras) first began to meet, to sing, to pray, to say mass, to preach, to baptize, till the King, being converted to the faith, allowed them to preach openly and rebuild and repair all churches in all places, when he . . . . . . believed and was baptised."

Ethelbert was baptised perhaps by Bertha's chaplain, Bishop Liudhard, or by Augustine himself.

C.

Mr. Kemble says :

"It is probable that from the very earliest times Kent had at least two Kings, whose capitals were respectively Canterbury and Rochester, the seats of two bishoprics. The distinction of East and West Kentings is preserved till the very downfall of the Saxon monarchy: not only do we know that Edric and Lothere reigned together, but also that Widred and his son Ethelbert the Second did so. . . . . . Sigred deliberately calls himself King of half Kent."

D.

The record says "Sailed from Lympne to Appledore." The Rhee Wall would hinder a direct passage, so we must suppose that by "Lympne" is to be understood the mouth of the Limen.

E.

The battle was perhaps fought at Twitton. When the South-Eastern Railway was being made here human skeletons with fragments of swords and armour were found.

F.

It is interesting to note a possible association between the Lathes of Kent and the Three Lothians of Scotland. This district was settled by Jutes soon after the middle of the fifth century, under the traditional leadership of Octa, son of Horsa, and his brother Ebusa. Less than two centuries later we find another association between the two distant Kingdoms of Kent and Northumberland in the marriage of Ethelburga of Kent with Edwin of Northumberland, and the consequent conversion of the latter Kingdom to Christianity.

G.

Some of these Boroughs consisted of a single dwelling. There is a fine, but sadly dilapidated and degenerated old house near Charing which is still known as the Borough of Sand Pett.

IV.—NORMAN KENT.

ON September 28th, 1066, William Duke of Normandy landed his army of invasion on the Sussex Coast near Pevensey, but the first blood in this momentous enterprise was drawn by the Kent men, for William, in order to make a diversion, ordered a detachment of his fleet to disembark troops at Romney, and the Romney men repulsed it with great loss.

At the Battle of Hastings the Kent men were placed in the van and throughout the day bore the brunt of the fighting. Whether, as we Kent people like to believe, this occupation of the place of honour was in satisfaction of a historic claim of the Kent men to strike the first blow in battle, or whether, as some modern dissectors declare, it was merely in accordance with a general rule of the times that the fittest people to be entrusted with the key to a position were the natives of the neighbourhood, we are not going to attempt to decide.

It is sufficient for us that the Kent men occupied the position of honour on the field of Senlac, and that right heroically they held it.

William's first steps after his victory were to establish his base and march on London before the scattered English could recover themselves. He marched Eastward, inflicted condign punishment on the town of Romney for having dared to oppose him, summoned Dover which at once submitted and had to put up with the excesses of his soldiers for eight days, to Canterbury which followed Dover's example, and so on to London.

It was during this march from the Coast to London that the famous Swanscombe Wood episode is said to have taken place. Briefly it was this. Swanscombe is between Gravesend and Dartford, and here the Conqueror and his men were confronted by the appearance of a vast moving wood. As he halted, amazed and affrighted, so says the legend, the wood resolved itself into an army in battle array. From the ranks stepped forth Stigand, Archbishop of Canterbury and the Abbot of St Augustine's, and these demanded the recognition of the ancient Danish Gavelkind system of tenure as had existed heretofore and a partial restitution of territory, with the alternative of being attacked.

William, it is said, at once yielded to *force majeure*, and from this circumstance arose the proud county motto, the firm belief that Kent alone of all England defied the Conqueror and retained her rights, and innumerable ballads and sayings glorifying Kent in general and Swanscombe in particular.

We are not of those whose delight it is to shatter the darling creeds of the people, to shred the heroism or romance or beauty off every attackable legend simply because it is ancient and improbable, or to tear the pleasing garment which Time weaves around facts as well as buildings and expose its nakedness with the grim glee of an anatomical operator. But we confess to absolute scepticism about the Swanscombe affair, because in the first place William had done and was doing his work far too thoroughly to allow the possibility of the existence of an army sufficient to crush him; and in the second place William was not the man to be frightened by a trick which he must have known was a favourite one with Danish warriors, and was far ahead of his age, as he oft showed, in his contempt for superstition. Still, the story is widely believed, and has the support of Mr. Jas. R. Scott, F.S.A., who tells us that Swanscombe is Sweyn's Camp, and that the chief mover in the business was Sweyn Godvinson, grandson of the great Earl Godwin, whose father was Sweyn the Outlaw, cousin of the "young Siward" who had moved Birnam to Dunsinane against Macbeth thirteen years previously.

At any rate, the legend became so deeply rooted in the Kentish mind, that, according to Drayton, three hundred and fifty years later Erpingham's Kentish bowmen at Agincourt bore as the device on their banner an armoured arm coming out of a wood, above the motto "Unconquered." To London William proceeded without opposition, except for a gallant sally of the Londoners, which was repulsed. Kent submitted without a blow, not because the spirit of Kent was wanting, but because William at Hastings had destroyed what was practically the whole fighting force of the South Eastern Counties, hence the utter emptiness of such boasts as that Kent demanded and won from the Conqueror independence. No unbiassed county man can read his history thoroughly without being ashamed of the Chauvinism which prompts such utterances.

Our greatest historian of this period says :

"William did not abolish the old Kentish laws, but that is because he did not do so anywhere else ; nor is there anything to show that he treated Kent better or worse than the rest of the Kingdom."

And again :

"The little legislation of William's reign takes throughout the shape of additions. Nothing old is repealed ; a few new enactments are set up by the side of the old ones."

We may be sure that if any other county had special customs and laws of its own, such as the Gavelkind tenure of Kent—which, by the way, was by no means limited in observance to the County of Kent—(see *Note A at end of Chapter*) William, in pursuance of his glove and gauntlet policy, respected them. As for the difficulty raised in solving the question, why did William treat East and West Kent so differently, disinheriting all the Manor-

ROCHESTER
CASTLE

holders of two West Kent Laths, and allowing those of
the four East Kent Laths to remain as in the days of
Edward the Confessor?—It may be answered that he no
doubt acted to people according to their deserts. East
Kent let him alone and he let it alone. If the Swanscombe affair is to be accepted as a historical fact it would
seem that, inasmuch as Swanscombe is in West Kent,
William so far from being terrified into submission by the
apparition, punished the district for its presumption.

At any rate, the broad fact remains that Kent was not
only just as thoroughly subjected as any other part of the
Kingdom, but that during its subsequent history under
William's rule no such heroic episode is recorded as the
magnificent defiance hurled at the whole might of the
Norman crown by Hereward the Wake and his men in the
fens of East Anglia.

It is interesting to note that the first act of reward
made by William was the endowment of the new Abbey of
Battle with the Royal Manor of Wye, near Ashford,
with its lordship over twenty-two hundreds, and privileges
extending to Folkestone, Chart, and Milton. His next
act was to make Odo, Bishop of Bayeux, Earl of Kent
and Custos of the Southern ports, whilst Hugh de
Montfort was made Governor of Dover Castle. These
two officials abused their power so brutally that in 1067
the Kent men assembled at their ancient folk-mote
meeting place, Penenden Heath, and considered what
should be done.

They decided upon the worst possible course, and
invited Eustace, Count of Boulogne, the same who had
been so roughly received at Dover, and who only hated
the English less than he hated William, to help them.
Rochester Castle was attacked, but the patriots were
defeated, and the one effort made by the men of Kent to
kick against the authority imposed on them failed.

One of the first recorded trials in our history took place
in Kent in 1072. Archbishop Lanfranc complained that
Odo of Bayeux, as Earl of Kent, had appropriated lands

belonging to the see, whereupon William called a meeting of Kent men, not of Normans, on Penenden Heath to decide the issue, and, when the meeting gave judgment against Odo, William endorsed it and ordered it to pass as law—a significant act when it is remembered who and what Odo was.

By this trial Lanfranc won back Reculver, Sandwich, Maidstone, Lyminge, Saltwood, Newenden, Preston, Sandhurst, Erith, Orpington, Hayes, and Eynesford, besides other manors. He devoted to religious uses the ecclesiastical wealth thus regained, and particularly embellished Canterbury Cathedral and St. Alban's Abbey.

Bits of Lanfranc's work at Canterbury still exist. In the nave is his plinth in the North and South walls, with blocks of Caen stone, not *in situ*. The same in the Western Transepts. In the Cloisters' Eastern wall, a doorway near its North End, and above that doorway, three windows of the old Dormitory (now the Library) are ascribed to Lanfranc. (Scott Robertson)

Until we reach the reign of Stephen there is nothing noteworthy in the history of Kent, except the rebellion of the barons, headed by Odo, against William Rufus, during which Rochester Castle underwent a memorable siege.

Kent however comes to the fore in the turbulent times of the last Norman Monarch. Briefly, the cause of the ceaseless war of this reign was the succession to the crown. Henry the First, contrary to the idea of the age which regarded a monarch as necessarily a soldier, wished that his daughter Maud should succeed him to the crown of England, and relied upon his nephew Stephen to see that his wish was carried out.

Stephen however had his own designs, and, directly Henry was dead, declared on oath that Maud had been disinherited by her father, and that he had been named heir. Landing in Kent, he was refused admission to Dover, but went on to London, and by the help of his brother the Bishop of Winchester, seized the late King's treasure there, and with the support of the barons, who saw a chance of being more independent under a prince with no firmness of character and a bad title than they had been under the first three Norman Kings, was crowned with his high-spirited wife Matilda at Winchester.

Maud, however, was not going to be cheated of her rights in this flagrant manner without a struggle. She invaded Normandy and was repulsed, but she had powerful allies over the water in her Uncle David of Scotland, and her half-brother, Robert of Gloucester. The former invaded England but was crushingly defeated at the battle of Northallerton or the Standard in 1138. To the latter Stephen made overtures against Maud, but although he had taken the usual baronial conditional oath he foresaw danger, fled to Normandy, and renounced his homage.

Stephen then quarrelled with the Bishops of Salisbury, Lincoln and Ely, destroyed their castles and seized their property, whereupon Henry of Winchester and the clergy deserted his cause, and in this extremity London and Kent alone stood up for him. Maud and Robert of Gloucester came over to England with mercenary troops, and everything went against Stephen ; he lost Dover and Leeds Castles, and finally was defeated and taken prisoner at the battle of Lincoln, 1141.

Maud, who treated the captive monarch with great indignity, was declared Queen at Winchester, and crowned by Stephen's brother, Henry, Bishop of Winchester.

Matilda set nobly to work to aid her imprisoned husband. London and Kent loved her just as they hated the arrogant Maud, whom they regarded as the representative of the Norman party. With her young son Eustace, and under the protection of William d'Ypres, Earl of Kent, she went into Kent, whence, after assembling an army, she marched on London where was her rival, Maud. Maud, who was fast alienating her supporters, fled to Oxford, closely pursued by the army of Londoners and Kent men, and thence to Winchester, which was immediately besieged. With great difficulty she escaped from Winchester, but in covering her flight the Earl of Gloucester, Maud's half brother, was captured. As a contrast to the manner in which Maud had treated Stephen after the battle of Lincoln, Matilda behaved to her captive in the most kindly and generous way, and removed him to Rochester Castle.

After much haggling and disputing, however, an exchange of prisoners was effected, Matilda was re-united to Stephen, and the Earl of Gloucester went to Normandy to get aid for the renewal of the war. This was in 1141.

Stephen at once marched to Oxford, where was Maud, and with his army of Londoners and Kent men so nearly captured her that she only escaped by dressing herself in white, and during a snow storm getting away on foot to Abingdon, six miles away, whence they rode to Wallingford. Here she met the Earl of Gloucester with reinforcements from Normandy, and her son Prince Henry— afterwards Henry the Second.

The tide of fortune turned for a while against Stephen, who was defeated in 1143 at the battle of Wareham, but the death of the Earl of Gloucester deprived Maud of her chief support, and she herself retired to Normandy in 1145.

But this did not prove to be quite the end of the struggle. War threatened to be continued by the rising royal generations in the persons of Stephen's son Eustace and Maud's son Henry.

The latter landed at Dover, whence, after rebuilding the keep of the Castle, he advanced through Kent to Wallingford on the Thames. Here he met Eustace. A battle seemed imminent, but according to Matthew Paris, a romantic appeal on the part of Maud brought about the settlement of a peace by which it was arranged that Stephen should remain King during his life, and that Henry should succeed him.

As Maud was in Normandy at the time it is not very clear what hand she could have had in the matter.

2

Eustace was so disgusted at this arrangement that he refused to agree, took himself and army off to Bury St. Edmunds, burning and destroying as he went, and soon after died " by the favour of God." This was 1152. The next year matters were finally settled, Henry swore fealty, and the barons allegiance to both, but the air was full of treachery and uncertainty. A plot of Stephen's son William and the Flemings against Henry being frustrated by an accident to William on Barham Downs drove Henry from the Kingdom, but in 1154 Stephen died. He was buried at Faversham in the Abbey he had founded, where lay the ashes of his gallant, faithful wife and of his son. A fine canopied tomb is pointed out as their resting place, but the contents were taken out and thrown into the Creek some four hundred years later, for the sake of the coffin lead.

REMARKS ON NORMAN KENT.

The chief terror of the Norman period was caused by the illimitable practise of building *private* castles, of which, says Mr. Pearson, few, if any, existed before the time of Edward the Confessor, when the Norman influence was beginning to assert itself in England. The lord of a private castle exercised life and death over all around him, and if under the Conqueror he dared not actually defy the sovereign, under Stephen his was an *imperium in imperio*, and he was practically an independent potentate. Of the misery thus caused it is impossible to form any idea at this distance of time, but we need not doubt that the following description of England in Stephen's reign given by the Saxon Chronicle applies as well to Kent as elsewhere :

" The nobles and bishops built castles and filled them with devilish and wicked men and oppressed the people, cruelly torturing men for their money. They imposed taxes upon towns, and when they had exhausted them of everything, set them on fire. You might travel a day and not find one man living in a town, nor any land in cultivation. Never did the country suffer greater evils."

Of these castles we have still many substantial remains, but it should be borne in mind that the following list by no means represents the extent of the evil in our county, inasmuch as it was one of Henry the Second's first tasks to destroy the private castles erected under his predecessors, so that the very sites of many of these strongholds have yet to be discovered.

Dover and Canterbury were Royal castles. Best known amongst the private castles are Rochester, Leeds, Salt-wood, Folkestone, Chilham, Tunbridge and perhaps Allington and Eynesford.

At the Conquest there seem to have existed as flourishing independent communities only five religious houses—Christ Church and St. Augustine's (Canterbury), Rochester, St. Martin's Dover, and Lewisham, which, by the way, was an alien priory, belonging to Ghent. Ten other large foundations had either been destroyed, or had been absorbed as Lyminge and Reculver were absorbed by Christ Church. But during the Norman period religious house founding went on apace, and by the end of Stephen's reign we find the Abbeys of Boxley, West Malling, Faversham, and Minster in Thanet, Higham Nunnery, of which Stephen's daughter Mary was the first prioress, and the Priories of Leeds, Folkestone, Dover, Lesnes, and Davington. Minster in Sheppey Nunnery, which had been destroyed by the Danes, or at any rate had been abandoned, was re-constituted in 1130.

The best specimens of Anglo-Norman ecclesiastical architecture in Kent are the West Front, the Nave (except the last two east bays) and the Crypt of Rochester; at Canterbury part of the choir, the plinths of the North and South walls, the whole of the Great Crypt, the outer walls of the choir aisles, the eastern transepts, the chapels of St. Andrew and St. Anselm, the Treasury, the Transept

NORMAN STAIR
CANTERBURY

towers and many bits about the Cloisters, the Infirmary ruins and the monastic buildings.

The best purely Norman churches are at Barfriston, St. Margaret at Cliffe and Patrixbourne, and a long list can be made of churches which present features of Norman work, such as towers, doors, pillars and windows.

Although it may be deemed extraneous to a strict and literal History of Kent, a short sketch of what the Feudal System under our Norman Kings was is here appended.

It must be premised that the Normans who conquered England did not bring the Feudal System as afterwards perfected with them. It followed upon the publication of Domesday Book, when at Sarum the principal landowners came forward and offered to become feudal vassals in 1086. Amongst the Anglo-Saxons there was little of the *spirit* of feudalism, and none of its after-elaboration. In the *spirit* it existed in Normandy, and with the spirit existed to some extent the tenures. But the perfection of the system is due to William and his successors.

There were four kinds of service :

    1.—FREE : to serve in the wars, etc.

    2.—BASE : to plough, dig, etc.

    3.—CERTAIN : to pay a stated annual rate, etc.

    4.—UNCERTAIN : to wind a horn upon invasion by Scots, etc. *(See Note B at end of Chapter).*

Land was of two kinds :

Allodial Land was that in which a man had full and entire property.

Feudal Land was that which a man held of another, in return for the performance of one or other of the three following tenures.

    1.—Knight Service. 2.—Free Socage. 3.—Copyhold.

Knight Service contained the following " incidents : "

    (A).—*Aids,* for which the lord might call if he wished to marry his eldest daughter, to ransom himself if taken prisoner, or to make his eldest son a knight.

(B).—*Reliefs*, due from all on inheriting land.

(C).—*Fines for Alienation*, or if tenant died without heir, lord took lands.

(D).—*Escheat and Forfeiture*, as by being attainted for treason.

(E).—*Primer Seisin*, the King received of heir when a tenant in chief died a certain proportion of the year's profit, except when land was held in *Gavelkind*, when no wardship could be claimed by lord.

(F).— *Wardship*, custody of body and lands of heir until of age.

(G).—*Marriage*, the lord had the right of nominating a wife to his male ward, or a husband to his female.

Escuage or Scutage, pecuniary payment in lieu of military service. The abuse of this helped to wreck the Feudal System, for military service often becoming irksome or distasteful men escaped it by this payment.

Free Socage (now Freehold)

Was a tenure by any certain service not being knight service. It comprised the following varieties :

1.—*Burgage*, when the king was lord of an ancient borough in which tenements were held by a rent certain. There was very little Burgage Tenure in Kent.

2.—*Borough English*, by which the youngest son succeeds.

3.—*Gavelkind*, by which the lands descend to all sons alike, are not alienated for attainder for felony, and the tenant may alienate his estate at the age of fifteen. *(See Note C at end of Chapter)*.

Copyhold :

Villeins under indulgent lords gradually gained lands which they enjoyed for a long time, and so were inviolable, although their tenants could only show a roll.

Other tenures were *Heriots,* by which on the death of a tenant the lord received the best beast on the land, and

Francalmoign, whereby a religious corporation held lands of a donor for ever with no burden but that of the

Trinoda Necessitas, i.e., repairing highways, building bridges and repelling invasion.

Generally, the results of the Norman Conquest were :—

1.—Separation of Civil from Ecclesiastical Courts brought about by William's avarice, by his anxiety to get rid of those who understood Saxon law, so as to ensure the supremacy of Norman, and by his friendship with the Pope.

2.—Forest Laws established—hence our Game Laws.

3.—Diminution of the influence of County Courts and institution of the *Aula Regis,* the proceedings whereof were in Norman French.

4.—Introduction of Trial by Combat.

5.—Institution of Feudal Tenures.

NOTES ON NORMAN KENT.

A.

The special features of Gavelkind in Kent were :—

(1) Husband inherits half his wife's property on her death till he marries again, whether there be children or not. Wife the same on husband's death.

(2) Tenant in Gavelkind kept in ward one year longer than was usual in other tenures : i.e. : till fifteen.

(3) Lands in Gavelkind not forfeited by felony :
   " The father to the bough,
   The son to the plough."

(4) Tenant had power of devising lands by will, before the statute of Henry VIII. was passed for that purpose.

(5) Property descends to all sons alike, and if there are no sons to the daughters.

(6) Tenants in Gavelkind claimed the privilege that trials respecting lands in Gavelkind should only be heard before juries of tenants in Gavelkind.

B.

Grand Serjeanty was one of these uncertain services. The following are some Kentish examples.

The Manor of Shorne was held by the service of carrying a white banner for forty days when the King marched into Scotland. That of Seale by blowing a horn at the approach of the enemy. That of Bekesbourne by finding one ship for the King when he crossed the seas, and paying three marks. The manors of Copeland and Atterton in the parish of River, near Dover, were held by the extraordinary tenure of supporting the King's head whenever bad weather occurred during his passage between Dover and "Whitsand" (Wissant). This was observed until the end of the 16th century. The manor of Seaton in Boughton Aluph was held by providing a man to lead the King's greyhounds whenever he went to Gascony, until the leader had worn out a pair of shoes worth fourpence bought at the King's cost. Certain tenants held lands of the Archbishop of Canterbury by Grand Serjeanty. Thus the Badlesmeres held Hothfield by attending the Archbishop at his enthronisation with water to wash his hands, the basin and ewer being the tenant's perquisites, and also by being Chamberlain to his Grace the same night, the bed being the tenant's perquisite. The manor of Horton and the estate of Chartons near Farningham were held respectively by the services of acting as cup-bearer and chief carver at the enthronisation banquet.

Bilsington Inferior was held by the service of carrying the last dish of the second course to the King's table at the Coronation banquet, and presenting him with three maple cups. Bilsington Superior, by serving the King with his cup on Whit Sunday.

Grange in Gillingham was held by the finding of a ship and two armed men for the Cinque Ports fleet.

The manor of Ashton was held by guarding and carrying the King's falcons.

Instances of Petty Serjeanty, which primarily consisted in the offering of anything pertaining to war, are found in the case of Eastbridge, which was held by one sparrow-hawk; of two Boxley manors held by finding a horse of a certain value, and one wallet, and one skin of wine whenever the King marched to Wales; of Wilmington in Boughton Aluph, by the presentation of a meat hook to the King whenever he should come into the manor; of Oxenhoath, Lullingstone, St. Mary Cray and others by the presentation of one pair of gilt spurs annually; of Footscray, which was held by Walter Abell in the fourteenth century, by the providing of one "sure sparrow-hawk."

C.

Gavelkind was one of the tenures which the Real Property Commissioners in 1832 proposed to abolish. It still however survives, although much disgavelling has been going on of late years.

V.—PLANTAGENET KENT.

PART I.—THE REIGNS OF HENRY II., RICHARD I.,
JOHN, AND HENRY III.

A. HENRY II. 1154-1189.

THE interest of Kentish history under the first
Plantagenet King, Henry the Second, grandson of
Henry the First, is concentrated upon the quarrel
between the King and Thomas à Becket.

The key of the quarrel was the question as to whether
the Church was to enjoy its ancient privileges—privileges
which encroached sorely upon the royal power—or not.
The Kent men stood up for Becket throughout, and this
despite the fact that one of the new King's first acts was
to humble the power of the great barons, until now the
most dreaded and implacable enemies of the people, by
razing their castles to the ground. We have seen that the
Norman Churchmen in high office could play the parts of
oppressors and tyrants as effectively as did the lay barons,
but this was because the churchmen, rewarded by the
Conqueror with temporal power, were *de facto* ecclesiastics
in little else but name. Abbots and Bishops owned
castles and led armies, and their ecclesiastical titles and
garb were but cloaks to enable them to enrich themselves.
At the same time there was a bond between churchmen
and people which did not exist between baron and people.
If the abbot or bishop wrought mighty wrong, the institutions with which they were connected were the only

fountains of charity and help at which the poor, the oppressed, the sick could quaff freely, and in an age when superstition and ignorance went hand in hand to an extent hard to be realised nowadays it may readily be imagined that the bulk of the people, with the choice of two evils, preferred the lesser.

But there was more than this in the sturdy partisanship of the Kent men for Becket. There was firstly, his endearing personality, which differed wondrously from the personality of such men as Odo, Bishop of Bayeux, and the stoled and mitred tyrants of the first two Norman Kings. Finally, there was growing up in Kent a yearning for the personal freedom which, the Kent men learned as their commercial intercourse with the Continent grew closer, was being won by their own class in Flanders and France, and this personal freedom seemed more likely to be theirs under the Church than under a King who was palpably bent upon crushing Church, Baronage and People into one plastic mass to be moulded or shredded at will.

In her little book on this reign Mrs. Green says:—" The men of Kent were stout defenders of their customary rights ; they clung tenaciously to their special privileges— (whatever these may have been !) they had their own views of inheritance, their fixed standard of fines . . . . they were a very mixed population, constantly recruited from the neighbouring coasts. They held the outposts of the country as the advanced guard formally charged with the defence of its shores from foreign invasion, which was a very present terror in those days . . . . And it seems as though the shire very early took up the part it was to play again and again in mediæval history, and even later, as the assertor and defender of popular privileges."

Thomas à Becket was personally known and personally beloved by the people of Kent. He had a singularly gentle and winning manner, he was magnificent, and he was an Englishman. When, after his elevation to the Archbishopric of Canterbury—the first Englishman since the Conquest to fill that position—business took him from place to place, he travelled magnificently and slowly, magnificently as became the first subject in the land, slowly because it was impossible to travel otherwise on the Kentish roads of Henry the Second's time. He had a splendid palace at Canterbury, and Castles or manor-houses—palaces really, although not so called—at Ford, Charing, Lyminge, Otford, Teynham, Gillingham, and perhaps Saltwood.

Around Otford in particular memories of the great Archbishop still cling. We may see the well called after him, one of the obligatory places of halt for the pilgrims along the sequestered old way to his shrine: we may follow the path still called St. Thomas' Walk, and some old villagers still pretend to believe that nightingales never sing at Otford because they disturbed Thomas at his devotions, and that no blacksmith can flourish at Otford because one mis-shod the Archbishop's horse. *(See Note A at end of Chapter).*

To understand aright the fatal quarrel between King and Archbishop we must bear in mind that at this time the Church had jurisdiction not only exclusively over the clergy, but that it exercised wide powers over the laity, and that, without doubt, under cover of this a great many crimes passed unpunished, and what touched Henry far more nearly, a vast amount of wealth which would otherwise have gone into his coffers passed into ecclesiastical treasuries.

This is a History of Kent, but the histories of à Becket and the Kent of his day being inseparable, as brief as possible a *résumé* of the quarrel must be permitted. It may be divided into five stages :

(1)   Thomas resigned the Chancellorship with which Henry had invested him in the hope that Church and State would thus be brought closer together, and declared that his life and work were henceforth for the Church alone. This much displeased the King.

OTFORD

BARBACAN
SANDWICH

(2)   Thomas refused on ecclesiastical grounds to allow Henry to marry his brother to Stephen's daughter-in-law.

(3)   Thomas refused to consent to the King's plan of appropriating local revenues in the shape of land tax for his own use.

(4)   Thomas pressed the recovery of Tunbridge, Rochester, Hythe and Saltwood Castles as belonging to the See of Canterbury.

(5)   The important one : Henry pressed the principle that ecclesiastics should be punished by the Common Law for offences committed against the Common Law.

During the course of our history we have often occasion to note what prominent parts have been played in it by places which are now insignificant : for instance, the fighting of two important battles at Otford, and the ancient importance of the town of Wye : *(See Note B at end of Chapter)* and we may here record that one of the first circumstances which fanned Henry's wrath into flame on the question of ecclesiastical supremacy was the action of Thomas in excommunicating a priest whom Henry, through the patron of the living, William of Eynesford, had appointed to the church at Eynesford.

That Thomas had not entirely thrown off the soldier when he assumed the mitre, and that the old fighting blood of his profession was not stagnant within him, was evident by the promptitude with which he laid siege to Tunbridge Castle, when the possessor declined to admit his claim to it, as belonging to the See. Indeed, throughout his career he was a dealer of buffets rather than a weaver of webs, and it was this sturdy English spirit which played no small part in his popularity, and no doubt doubly sanctified him in the eyes of the simple folk when they learned that to the last moments of his life, in the winter gloom of the Cathedral transept, he stood defiant with uplifted cross before his assassins whilst his terrified comrades ran for their lives.

In order to settle the great question of the interference of the civil authorities with ecclesiastical offenders, Henry summoned a Council at Winchester. In reply to the King's command the bishops all said, "We will obey in all things save our order." The King burst out into a violent rage, before which the prelates quailed and backed out of their sturdy position. Thomas alone remained firm, until, at the prayers and entreaties of the bishops who foresaw that opposition to the King spelt their ruin, he yielded and declared that he would obey the customs of the kingdom.

Instantly the King called a Council at Clarendon to clinch matters. Then, Thomas, ashamed at having yielded, took up his old position of defiance. The King raged, the barons drew their swords, and for a moment it seemed as if the tragedy in Canterbury Cathedral was about to be anticipated.

Thomas yielded again, and declared himself ready to obey the customs of the Kingdom.

"Let the customs of the Kingdom be written down!" cried the delighted King.

The result was the Sixteen Articles known as the Constitutions of Clarendon. This was in 1164.

As these Constitutions established exactly what Thomas had been combating, and generally attacked the power of the Church, Thomas refused to sign them, or, if he did sign them, refused to get the Pope's sanction to them, and threatened to appeal to Rome. The King's anger was so terrific that Thomas attempted to escape to France from Romney, which belonged to the Archbishopric, but failed.

His disgrace followed, and when he obeyed the royal summons to attend the Council at Northampton marked humiliations were heaped upon him. At this Council a case came up against Thomas in which the great vexed question of the competency of non-ecclesiastics to pass judgment upon an ecclesiastic had to be settled. No decision being arrived at the King broke up the Council in anger. It is unnecessary to detail the bickerings, and disputes, and quarrels which followed. Suffice it to say that at length Thomas contrived to escape to the Papal Court at Sens.

During his absence the famous Assize of Clarendon was passed,—a series of laws framed as a complete reform of the system of administering justice, of which one of the most important was a hard hit at the principle of ecclesiastical Privilege of Order, as it laid down that no privilege of order could harbour an offender against the King's officers. This was in 1166.

Thomas was now made Papal Legate for England, and at once exercised his power by excommunicating Henry's chief agents. Henry retaliated by virtually deposing Thomas from the Archbishopric, and by making it penal for anybody to admit his supremacy. So the miserable quarrel continued—Thomas fulminating excommunications from Sens, Henry hurling back defiance.

At length, from political motives, Henry performed an unheard of act—caused his boy son Henry to be crowned by the Archbishop of York. This roused the Church party, and Henry was probably convinced that he had gone too far as he met Thomas in Normandy, and to all appearance arranged amicably for his return to England in full possession of his dignities.

Thomas, with a pathetic farewell to the Bishop of Paris—" *Vado in Angliam mori,*"—returned, not because be believed in the King's sincerity, but from a stern sense of duty, and with a determination to do it, and at once excommunicated all who had taken part in the late coronation.

He landed at Sandwich and proceeded straight to Canterbury. Lyttelton thus describes the journey : " On the road thither he was met by all the poor of the country, who in great multitudes attended him to the city. The parish priests also came in solemn pomp to meet him with their crosses in their hands, and the pageantry was closed by the monks of Canterbury, who received him into their convent with the ringing of bells, the music of organs, and with hymns of praise to God."

On Christmas Day, 1170, he preached in the Cathedral, and publicly excommunicated Robert and Randolph de Broc, who had been foremost in persecuting him. Henry was in Normandy when all this news reached him, and, bursting forth into one of his characteristic furies, he uttered the historic words which sent four knights across the sea to Hythe, to Saltwood Castle, where they arranged their plan, and along the old Roman Stone Street to Canterbury, where, on the night of December 29th, 1170, they accomplished their master's vengeance.

All night "Becket's" body seems to have lain in the transept still known as the Martyrdom, although retaining scarcely any of its original features, but the next day the monks, fearful of a threat uttered by Robert de Broc that if the body was not removed it would be torn asunder and cast into the dung pit, took it away secretly to the remotest chapel East of the apse of Ernulf's crypt, but again it was removed behind the chapel of Our Lady.

Miracles began to be performed at once, but for twelve months the Cathedral remained silent, bereft of its hangings, and desolate. Henry's remorse amounted almost to loss of reason, and for weeks he shut himself up, refused to see anybody, and passed his time in prayer and penance.

On December 21st, 1171, the Cathedral was re-opened for divine service, and pilgrimages from all parts, not only of England, but of Europe, became the rage, and even the erstwhile foes of Becket did penance. In 1174 the King in person performed penance. He walked barefooted from St. Dunstan's to the Cathedral, and placing his hand in one of the apertures of the tomb, which was still in the crypt, he was flagellated, and passed the night there.

He repeated the penance next year with his son, again in 1178, and again in 1181.

With the death of Thomas à Becket we may close our survey of Kent during this reign. The county seems to have been free from disturbing influences, and, from the number of charters granted to towns during the next hundred years, we may suppose that it was not only slowly and surely regaining its old unique industrial character, but extending its foreign trade. Sandwich, Dover, Hythe, and Romney were its principal ports, although Fordwich, then accessible for ships of burthen from the sea, was a place of importance, and even at the time of the Domesday survey possessed ten mills and seven fisheries. The Weald too was gradually being opened up, *den* place names began to be frequently mentioned, but, as the earliest allusion to the Wealden iron industry dates from the thirteenth century, we must suppose that the Roman methods of extracting metal from ore—so rough that the early Sussex workers often found that it paid them better to treat the *scoriæ* of the Roman furnaces than to dig out fresh ore—had been forgotten, and that what at a later period made the wealth of this country was left untouched.

B. RICHARD I. 1189-1199.

The reign of Richard the First, so far as Kent is concerned, may be treated in a few words.

In 1189 the King held a great Council of the Realm at Canterbury, at which William King of Scotland attended, and Richard renounced sovereignty over that Kingdom. After this the King started from Dover for the Crusades. He returned after his captivity in Germany, in 1194, and by way of thanksgiving for his escape walked from Sandwich to Canterbury in penitential garb.

C. JOHN. 1199-1216.

The bad King John—for even this whitewashing age has been obliged to leave John as black as it found him— had some important dealings with our county.

In 1201, in order to spite the Archbishop of Canterbury by putting him to vast expense because the King con ceived that he kept Christmas in a style more befitting a monarch than a subject, he had himself crowned a second time. In 1203 John kept Christmas in high state at Canterbury. He was frequently at Chilham Castle, then a Royal manor, but with the Palace at Eltham, called by his name, he had no more to do than had Julius Cæsar, for the very sufficient reason that it was not built.

The death of Archbishop Hubert at the Teynham Manor House in 1203 brought about the troubles of this reign. Every election to the Archbishopric of Canterbury was an occasion of bitter dispute between the Bishops and the monks of Christ Church. Upon this occasion the monks quietly elected their man and sent him off to Rome to receive the Papal confirmation, and the Bishops, with whom was the King, elected their man, John de Gray, justiciary and bishop of Norwich.

Pope Innocent the Third, who resented the Royal and Prelatical election as an act of tyranny on the part of the Crown, when appealed to set both candidates aside and insisted that Stephen Langton, an Englishman, should occupy the high position. Such interference with the rights both of the English Church and the English Crown aroused the wrath of the nation, and John, for once backed up by all parties, refused to elect Langton and defied the Pope.

Thereupon the Pope placed the whole Kingdom under an interdict—no mere harmless fulmination in those days, —and for four years there was a suspension of all public religious performances throughout the land. John then threatened retaliation, whereupon the Pope first excommunicated him and then published a crusade against King and people, and selected Philip of France to lead it.

John's answer to this was to assemble an army of 60,000 men on Barham Downs, at the same time that the Cinque Ports Fleet, ever faithful to John, sailed across the Channel, met the French Fleet, fought it, and burned a hundred ships. This naval battle in 1213 is believed to be the first recorded in our annals in which manœuvring under canvas was resorted to to any extent. Mr. Clark Russell says that the battle afterwards fought by Hubert de Burgh off Deal was the first thus signalised. At any rate, the development of our national navy may be fairly considered to have been begun in this reign.

But the kingly spirit which had prompted some such noble answer to the Pope's legate as that which Shakespeare puts into the mouth of John, beginning :

" What earthy name to interrogatories
Can task the free breath of a sacred King ? "

was failing. John could place no reliance upon the huge army on Barham Downs, composed largely as it was of Welsh and Flemish mercenaries. He was fast alienating the barons by his brutal and arbitrary behaviour. The men of Kent were true to him, but the men of Kent were but a fraction of the armed force of the Kingdom. He was terrified at being alone in his defiance of the tremendous power of the Holy See, backed as it was by the armies of the ablest monarch in Christendom.

He had an interview with Stephen Langton—probably at Chilham Castle, and upon the news that Pandulph, the papal legate, was over the water, he invited him to England.

The first meeting between King and Cardinal was held in April, 1213, at Ewell, a grange belonging to the Commandery of Knights Templars at Swingfield—a fact still memorialised by the name Temple Ewell, which is sometimes used, and that of the Temple Farm hard by, whilst, according to Mr. Moore, a spot close to the latter is called Jerusalem.

On May 25th, 1213, John had a second interview with Pandulph ; this time at the *domus* of the Knights Templars on or near Bredenstone Hill, near Dover, the result being that he laid his crown and sceptre at Pandulph's feet, received them back as vassal of the Pope, agreed to the installation of Stephen Langton as Archbishop of Canterbury, and to pay 1,000 marks annually as the rental of England and Ireland.

A roar of rage and shame burst forth from end to end of England at the news of this dastardly act,—and yet, like more than one other event which at the time seemed a national calamity, it proved in a double sense the salvation of England.

The barons, backed for once by the people, except those of Kent, fiercely denounced him. The first result of their defection was the defeat of John by the French at Bouvines in 1214, and the second was the granting of the Great Charter.

If it is impossible to over-estimate the importance of the latter, the value of the former is scarcely less remarkable. " It must be remembered that from 1066 the English were ruled by an alien race, and that England was far more an appanage of Normandy than was Normandy of England. It seemed probable that the Norman Kings of England would reduce the whole of France under their sway, and establish an empire extending from the Scottish Border to the Pyrenees. Had they done so England would never have had a separate existence, but would have been a province of France. She owes her escape from this calamity to an event which some historians have represented as a misfortune—the separation of England and Normandy. Had John been like his predecessors and Philip Augustus like his the Plantagenet dynasty would have ruled the united Empire of England, Ireland, France, and probably Scotland. But just at this conjuncture France was ruled by a prince of great vigour and ability, England by a trifler and a coward.

John was driven from Normandy, and the Norman nobles, compelled to choose between England and the Continent, shut up by the sea with those whom they had hitherto oppressed and despised, came to regard England as their country and Englishmen as their countrymen. The two races, so long hostile, soon found that they had common interests and common enemies ; both were alike aggrieved by the tyranny of a bad King; they began to draw near to each other in friendship, and the first pledge of their reconciliation was the Great Charter, extorted from a tyrant by their common exertions, and framed for their common benefit."

We have quoted the above at length from Macaulay, as bearing upon the history of our county, inasmuch as in Kent was struck the blow which freed England from the tryanny of a brutal and incapable King by alienating his barons and his people. If John had continued to defy the Pope there is little doubt that Philip Augustus would have landed, have marched through the island, and have tightened the bonds which made England an appanage of Normandy.

It is interesting to note with reference to the Great Charter that the copy familiar to all who have visited the MSS. Room in the British Museum is that which Sir Edward Dering gave to Sir Robert Cotton, and which had been found in Dover Castle in 1630, whereto it had been taken by Hubert de Burgh, Chief Justiciar of England and Governor of the Castle.

It is hardly necessary to say that John had not the smallest intention of observing a Charter wrung from him *vim et armis*. If he had lost the support of the barons and of the majority of Englishmen by his action at Ewell, he had gained the Pope, and the Cinque Ports Fleet was still true to him. John applied to the Pope, who excommunicated the barons and released John from his obligations to them, which had no effect, and enlisted an army of Flemish mercenaries which alarmed the barons and set them on the war path. They seized Rochester Castle, which was immediately besieged by John, but the defence, despite the lack of assistance from London, the baronial head-quarters, was gallant, and three months elapsed ere starvation effected what arms had failed to do.

A miserable war between King and barons followed, but as Kent was with the King she seems to have escaped the desolation and misery which accompanied the campaign in other counties. Fortune favoured John for once, and the barons in despair invited Louis, eldest son of the King of France, to be King of England, and in 1216 he set sail for England with 700 ships. Stormy weather and the Cinque Ports fleet kept him in check for a while, but he at length landed at Stonar, took Canterbury and Rochester, and then John, unaided by the fulminations of his ally, the pope, against Louis, lost the support of the Kent men (except the garrison of Dover Castle) who declared for Louis and the barons.

Louis went on to London, and although not actually crowned, practically reigned as King of England.

Dover Castle, under the care of the gallant Hubert de Burgh, still held out for John, as did the Cinque Ports fleet, and Louis tried every means to reduce it, but without success. Perhaps, without being accused of too much county bias, we may agree with Lambarde that this fidelity of the Kent men to John in no small degree contributed to the maintenance of the position won by England when she lost the battle of Bouvines—independence of Normandy. At any rate the tide of luck seemed to be turning in favour of John when he died, 1216.

D. HENRY III. 1216-1272.

Although John had named his son Henry as his successor, and the majority of the baronage supported him, Louis the Dauphin had by no means abandoned the quest on which he had come. He went to France for reinforcements, but the Cinque Ports fleet instantly prepared to prevent his return. He, however, contrived to land at Stonar, burned Sandwich, and again attacked Dover Castle and with no more success than before. In the meanwhile other troops of his had been badly defeated at Lincoln, and he was forced to ask for further reinforcements from France. Eighty ships accordingly were assembled at Calais under Eustace the Monk, and put to sea with the intent of rounding the North Foreland and proceeding to London. Hubert de Burgh heard of this and appealed to the Cinque Ports, saying, " if these people land England is lost ; let us therefore boldly meet them, for God is with us, and they are excommunicate."

At Dover were sixteen large ships and some smaller.

These the townsmen and fisherman got out, and Hubert de Burgh's men at arms formed their crews. The little fleet was manœuvred so as to get between the Frenchmen and Calais; Eustace naturally imagined that the English object was the plunder of Calais, and laughed, for he had left that port well protected. Hubert's real plan, however, was to secure the windward position, in which he succeeded, came to close quarters, with the result that the Frenchmen were massacred, and that of their eighty ships only fifteen escaped.

Froissart thus describes a sea fight of the period : " The bowmen and archers began the engagement with a volley of arrows; as soon as their ships came in contact they were fastened together with chains and hooks; powder of lime was scattered in the air that it might be carried by the wind into the eyes of the enemy, and the English, leaping on board with axes in their hands, rendered the ships unmanageable by cutting away the rigging."

This great victory is thus spoken of by Mr. Hannay : " The trial stroke of the English navy was a master stroke. No more admirably planned, no more timely, no more fruitful battle has ever been fought by Englishmen on water. It settled for ever the question how best this country is to be defended. In after times, during the Armada year and later, there have been found men to talk of trusting to land defences; but the sagacity of Englishmen has taught them to rely on the Navy first, and that protection has never wholly failed us in six hundred and eighty years. The battle is curiously similar to the long list of conflicts with the French which were to follow it. The enemy is found carrying out a scheme of attack on our territory, and so intent upon his ultimate object as to neglect to attack our ships first. Hubert de Burgh, acting exactly as Hawke, Rodney, Hood, or Nelson would have done, manœuvres for the " weather gage," the position to windward, falls upon the Frenchman on his way, and wrecks his carefully laid scheme at a blow."

It is a proud fact never to be lost sight of by a true Kent man that the foundation of our magnificent naval dominion, and hence of our colonial empire, was laid by these gallant if somewhat unscrupulous thirteenth century men of the Cinque Ports.

For two hundred years the Cinque Ports navy was practically the Royal Navy of England, and the only bulwark against foreign invasion; for a still longer period the chief military ports of the Kingdom were those of Kent; and almost to our own era the chief material for the construction of our national " wooden walls " was obtained from the forests of the Kent and Sussex Weald. (See Appendix C.   The Cinque Ports).

After the naval victory mentioned above, Louis, having obtained a loan from the City of London, returned to France for good.

When William, Earl Mareschal, who had been appointed Regent of the Kingdom, died in 1219, he was succeeded by Hubert de Burgh, who now reached the apex of his chequered career. Too much of a patriot to suit the easily influenced young King, and accused by the jealous barons of extortion and avarice, he found himself attacked on all sides, and after an almost absolute rule of more than eight years as Justiciar, Earl of Kent, Constable of Dover Castle, Warden of the Cinque Ports, Warden of the Welsh Marches, and lord over many Castles, he was arrested, imprisoned, and finally released, to die in obscurity in 1243.

We may note by the way how closely associated with our county were the three men who stand out prominently in these dark reigns of John and Henry III. as patriots and champions of English freedom—Stephen Langton, Hubert de Burgh, and Simon de Montfort.

In 1220 the remains of St. Thomas à Becket, together with some four hundred relics, prominent among which was the arm of St. George, were " translated " with great pomp from the new West Crypt to the magnificent shrine in the Trinity chapel. There were present the King,

Pandulph the Pope's legate, Archbishop Langton, the Archbishop of Rheims, Hubert de Burgh, bishops, and "four great lordlings," and these carried the coffin and set it in the shrine. Until the fourteenth century the shrine stood alone in the Trinity chapel, but later it had for neighbours the tombs of the Black Prince, Henry the Fourth and his wife, and Archbishop Courtenay.

After the "translation" there was a sumptuous entertainment at the Archbishop's palace ; the Archbishop supplied hay and oats for the horses of all who came from London, and the conduits in Canterbury streets ran wine.

This year more than £20,000 was received in offerings at the shrine.

Passing over several years, uneventful so far as the County of Kent is concerned, but marked by misery and disaffection amongst all classes, and an utter lawlessness, we come to the year 1258, when the famous "Mad" Parliament of Oxford was held. A sinister sign of the times was that the barons who attended came fully armed and accompanied by their retainers, by which show of force they wrung from the King an oath to maintain the statutes of the Great Charter, and, what was especially significant as a proof that the process of cutting England adrift from the Continent had been completed, that the Castle of Dover and others, and the Cinque Ports should henceforth only have Englishmen for Governors.

In addition to these, the principal of the Provisions of Oxford, as they are called, were :

    1.—Supply to depend upon redress of grievances.
    2.—Four Knights to be chosen by each county to point out the local grievances.
    3.—Three sessions of Parliament to be held every year.

But the King had no more intention of keeping these Provisions than had his predecessor of keeping the Great Charter, and on the plea that his oath had been extorted from him by force he got the Pope to abrogate it.

The barons flared up. On their side they had been

acting selfishly and foolishly in aiming at the establishment of an aristocratic despotism, but that laws solemnly made and ratified should be cast aside at the whim of an unpatriotic King was too much. Simon de Montfort here comes to the front ; hitherto he had been regarded as a scheming ambitious foreigner, but as Earl of Leicester, and as being related to the King by his marriage with Henry's sister, widow of the late Earl Mareschal, he was powerful, and he was elected popular leader.

Henry prepared to assert his claims by arms, and the barons acted correspondingly.

Before war actually broke out an attempt to settle the dispute was made by referring it to the judgment of the King of France, but as he decided entirely against the barons, annulled the Provisions of Oxford, and gave all the power back to the King which they had denied him, the barons determined upon war.

De Montfort had been elected leader, but a strong feeling amongst the barons that he had other aims than those he professed to champion, drove him into exile, from which he was recalled in 1262.

It is not to our purpose to detail the miserable condition of war which came over the land on the top of a miserable condition of peace. Kent and the Cinque Ports stood by the barons ; Rochester Castle, held for the King, was unsuccessfully besieged, Tunbridge Castle was taken by him, the land was abandoned to freelances and outlaws, and as the Royal Armies swept through Kent into Sussex they perpetrated every excess, for, although the people were universally against the King, he was in possession of most of the strong places, except the Cinque Ports.

In 1264 De Montfort and the barons utterly defeated the Royal Army at Lewes ; Henry was taken prisoner and passed into the personal charge of De Montfort; his sons Edward and Henry were held as hostages for the observance of the Provisions of Oxford, and Earl Simon held Court in almost regal state at Canterbury In

December a Parliament was called which is for ever
remarkable as being the first genuinely popular national
assembly, the first occasion when burgher and trader,
baron, knight, and bishop, sat side by side. Whether
De Montfort's Parliament shewed us, as Mr. Green
thinks, "the large and prescient nature" of his designs, or
whether, as Mr. Hallam thinks, by summoning two
citizens from each borough and thus appealing to the
people rather than to the barons, he was endeavouring to
ingratiate himself with his own faction, mindful rather of
personal gain than of public weal, it is not easy to judge.
The writs are still extant by which each sheriff is directed
to return two lawful, good, and discreet Knights for his
shire.

Instantly at the news of Lewes, Eleanor the spirited
queen of Henry, the "noble virago" as Matthew of
Westminster calls her, spared neither trouble nor expense
in order to rescue him, and gathered together on the
opposite coast an enormous army. To meet the threatened
invasion De Montfort assembled by edict to every city,
town, and village, an army on Barham Downs, "so great
a multitude both of horse and foot united in one mass,
powerful for war against the foreigners, that you would
not have believed it to exist in England," but the Queen's
army was wind-bound and dispersed, and De Montfort's
levies did the same.

At length Prince Edward escaped from confinement;
many of the barons deserted De Montfort, partly because
they resented his too stern and literal sense of justice,
partly from sympathy with fallen royalty; the royal army
defeated the younger De Montfort at Kenilworth before
his father could reach him with reinforcements, and
marched on to meet the old Earl, who, with King Henry
in his train as a hostage, was hurrying from Wales.

At Evesham Simon de Montfort was amazed to see the
Royal Army with Prince Edward at its head, and saw
that he was entrapped, for the Avon forms a loop round
the town on three sides, whilst the fourth is blocked by a

hill called the Green, down which poured the royal troops on the ominously dark morning of August 4th, 1265. "By the arm of St. James, they come on well!" exclaimed the old warrior, "but it was from me they learned it! Let us commend our souls to God, for our bodies are the foes!" What followed was more of a butchery than a battle. "The murder of Evesham," Robert of Gloucester calls it. De Montfort, fighting valiantly to the last, was killed, and his head carried on a pole to Wigmore. Of his forces killed an old rhymer says :

"The number non wrote, for tell them mot no man,
Bot He that alle wrote, and alle thing ses and can."

Under the title of "Sir Simon the Righteous," De Montfort long reigned affectionately and reverently in the memory of the people, and many healing miracles were performed upon people afflicted who were encircled with his "measure" or girdle. Mr. Furley gives a list of twelve Kentish people thus cured.

De Montfort was described as "too great for a subject, which had hee not beene, he must have been numbered amongst the worthiest of his time."

There is a remarkable poem extant, written after the Battle of Lewes, in which the barons give as their motives for war the necessity of reform. A stanza translated from the Latin runs :

"May the Lord bless Simon de Montfort, and also his sons and his army who, exposing themselves magnanimously to death, fought valiantly, condoling the lamentable lot of the English who, trodden under foot, had languished under hard rulers, like the people of Israel under Pharaoh, groaning under a tyrannical devastation."

So Henry was established on the throne : he kept the Christmas of 1271 at Eltham, now a royal palace, and died in 1272.

NOTES ON PART I.

The miserable condition of the people of England, which was especially marked during the turbulent reign of John, reached its climax in the reign of Henry III. The groans of the lower classes were vented throughout these two reigns in passionate outbursts of satirical poetry in which the vices and extravagance of the nobles, the venality of the judges, and the alternate oppression from the Wolves and the Foxes, as the Barons and the clergy were aptly termed, were fearlessly scathed. Utter lawlessness prevailed throughout our country districts. "Nobody," says Canon Jessopp, speaking of Norfolk, and we may probably apply the words to Kent, "nobody seems to have resorted to the law to maintain a right or to redress a wrong till every other method had been tried. The law of the land was hideously cruel and merciless, and the gallows and pillory, never far from any man's door, were seldom allowed to remain long out of use. The ghastly frequency of the punishment by death tended to make people savage and blood-thirsty. It tended also to make men absolutely reckless of consequences when once their passions were roused."

And yet this was the century of the Great Charter, of the first popular Parliament, and of the revival of religion !

The two remarkable revolutions in the reign of Henry III. are the development of the English language, and the coming of the Friars.

By the loss of Normandy under John the barons were compelled to regard England as their home. Hence the gradual dying out of the Anglo-Norman language in home life. It was still retained at first as the tongue of the Court and the Law, but even at Court it gradually gave way to Central French, a distinct language from Norman French, and during the latter half of Henry III.'s reign the Law Reports were in Latin, although the Royal Proclamation of 1258 is in French and English. Although French was the language of the upper classes, private documents were in Latin, and in schools English was much used. Even in the reign of Henry II. there is evidence of Normans of high birth being able to speak English, and a Knight of that period was even obliged to get a tutor to teach his son French.

Little by little French became the tongue of a very few, and the exact equivalent of Chaucer's French of Stratford atte Bowe is found in the thirteenth century expression " He speaks the French of Marlborough."

So when Edward I. ascended the throne England was English from top to bottom. Hitherto, under the reigns of Richard, John, and Henry III. the body of the nation was English but the head was alien ; Edward was contemporaneously described as Edward the Fourth of the English, and Edward the Third of the sovereigns of Britain.

When the first Dominican Friars landed in England in 1221 they came to supply a long and sorely felt want. Hitherto the spiritual necessities of the people had been ministered to, when they were ministered to, by the Monks. But the Monks never left their buildings ; it was no business of theirs to go abroad in the exercise of their calling ; their notion of duty was to follow the routine of the monastery and not to be concerned with anything that went on outside its stately walls unless it touched their purses or their stomachs. If an ailing or starving wretch came to the monastery gates they physicked or fed him, but it was no part of their work to go out into the highways and ditches and find the halt, the maimed, the blind, and the distressed, and such an act as a hut bedside visitation would possibly have been considered derogatory to the dignity of the order, and as unbecoming the performer's gentle birth.

After the interdict placed on the Kingdom during John's reign, when for eight years the practice of religion was actually suspended throughout the land, the Monks relapsed into a condition of indolent sybaritism, so that the condition of the people, especially in the awful slums of the thirteenth century towns, was one of utter heathendom.

The Dominicans (Preachers or Black Friars) came in 1221 ; in 1224 the Franciscans (Friars Minor or Grey Friars) followed, and these little bands of noble, devoted men spread themselves abroad over the face of the dark, faithless, uncared for country, treading literally in the footsteps of the Apostles in that they took no money in their purses, no food in their scrips, and were bound to live and sleep unsheltered, to do the great work of moving the hitherto untouched hearts of the scum of the population in the truest spirit of their names—Mendicants. *(See Note C at end of Plantagenet Kent.)*

We may note here that it was in Canterbury that the Franciscan vanguard of nine men were first received and encouraged and made their mark. Simon Langton, the primate's brother, befriended them, so did Sir Henry de Sandwich and Lady Inclusa de Baginton (Birchington ?), and from Canterbury they went to London and to the Universities. With their later degeneracy we have nothing to do, but the movement was notable if only for the principle it accepted, that the religious strength of a nation should be looked for in its masses, and not as hitherto confined to its classes.

The reign of Henry the Third affords another instance of benefit accruing from apparent calamity. If England had not been conquered by William, if Normandy had not been lost by John, if a strong prince like the first Edward had succeeded John, our *insularity*, the very secret of our national prosperity and glory, would have been a fact of much later time if it had ever become a fact at all. Briefly the salient points of the reign were :

1.—Normans and English became united.

2.—A strong hankering manifest after the laws of Edward the Confessor.

3.—Growth of the spirit of representation.

4.—In 1258 the first instance of supply being made to depend upon redress of grievances.

5.—The struggles of the barons to establish a check on royal authority produced Parliament.

And still, it is hard to believe with Hallam that "from the reign of Henry III. at least, the legal equality of all ranks of freemen below the peerage was to every essential purpose as complete as at present," although we know that slavery was declining. Still the improvement in the condition of the slaves was due rather to their development of powers of combination than to concessions made them by masters and laws.

A notable characteristic of the reign of Henry III., and one which had no small share in fomenting discontent among the miserable masses of the people, was the spread of luxury amongst the governing classes. The King set the example, for he was an outrageous dandy. "The most sumptuous and splendid garments ever seen in England," says Miss Strickland, "were worn at the Coronation of the young queen of Henry III." On this occasion the King himself was arrayed in a tissue of gold. From the Court the rage spread to the nobles. Such was the excess to which table gluttony was carried that a sumptuary law was passed that no more than two dishes were to be served at a meal. As the old-fashioned castle became to be felt inconvenient and uncomfortable as a dwelling place, the keeps were either much enlarged or altogether relinquished as residences except in time of siege, whilst more convenient apartments were erected in the entrance towers, a new arrangement which may be observed in Tunbridge Castle.

Painted glass was probably first used in English churches during this reign, perhaps at the building of the Lady Chapel of Westminster Abbey. The famous old windows in Canterbury Cathedral—the two in the North Aisle of the choir, in Trinity Chapel, the centre window of Becket's Crown, and the great west window, are believed to date from this period.

Glass windows even in the houses of the wealthy were not yet dreamed of. Here may be noted by the way that the sciences of glass window making and of building in brick seem to have utterly died out with the departure of the Romans. There is no brick domestic building extant in good repair older than the reign of Henry VI., but Queen's College and Clare Hall, Cambridge, and part of Eton College date from Edward IV. Even in the reign of Elizabeth glass windows were such costly rarities that noblemen carried them from place to place when they shifted their residences.

PART II.—THE REIGNS OF EDWARD I., II., III., AND
RICHARD II.

EDWARD I. 1272-1307.

If the History of England, according to Lord Macaulay,
properly begins with the reign of John, the history of
Englishmen in the strictest sense of the word begins with
Edward I.   Later on we shall give instances of the growth
of the English language as evidence of this ; at present,
speaking more generally, we see for the first time the
wearer of the English crown an Englishman by birth, by
appearance, and, above all, by character.

As Mr. Green says : " He is the first English King since
the Conquest who loves his people with a personal love,
and craves for their love back again, and it was this
distinction of character which earned him so fairly his
title of the English Justinian."

The early part of this reign was occupied with the
conquest of Wales, and Holinshed tells us that the Cinque
Ports fleet went to Anglesey, where " they bore themselves
right manfully."

Still, proud as we may be of the county's share in the
building up of the British Navy, we must not shut our
eyes to the fact that these Cinque Ports sea-dogs were sad
rascals, and that they as completely ruled the "narrow
seas " by piracy as did the West Country buccaneers of a
later date the Carribean and its approaches.   In fact this
piracy was so rampant that the prices of foreign goods in
England were enhanced, and the Ports themselves were
little better than nests of chartered sea robbers.   The
Cinque Ports ships were always fighting somebody : if not
a Frenchman or a Spaniard, then a Yarmouther, and one
of the last acts of Edward before he became King had
been to call a meeting of the Cinque Port barons at Shepway to punish them for acts of piracy.

In 1293 this piracy practice brought about a national war, and exemplifies the extent to which private warfare was carried. There was a row in a Norman or Gascon port between English and French sailors, the result being that a man was killed, and the Englishmen chased to their ships. Soon after the Frenchmen captured two out of six English ships, hung their crews together with dogs, and paraded the Channel defying the Englishmen. The four English ships which had escaped reported the matter at Dover ; Cinque Ports ships went over to Normandy, raided the shores, and accepted a challenge from the Frenchmen to fight the matter out in mid channel. This resulted in the defeat of the French and in declaration of war between the two countries.

Two years later the French sent a fleet of two hundred ships against England. Five galleys were detached to reconnoitre off New Romney, and one of them landed men at Hythe. The Kent men made a show of flight, but at the right moment turned, slew two hundred and fifty of the invaders, and burned their ship.

For this the French admiral landed at Dover and sacked the town and priory, but the country people, who seem always to have been in some sort of training for this kind of work, assembled and drove the French back to their ships with the loss of 800 men.

On the whole we have a right to believe that there was not a livelier neighbourhood in all England at this period than our Kentish coast, and we do not even except the Borderland of England and Scotland.

Between the years 1280 and 1287 England was afflicted by a series of disastrous inundations, storms, and frosts. It was during the last year that the great change in Romney Marsh, to which we alluded to in the chapter on Early Kent, took place, by which the fate of Romney as a port was sealed.

In 1293 fifty Kentish gentlemen accompanied Edward to the siege of Caerlaverock in Scotland (said to be the original of the Castle of Ellangowan in *Guy Mannering*), and were knighted for their services, which seem to have consisted chiefly in jousting with each other and with champion knights of the foe, for a regular sit-down siege, such as was that of Caerlaverock, was something of a picnic for the host outside the walls, however rough it may sometimes have been for the people inside.

Although not a peculiarly Kentish matter, it is impossible to pass over the reign of Edward I. without some consideration of his claim to the title of " the English Justinian."

In 1279 a severe blow was dealt the temporal power of the clergy by the Statute of Mortmain, by which religious bodies were forbidden to hold lands without royal permission. Hitherto, land held by a Corporation—religious or secular—not being capable of wardship or marriage, paid nothing to the lord, was in fact held in *mortuâ manu*. The monks by their influence over dying men contrived to get an enormous amounty of property into their hands, which contributed nothing to the military service of the country. Moreover, Corporations rarely parted with their lands, so that the business of transfer became quite stagnant. But for this law it seemed likely that the greater part of the land in the kingdom would become church property.

In 1282 was passed the Statute of Merchants. This enabled traders to recover debts by appropriating the rents of a certain portion of debtors' lands.

As regards the County of Kent, Edward's mercantile legislation was most important. The foreign trade was developing by leaps and bounds. The development of town life was equally remarkable. Trades' Guilds were being formed everywhere. There was constant intercourse with Flanders, especially Bruges, with Gascony, the Rhineland, and Spain for wines; with Venice, Lombardy, the Hanse Towns, and the Levant; the coal trade of the North was becoming important; foreign merchants were afforded every encouragement and protection, and the outcome of all this activity and enterprise was that the merchants became a power in the land in that they shared with the Lombards, who had replaced the expelled Jews, the distinction of being the Royal bankers. This was the age which produced Whittington, Canynge of Bristol, and the De la Poles, afterwards Dukes of Suffolk. In fact, although the Soldier still led Society, the Merchant, in an age of which one of the chief characteristics was a general feeling of revolt against clerical predominance in politics and society, was edging out the ecclesiastic.

The Statute of Quia Emptores, 1290, was a retrograde Act aimed at limiting the power of the new classes of yeomen and squires who were springing up with the spread of commerce, inasmuch as it obliged sub-tenants to hold directly of the lord and not of a tenant. It restricted, in fact, subinfeudation.

The Statute of De Donis enacted that land given to a man and the heirs of his body should go to his issue in regular succession so long as any existed, and on failure of issue would revert to the donor. This established entails, and was obtained by the nobility who wished to perpetuate their possessions in their own families.

In the same year, 1285, was passed the Statute of Winchester, by which public order and security were secured by what was virtually a revival of the old system of Frank pledge—districts being held responsible for crimes committed within their limits ; watch and ward established in cities and towns, and highways ordered to be cleared for a space of 200 feet on either side.

But the chief claim of Edward I. to be called the English Justinian is based upon the following all-important principles established in Parliament :—

1.—No tax to be levied without consent of Parliament.

2.—Taxation to be dependent upon redress of grievances.

3.—" Aids " to be granted not by free tenants only, but by all free men.

4.—Taxation and representation inseparable.

And, by the Parliament of 1295, came a revival of the principles of Le Montfort's famous Parliament :—

1.—Knights of the Shire admitted. Hitherto they had been mere local deputies for taxation purposes.

2.—Boroughs represented : a distinct gain for the Crown, inasmuch as the burgesses as proper representatives made grants far more readily and generously than they had yielded to exaction.

3.—Clergy represented. But they did not appreciate it, held aloof at first from taking any part in parliamentary proceedings, and finally kept away altogether.

In 1287 was passed the Confirmatio Cartarum, by which all private property was secured from royal spoliation, and placed under the safeguard of the Great Council of the Realm ; and it was re-made law that no "aids" should be levied without the consent of this Council.

It is needless to say that all and every one of these wholesome and advanced provisions were broken in after times, but the credit of their conception and carrying through remains with these thirteenth century Englishmen, and with the great King who in an age of Divine Right of Kings fostered them and made them law.

In 1299 King Edward married his second wife, Margaret of France, at Canterbury, in that part of the Cathedral near the Martyrdom. Amongst his offerings at the shrine during his numerous visits was the crown of Scotland which had been found amongst the baggage of John Balliol at the time of his banishment.

In the same year the King made a progress through Kent, and the operation of the Statute of Winchester seems to have been satisfactory, if the comparatively rapid progress of the King be a criterion. Thus, he went from Canterbury to Dover in one day, and from Dover to Wye in one day. Thence he went on to Charing, Smarden, Cranbrook, Sissinghurst, Mayfield, Wateringbury, Leeds, and arrived at Canterbury on the twenty-fourth day.

In the same year, during the war with Scotland, the Cinque Ports Fleet engaged the enemy in the Solway, captured 28 ships, and routed 16,000 men.

In 1302 the King made another journey through Kent, going by Newenden, Ashford, Dover, and Canterbury, and is said to have given away three pounds, modern value, in charity each day.

In this year the Kentish clergy stood up against the demand of the King for a half of their possessions so that he might carry on the French war. The result was that the Vicar of Tenterden and sixteen others were arrested and imprisoned, undaunted by the fact that even the Archbishop's horses had been seized by the King.

In 1305 Prince Edward was banished from Court for some indiscretions in which he and his friend Piers Gaveston were concerned, and spent much of his time at Wye, Chartham, Canterbury, Ospringe, and Sutton-at-Hone.

During this reign Eltham became a royal palace, for, although Henry III. had spent the Christmas of 1270 there, it belonged to Beke, bishop of Durham, who, if he did not build it, much enlarged and beautified it, and gave it to Eleanor, Edward's queen.

Some of the finest English castles were built during this reign, but in Kent the only two now existing of that date seem to be Allington and Cooling.

EDWARD II. 1307-1327.

Edward stayed at Wye Manor House until the funeral of his father, and, according to Lambarde, kept the Christmas of 1307 there.

The first five years of the King's reign were spent in a continual contest between King and nobility about Piers Gaveston, the royal favourite, who was created Earl of Cornwall and placed at the head of affairs. The barons, now too English to view unmoved the honours heaped wholesale upon a foreigner who had only the qualities of a tournament Knight to recommend him, did not relax their efforts until Gaveston was exiled. But, upon Edward yielding to the complaint of the Commons of England about certain grievances, the favourite was recalled.

In 1307 there was one of those national outbursts against particular sects or communities as characteristic of modern as of old times, which resulted in the expulsion from England of the Knights Templars. There is much in common between this outburst against the Templars and that of a later age against the Wandering Friars. Both bodies were actuated at the commencement of their careers by principles of the sincerest virtue : both were bound by the strictest rules of abstinence and self-denial : both went astray from the simple paths they had marked out, became intoxicated with success, became wealthy, worldly, powerful political bodies, and lost sight of their original *raison d'être*. Both fell with a mighty fall.

The chief accusation brought against the Templars was that they had dealings with the supernatural world, and in evidence the rector of Godmersham said that a Templar had told him : " We have three vows, known only to ourselves, God, and the Devil." Their master was imprisoned at Canterbury, their houses put down, and their estates forfeited. The localities where they settled are still often recognisable by names such as St. John's near Ash, Temple Manor near Dartford, Temple Ewell and the neighbouring Temple Farm, St. John's Hole at Rodmersham, Temple Stroud and perhaps Temple House at Kennington.

In 1308 the King and his queen, Isabella of France, were at Dover, and during the preparations for the coronation resided at Eltham. The outrageous conduct of Piers Gaveston now brought about his ruin, he was executed, and the King took this so much to heart that he retired to Canterbury in sulky dudgeon. In 1312 Edward, afterwards King, was born, and in 1316 John of Eltham, at which place he was baptised. The Twelfth Night festival of this year was kept at Eltham with unusual magnificence.

GATEWAY
LEEDS CASTLE

In the meanwhile the Cinque Ports sailors were distinguishing themselves in their usual high-handed lawless fashion. They compelled foreigners to acknowledge English supremacy in the "narrow seas," a very flagrant instance of this being the case of a Fleming who was wronged by English sailors—probably robbed and thrashed—at a spot which was not within English dominions but which was washed by "English Sea," which acknowledged fact rendered his appeal to Edward as Lord of the Sea fruitless. Another instance was that of the Spanish ship *Blessed Mary* of Fuenterrabia, which was driven ashore and plundered by men of Romney, Rye and Winchelsea, and, when enquiry into the matter was ordered to be made, the Cinque Ports people prevented it by force. About this time the ship's rudder was invented : a second mast with fighting tops was introduced, and the elevated stern stage which afterwards became the poop.

The chief event of this reign connected with the history of Kent was the rebellion of Lord Badlesmere. After the death of Piers Gaveston the King took unto himself another favourite in the person of Hugh le Despenser, and his repetition of the old favouritism aroused the resentment of the barons, who were under the leadership of the Earl of Lancaster.

Badlesmere was a man in high office, being Warden of the Cinque Ports, and Governor of Bristol, Chilham, Tunbridge and Leeds Castles, which last he had got by exchange from the King, it having belonged to Edward I. as forming part of the dowry of his widow, Queen Margaret.

Edward, with the idea of strengthening himself as much as possible, wanted to have Leeds back. But Badlesmere, hearing of this, threw a garrison into it, and, leaving Lady Badlesmere under the charge of Sir John Colepeper, who no doubt had his instructions, proceeded to Canterbury, where he recruited men under the standard of the baronage.

Edward sent his queen, Isabella, the " she wolf of

H

France," under the pretext of a pilgrimage to Canterbury, to ask a lodging at Leeds. Lady Badlesmere, however, noting that the Queen was attended by a very much more warlike following than was consistent with a religious errand, refused her admittance, shots were fired from the castle, and some of the royal retinue slain.

The insulted Queen applied for redress to the King, who at once marched on Leeds, and Lady Badlesmere surrendered after showing fight for awhile. Badlesmere was depending upon Lancaster, who had formed an alliance with the Scots, but the King marched against him, defeated him at Boroughbridge in 1322, took a signal revenge by executing Lancaster, Badlesmere and Colepeper and so crushed the rebellion.

The remainder of this reign is the continued record of misery. Famine occasioned disturbances amongst the peasantry, who were in constant revolt ; the men of Kent held several meetings on Penenden Heath upon the subject of " aids " in payment of the knights of the shire at the rate of four shillings per diem, an imposition from which they considered the prevalent tenure of Gavelkind absolved them, and so, when the King was deposed and met his frightful death in Berkley Castle, the nation had sunk to the lowest estate.

EDWARD III. 1327-1377.

Bannockburn rankled deeply in the proud English heart, and the young King's first attention was to his unruly neighbours over the Border. But, if the mind of the people was bent upon avenging the defeat, the Kent men at any rate were in no mood to submit to a partial levy of contributions towards the war. And so in the very first year of the reign the Prior of Christ Church, Canterbury, was summoned to help the bailiffs and citizens in sending twelve men-at-arms to Newcastle against Bruce. He refused, pleading that lands held in francalmoigne were not liable to military burdens. The bailiffs and citizens of Canterbury held a meeting and passed a series of resolutions by which the monastery was practically boycotted and outlawed, for they rightly held it shame that the wearing of a tonsure should absolve a man from contributing to the national defence. The monks were locked in and threatened to be thrashed if they so much as showed their noses, no supplies were allowed to be sent in, and strangers were even forbidden to leave offerings at the shrine of St. Thomas.

The matter was smoothed over, but is important as one of the many evidences of the fast growing feeling against clericalism. Another is the fact that whereas in the 13th century no less than 296 new religious houses were built in England, in the 14th the total was but 64.

War with France—the famous Hundred Years' war— raged throughout this reign. Edward's claim to the French throne was utterly untenable, for the three sons of Philip le Bel had died without leaving male issue, but had left daughters. Edward claimed through his mother, a daughter of Philip, asserting that he as a male grand-child stood nearer to the succession than the females, although they were daughters of sons of Philip, and although the Salic law had been set aside.

The first part of the war was glorious to our arms both ashore and afloat.

In 1340 the English fleet gained a great victory over the French under Philip of Valois, at Sluys. There are three different accounts of the extent of the defeat, so we give them all. Hume says that 240 English ships defeated 400 French with 40,000 men on board, taking 230 ships and slaying 30,000 Frenchmen! Froissart places the French fleet at 120 large ships with 40,000 men; whilst a letter from Edward to his son speaks of 190 ships as the French fleet, of which all but 24 were taken, and adds that there were a great many English ladies on board his fleet going to attend the Queen at Ghent.

In 1346 Edward collected a great fleet for the siege

of Calais. Haklyt writes of "the roll of the huge fleete of Edward III. before Calice," that it consisted of 1,738 ships and 15,000 sailors. To this the Cinque Ports contributed 105 ships and 2,200 men, but already the western ports are pushing ahead, for on the list of contributions the leading Cinque Port is but eighth on the list,— Sandwich with 22 ships, Fowey leading with 47, Yarmouth coming next with 43, followed by Dartmouth, Plymouth, Shoreham, London and Bristol in the order named.

The ships carried no ordnance, although cannon was used in the same year at Crecy, but Jack fought in complete armour with crossbows, pike, and, above all, slings.

The siege of Calais lasted a year : we do not re-tell the beautiful story about Eustace de S. Pierre, not because we are of those who don't believe it, for we do, but because it has nothing to do with our History. At Crecy the van of the English army was led by the Earl of Stafford, Lord of Tunbridge Castle, and Lord Cobham with his contingent of Kentish bowmen contributed no little towards the victory.

All this glory of course meant heavy expense, and it was to get the wherewithal to meet this expense that Edward granted the following three important enactments.

1.—The illegality of taxation without consent of Parliament (no new thing, but the endorsement of a law which had but been too often more honoured in the breach than in the observance.)

2.—No alteration of laws without the consent of Parliament (Laws were made by the King, *at the request of the Commons*, with the assent of the Lords. The division of Parliament into two houses really dates from the last reign, but the strong distinction in functions herein marked does not appear before).

3.—The right to enquire into public abuses and to impeach.

(Thus, Sir John Lee was impeached for embezzlement in his office of Steward of the Household).

In accordance with this, a levy was made upon imported goods, and especially upon exported wool. In this levy Kent stands second to Norfolk in the amount granted. This leads us briefly to consider the Kentish wool trade, which was first fairly established in this reign.

Cloth had long been made in England, but Kent, says Philipot in 1659, was one of the first places where *fine* cloth was manufactured. In 1337 weavers and clothmen, principally Flemings, were invited over to work up the raw material which had hitherto been sent over to Flanders for that purpose. The inducements offered by Edward's agents are amusingly practical enough to be quoted:

"You have to be up very early in the morning, and sit up very late at night, and work very hard all the day, and yet you get nothing better than herrings and mouldy cheese to eat with your bread. Now take our advice. Go over to England, and learn my countrymen your trade, and you will find yourselves welcomed wherever you go. Besides, you will be fed on beef and mutton till your stomachs are full; your beds will be good, and your bedfellows better, for the richest yeoman in England will not disdain to marry their daughters to you, and they are such beauties that every foreigner commends them."

Special enactments were passed for the protection of these foreigners, and after a Parliament at Rochester, summoned expressly that commercial affairs should be discussed by commercial men, the following statutes were passed September 27th, 1337 :—

1.—Felony to carry wool out of the kingdom.

2.—Only cloth made in England to be worn.

3.—No foreign cloths to be imported.

4.—A command for the proper treatment of the foreign settlers, and franchises granted them.

The result shortly was that the Kentish Weald became
as busy a hive of industry as was later on the Sussex
Weald to be busy with iron manufacture.

The Walloons, as they were called, came over in great
numbers, and made Cranbrook their centre, selected, no
doubt, on account of the beds of fuller's earth in its
neighbourhood, besides abundance of water and timber,
all requisites for the proper milling of cloth.

The tradition still lingers that when Queen Elizabeth
came to Cranbrook during her progress through Kent in
1573, and stayed at the *George* Inn, and received a silver
cup from the town, she walked to Coursehorne Manor, a
mile distant, entirely upon Cranbrook broadcloth.

Goudhurst, Tenterden, Hawkhurst, and Headcorn were
also busy manufacturing towns, and relics may yet be
ferreted out by the curious explorer in the shape of fine
old cloth-masters' houses, traditional factories, and ponds
formed by the damming up of streams.

These cloth-masters and their descendants, known as
the "Grey Coats of Kent," formed a much respected
political power in the land.

Broad minded as Edward had shown himself in not
merely encouraging this industry, but in inviting
foreigners by special inducements to come over and teach
his people to do what had hitherto been done abroad,
much of the benefit which should have accrued was dis-
counted by sundry vexatious petty regulations which
limited the manufacture of certain articles to certain
districts, and which restricted the individual action of the
manufacturers. The supervision exercised by the Government measurers, weighers, and "aulnagers," was very
irritating; the Statute of the Staple, passed in 1353,
limited the number of towns in England and Wales where
wool before being exported had to be weighed by the
Standard and sealed by the Mayor to fifteen, and in Kent
the only Staple towns were Canterbury and Queenborough,
so that great delay and inconvenience was caused to
manufacturers by having to send their goods to one of

these places before it could be sold or exported. Besides, there were numerous petty limitations and restrictions which tied the hands of manufacturers, such as the prohibition to carry on more than one branch of the trade, or to have more than one mill and two apprentices, and the strict definition of colours to be employed.

However, the trade flourished, and the wealth accumulated in the county must have been very great.

The year 1348 will ever be memorable in the annals of England as the year of the Black Death.

It entered Europe by a Genoese port in the Straits of Kertch, whither it was brought by the overland caravan route from China. It arrived in England in August, 1348, at Melcombe Regis in Dorsetshire, travelled rapidly through Dorset, Devon, Somerset, Bristol, Gloucester, and Oxford, and reached London in November, whence it spread to the Eastern and Southern Counties, and through Yorkshire even to the Welsh mountains.

It was not so bad in Kent as elsewhere—for instance, in the West Riding of Yorkshire where two-thirds of the parish priests died, or in Nottinghamshire where one half died, or in Norwich where the proportion was about the same, but it was bad enough to leave traces which have hardly yet been effaced altogether.

It has been estimated that during the years 1348 and 1349 about one half the population of England, say about 2,500,000 people, died of this plague.

The symptoms were sudden swellings in the groin, armpit, or neck, red spots on breast and back, vomiting, blood spitting, and delirium. The attack was appallingly sudden, the illness rarely lasted more than three days, and the only escape from it seemed to be to get on to water.

With regard to its progress in Kent. The diocese of Canterbury was peculiarly exposed to contagion, as through it ran the chief roads to the Continent, and it possessed the seaports of Dover and Sandwich. Three archbishops succeeded in a few months, and one at least is known to have died of the plague. " In 1348," writes

Stephen Birchington, "arrived the common death of all people . . . . and by this pest barely one third part of mankind were left alive. Then also there was such a scarcity and dearth of priests that the parish churches remained almost unserved, and beneficed parsons, for fear of death, left the care of the benefices, not knowing where to go."

It is however recorded that out of the eighty monks at Christ Church, Canterbury, only four died, this singular exemption being attributed to the purity of the Monastery water. Two Masters were appointed to the Eastbridge Hospital in a very short time. The Prioress of St. Sepulchre's, and the Prior of St. Gregory's died. At Sandwich the cemetery is described as filled to overflowing. Sir Thomas Dene of Ospringe died on May 18th, 1349, and in less than four months was followed by his wife and two daughters.

As to the Diocese of Rochester, William Dene, a monk, writes :

"The Bishop of Rochester out of his small household lost four priests, five gentlemen, ten serving men, seven young clerks, and six pages, so that not a soul remained who might serve him in any office. At Malling he blessed two abbesses, and both quietly died, and there were only left four professed nuns and four novices. The bishop remained at Halling and Trottescliffe, and, alas for our sorrow! this mortality swept away so vast a multitude of both sexes that none could be found to carry the corpses to the grave. Men and women bare their own offspring on their shoulders to the church, and cast them into a common pit. From these there proceeded so great a stench that hardly anybody dared to cross the cemeteries."

As chaplains and paid clerics refused to work except at higher salaries, they were ordered to under pain of suspension.

Dene goes on :

"So great was the deficiency of labourers and workmen

of any kind that more than one-third of the land all over the kingdom remained uncultivated. The labourers and skilled workmen were imbued with such a spirit of rebellion that neither King, law, nor justice could curb them. The whole people for the greater part ever came more depraved, more prone to every vice, and more inclined than before to evil and wickedness, not thinking of death nor of the past plague, nor of their own salvation. And priests, little weighing the sacrifice of a contrite spirit, betook themselves to places where they could get larger stipends than in their own benefices."

The results of this terrible visitation were far reaching and long lasting. The first great immediate result was the utter dislocation of the labour market. In Kent entire districts remained waste, and grass sprang up in the streets of once busy towns, partly on account of emigration, but chiefly simply because there were no hands to work. Combinations of labourers for higher wages, the refusal of tenants to pay the old rents, and their evacuation of holdings when rents were not reduced led to the passing in 1349 of the Statute of Labourers, by which it was enacted that everyone under sixty, man or woman, free or bond, not having a livelihood or ground to cultivate, should be obliged to serve any employer who should require them at the old rate of wages in the neighbourhood. Migration to other counties was forbidden, and those who broke their agreements were imprisoned and branded with F for "false."

This was followed by what is probably the first regularly concocted strike in our history, and by a constant flow of emigration. To counteract this latter an order was sent December 1st, 1349, to the Mayor and Bailiffs of Sandwich and Romney, "to stop the passage beyond the sea of them that have no mandate, especially if they be Englishmen, excepting merchants, notaries, and the King's envoys."

Other proclamations followed to the effect that harvesters and others were not to claim more than the old wages,

that Abbots and employers of labour would be fined for
giving higher wages, and that almsgiving to vagrants was
to be discontinued.

Another result was a tremendous rise in prices,
especially of fish. Dene writes that there was such a
dearth and want of fish that many who had been wont to
live well had to content themselves with bread and
pottage, and that in Lent there was such a lack of fish
that four herrings were ordained to be sold for a penny.

Another important result was that bailiff farming by
land owners died out, and that as there was no capital
available for the working of farms, the ordinary leasehold,
such as we now have, came in. Thus tenant farmers
became numerous, the famous class of the English yeoman
was created, the land passed out of the hands of the old
feudal owners, and in Kent to a great extent sheep grazing
and pasture took the place of arable land.

Necessarily the wool trade of Kent was for a time
entirely paralysed.

The church, as we have seen, was sorely smitten by the
Plague. Such service as was performed was done by
novices, and in many churches there was no service at all.
Many ordinations of seculars had to be made to fill up,
somehow, the vacant places; the abuse of pluralities grew
apace, and the effect upon the monastic life was such that
it really never recovered. "In short," says Cunningham,
"the steady progress of the twelfth and thirteenth centuries
was suddenly checked in the fourteenth."

William Dene, before quoted, after describing the sad-
ness of the poor old bishop of Rochester in his retreat
at Trottescliffe says:

"In every manor of the bishopric buildings and walls
fell to ruins, and in that year there was scarcely a manor
that returned £100. In the monastery of Rochester there
was also such a scarcity of provisions that the community
were troubled with great want of food." The Prior however, he remarks, always managed to live well. The
bishop visited Malling and Lesnes and found them so poor

"that from the present age to the Day of Judgment they can never recover."

In 1352 the Prioress and nuns of St. James outside Canterbury were freed from the tax of one-fifteenth granted to the King, on account of their poverty. Even Christ Church was badly hit ; it lost cattle worth £790, and 1,200 acres of abbey lands were inundated by the sea because there was no labour to keep up the sea walls.

In 1359 the scarcity of clergy, and the troubles arising from the replacing of priests by scamps of all sorts, led to the placing of the clergy under the Labour Laws. Even in the architecture of the period following the Plague we see the shadow of this tremendous calamity. Church building was stopped, and to this day we may note the effect in the unfinished cathedral at Siena, and at home in the wanting western towers and the Bachelors' Aisle of St. Nicholas, Great Yarmouth. It has been observed too that the Perpendicular Style happened to succeed the Decorated just at the time when the paralysis of labour was most complete, and that this is the style which calls for the smallest play of imagination and fancy. Late fourteenth century stained glass too is a rarity, for even the great west window of Canterbury, dating from this period, is but a heterogenous collection of old glass.

We have seen that one great result of the Black Death was the debasement of ecclesiastical life by the almost necessary introduction into it of incongruous and ill-assorted elements. The fruits of this were not long in showing themselves, for in 1360 Wycliffe began to preach against the abuses in the church generally and against the Mendicant Friars in particular, and the Lollards became a power in the land. We may perhaps find three chief causes for the early success of the new movement :

1.—The increasing bitterness of the contest between Crown and Parliament with the Papacy.

2.—The strong feeling amongst the laity against the extravagance and dissoluteness of the clergy.

3.—The general European upheaval caused by the progress of learning and the unwillingness of the lower orders to submit to bondage.

As we have said, Wycliffe's chief attack was directed against the so-called Mendicant Friars, who, however, had swollen into rich and important communities who practised everything but what they preached, and through them, against the Papal power. "The burden of Wycliffe's teaching," says Mr. Froude, "was the exposure of the indolent fictions which passed under the name of religion in the established theory of the Church." Wycliffe's points were specially the disposition by the Pope of all the benefices in church patronage, his claim of first fruits, and the intrusion of foreign priests into English livings, as exemplified by the Archdeaconry of Canterbury, one of the richest English benefices, which was held by an Italian. "Great houses make not men holy," said the Reformer, and against these vast nurseries of vice and hypocrisy he sent his preachers, who spoke to the people in their own English tongue, with such success that until well into the next reign Lollardry was at any rate connived at. No doubt, over-zeal carried Wycliffe's disciples sometimes too far, for Hall the Chronicler speaks of the Lollards as resembling the Elizabethan Puritans, characterised by the moroseness which proscribed all cheerful amusements, an uncharitable malignity which made no distinction in condemning the established clergy, and a narrow prejudice which applied Jewish law to modern institutions. We shall have more to say about Lollardry under the two following reigns, but we allude to it here as being one of the results of that convulsed state of society consequent upon the Black Death which was to culminate in the great popular rising under Wat Tyler in the next reign.

In 1346 was instituted the Order of the Garter, and on the original roll are the names of three Kentish Knights, the Earl of Stafford, Governor of Tunbridge Castle ; Lord Burgherst, Warden of the Cinque Ports and Constable of Dover Castle ; and Sir Walter de Pavely.

In 1350 there was a sea fight off Winchelsea, known in history as " Les Espagnols Sur Mer," at which the King and Black Prince were present, resulting in the defeat of the Spaniards and the capture of seventeen of their ships. The English archers contributed chiefly to this victory.

In 1356 was won the glorious victory of Poictiers, and the next year the Black Prince arrived at Sandwich with his prisoner John, King of France, whence he passed by Canterbury, where he had a magnificent reception, to London, into which he made the famous entry familiar to the most juvenile readers of history. From London the French King was brought to Eltham Palace, where he was feasted and treated, according to the chivalrous usage of the day, rather as a guest than as a prisoner. It is no doubt from this circumstance that the grand old hall now standing is still known as King John's Palace, although our King John had no more to do with it than Julius Cæsar, for it was not built until the reign of Edward IV.

Four years later the French King obtained his release by the Treaty of Bretigny. He came by Dartford, rested at Rochester, dined at Sittingbourne, supped and slept at Ospringe. Thence he came to Canterbury, halting at the Leper Hospital of St. Nicholas, Harbledown, at all of which places he left presents, and to the shrine of St. Thomas, whereat he and his son Philip made offerings of jewels and money.

Finding, however, that he could not honourably abide by the terms of the Peace he voluntarily returned and lived at Eltham.

In 1360 the French landed at Winchelsea, burned the town, and committed atrocities in the country round about as black as those which the Black Prince afterwards committed in Guienne. It was after this destruction of Winchelsea that Edward I. planned the new town on the block system, never completed, but of which the traces are distinct to-day. This was an exciting and anxious period for our Kentish coast folk. Never a week passed without the bells being rung and the beacons which stood on every

church tower being fired to give alarm of a French or
Spanish landing.   Every countryman was a soldier, every
longshoreman a fighting sailor, every religious house and
manorial hall an armoury and a barrack.

In 1361 the Black Prince married his old love, his
cousin Joane, daughter of Edmund of Woodstock, Earl of
Kent, known as the Fair Maid of Kent, although she was
a widow and thirty-five years old.   In commemoration of
this the Prince founded a chantry in the crypt of Canterbury, afterwards used as the Huguenot Church.   Two of
the ceiling bosses of this chantry are adorned with portraits
in stone of himself and his bride—a branch of sculptural
art which became popular at about this time.

In 1368 the King was at Stonar—then a rival port to
Sandwich—and thence he sailed with his four sons for
Calais, starting between daybreak and sunrise and arriving
the same evening, which was considered a smartish bit of
work in those days.   In 1376 the Black Prince died in
the Archbishop's Palace at Canterbury *(See Note D at end
of Plantagenet Kent)*, after having tried the effects of the
waters of the spring at Harbledown, just under the old Leper
Hospital, which is still called the Black Prince's well, and
is still reputed a curative of sore throats.   He was buried
in the Cathedral.   The next year died the King.   Unhappily his reign, which was marked by so much that was
great and glorious, closed in dishonour and shame—our
arms unsuccessful in France, and our masses at home only
waiting for the opportunity to assert themselves, the
Church in a degenerate condition, and the great nobles
preparing amongst themselves the explosive train which
was to burst over the country with such fearful force in
less than a century's time.

RICHARD II.   1377-1402.

It was a troublous inheritance for the boy of eleven
who now succeeded to the crown, and the storm which
burst would have put upon their mettle the ablest and
most powerful of his predecessors.

It had been long gathering; indeed, the Rebellion of Wat Tyler, to which we allude, may be included amongst the results of the Black Death thirty years before, as well as being what Mr. Froude calls "a mischievous comment on Wycliffe's doings." That it was inevitable is evident from the nature of its surroundings, for it is notable that at the time of the Rebellion the condition of the people, so far from being as miserable as it had been, was characterised by such an amelioration that landlords and labour employers were complaining of the continual craving for "bettering themselves," and of the increasing daintiness of their subordinates.

The nobles were suspicious of the King, hated the clergy, and eyed with suspicion the growing power of the merchants; the nobles and the leading clergy were trying to keep down the labourers and serfs; labourers and serfs were trying to rise; the friars, once the champions of the poor, were now their plunderers; the church was wealthy, but shared no burdens; Piers Plowman's Creed, circulated in purer English than were the contemporary writings for the classes, had produced a profound effect amongst the masses, hitherto uninspired by any writing by one of themselves, and, like all uninspired masses, lacking cohesion, and almost unable to put in black and white what they wanted.

Generally speaking, the main springs at work were:

1.—The progressive improvement of Society.
2.—There gradual diffusion of knowledge.
3.—The increasing pressure of taxation.
4.—The perpetuality of War.

The Poll tax of three groats per head, levied 1379-1380, as Mr. Green says, "not only brought the pressure of war home to every household, but goaded into action precisely the class which was already seething with discontent."

It was John Ball, a Yorkshireman, although Froissart calls him "a mad priest of Kent," who ventilated the popular feelings. He was a parochial chaplain, a sort of artizan among ecclesiastics, whose duty it was to take care of churches, and his sermon upon the slavish doctrine enforced by the Statute of Labourers, with its famous text :

> " When Adam delved and Eve span,
> Who was then the gentleman ?"

procured his imprisonment at Maidstone by Treasurer Hales.

In 1381 Commissioners were sent into Kent to find out why the Poll Tax had failed to produce what was expected of it, and these men, rough and ready Jacks in office, under the pretext of discovering the real ages of women, often insulted them. Leg, the Kentish Commissioner, and his fellow, went to the house of John Tyler, at Dartford, and thus insulted his daughter. Leg was knocked down and killed by the infuriated father. The incident has, perhaps, been exaggerated in importance, but it was the spark which set the combustible mass in a blaze, a tremendous ferment ensued amongst the confederacies of villeins to obtain relief from burdensome feudal customs, and Wat Tyler, of Maidstone, or "John Rakestraw and Watt Tegheler, of Essex," were chosen popular leaders.

One party of the insurgents seems to have gone to Rochester, where Sir Simon Burley had imprisoned a Gravesend man, whom he claimed as his bondsman, and this man was released. At the same time Ball was released from Maidstone, and the Essex men, who had really first opened the ball, hearing of the Kentish movement, hastened up as allies. Another party went to Canterbury, released the prisoners from the castle, entered the house of William Medmenham, a manor steward, burned his books and rolls, seized the sheriff, ill-treated, if they did not kill, obnoxious individuals, found the roll of the three great subsidies, burned it, plundered houses, and were in armed possession of the city.

On June 12th the Kentish contingent assembled on Blackheath, and being joined there by men of Huntingdon, Cambridge, Essex, Sussex and Surrey, numbered about one hundred thousand. Then the mighty tide rolled on Londonwards.

The insurgents, after their excesses at Canterbury, seem to have made their march in tolerable order, but the exceedingly ill-timed rebuff of the Earl of Salisbury at their request for an audience with the king, to the effect that they were not properly dressed or in a fit condition to approach royalty, put an end to their moderation. Some say that it was this incident which inspired the preacher Ball with the distich text for his sermon.

At any rate, arrived in London they proceeded to acts of violence. John of Gaunt was particularly hateful to them for his acts of tyranny and outrages of sanctuary, despite the gloss which Shakespeare has cast over his memory, and they burned his palace in the Savoy. They poured into the Temple, pulled down the lawyers' houses and burned their books, rolls and deeds; they burned the Fleet prison; they burned the monastery of St. John of Jerusalem at Clerkenwell; they seized Hales the treasurer and Archbishop Sudbury, who had imprisoned Ball, and murdered them.

It was Sudbury who in 1370, when Bishop of London, met a party of pilgrims bound to Canterbury, stopped them, and told them they were fools if they expected to get plenary absolution for visiting Becket's shrine, whereupon a Kentish knight, Thomas of Alden, prophesied a bad end for him. Wat Tyler's special grievance against him was prodigal expenditure of public money. He was beheaded on Tower Hill and his head set on London Bridge. Miracles were said to be performed at his tomb in Canterbury; his head is still shown in the vestry of St. Gregory's church at Sudbury, and that it may be his has been perhaps confirmed by an examination made of his coffin at Canterbury in 1833, when it was found that in the place of the head was a ball of lead. At Mile End the King managed to pacify the Essex rebels under Jack Straw, but Tyler liked not the security given, and at Smithfield met the King and made the following demands :

1.—Abolition of serfdom.

2—.Liberty of buying and selling in all fairs and markets.

I

3.—Reduction of land rents to a greater equality.

4.—General pardon.

From the nature of the first demand it would appear that slavery was not extinct in England. This was probably not so much a demand of the Kent men as of those from the other associated counties, for there was certainly less personal slavery in our county than elsewhere, not only on account of the peculiarly free character of the Kentish tenures, but from the fact that the greater number of Kentish villeins were in ecclesiastical service, and therefore not so liable to be treated as mere animals as if they were under lay lords. It was probably accepted as a legal maxim under Edward I. that everybody of Kentish origin was free from personal villeinage, and although the rule was not always observed, it was generally allowed. An examination into Gavelkind tenure will show that personal slavery had little or no chance of existence. The second demand was a blow at the monstrous abuse of the "rights" of certain corporations, communities, and individuals to control markets, at the monopolies of rich abbots and merchants, and their efforts to prevent freedom of trade, and to hinder by tolls the entrance of produce into towns.

This the King granted, and he acceded also to the demand that all warrens in parks and fields should be common—this was a hit at the severe game laws of the period.

Then comes the episode of the death of Wat Tyler and of the young King's presence of mind. Whether Wat Tyler's head had been turned by the apparently ready concessions made and he behaved insolently, or whether Sir William Walworth had an inkling that an order had been given by Tyler that at a given signal the King's people, but not the King himself, were to be killed, and thought to anticipate it by knocking the rebel leader down, cannot be decided. At any rate Tyler was knocked down and killed, the Kent men at once bent their bows and prepared to avenge their leader, and without doubt a bloody conflict would have resulted but for the cool gallantry of Richard, who rode forward, and exclaimed :

"Good people ! You want a leader ! I will be your leader ! "

This won the hearts of the crowd, and they peacefully followed the King into the fields and received his royal confirmation of the promises made.

The immediate danger over, however, the young King seems to have been persuaded that concessions extorted by force were unworthy of the royal dignity, revoked them, there was a general muster of the military tenants of the Crown, the rebels were hunted down and ruthlessly butchered, and John Ball, who had been the soul, as Tyler had been the arm, of the movement, was hung, drawn, and quartered.

The results of this famous Kentish rebellion were that the villeins were taught to combine for defence, and it led to enquiries into the tyrannies exercised over the people.

In 1382 Richard and his Queen, Anne of Bohemia, landed at Dover, whence they proceeded to Canterbury and Blackheath, where they were met by the Lord Mayor and citizens of London in full state.

It was in this year that Wycliffe was condemned by the National Synod under Archbishop Courtenay for his sermon against transubstantiation, his heterodox idea that an ecclesiastic who was himself in a state of mortal sin could and should have no control over the faithful, his assertion that Scripture prohibits ecclesiastics from holding temporal possessions, and that where repentance is sincere confession is useless.

No better proof however was lacking that Lollardry, although proceeded against, especially at Oxford, its hot-bed, was connived at during this reign than the fact that Wycliffe himself, its arch-priest, was allowed to end his days peaceably, having on the eve of his death completed his *magnum opus*—the Bible which bears his name.

The King kept the Christmas of 1386 at Eltham with great state.

In 1396 Parliament met at Eltham to discuss the
second marriage of the King with the "little Queen"
Isabella of France, and Froissart, who was present, speaks
enthusiastically of the magnificence of this Kentish palace
of the Kings of England. In the same year the marriage
was celebrated in the church of St. Nicholas in Calais.
There is nothing more in this reign connected with the
history of our county to detain us. How the King
during his closing years found himself friendless and alone
in his realm; how by the machinations of the unscrupulous
and powerful Henry of Bolingbroke, Duke of Lancaster,
he was confronted before Parliament by thirty-three
articles of accusation and deposed; how the Duke of
Northumberland by treachery obtained the Royal person
and confined him first in Leeds Castle, then at Flint
and lastly at Pontefract, are matters of national
history.

The last scene of his life, as told by Shakespeare, who
drew it from Holinshed, was royally magnificent. His
resistance to Sir Piers Exton and eight other assassins
was worthy of his warrior forbears; two of them he slew
ere Exton felled him from behind, and travellers two
centuries and a half later reported that tokens of the fray
were still visible in the chamber of death.

There are two other versions of Richard's death. One
is that he died of grief and self-starvation; the other
that his jailors starved him to death. Sir Walter Scott
alludes to a tradition that Richard escaped from Pontefract and got to Scotland, and, without absolutely
believing in it, adds that he deemed it worthy of grave
attention.

Under Richard our Navy was in a bad state; there
was no discipline on the ships, so that mutinies were
frequent, commanders were incapable, and provisioning
bad. In 1379 when Sir John Arundell's squadron was
overtaken by a storm, sixty *women* were thrown overboard! The French insulted our coasts, and the
Spaniards sailed up the Thames and burned part of
Gravesend.

ROOF OF HALL
ELTHAM

By the end of the Fourteenth Century, at which we have arrived, English became the established state and popular tongue. By a Statute of 1362 pleadings in the Courts of Law were ordered to be in English "because the French tongue is much unknown"; and yet this same Statute is in Norman French! By the year 1385 in all the grammar schools English was the prevailing language. Edward III., thoroughly English otherwise as he was, habitually spoke French. Indeed the few specimens of his English which have come down to us are the motto he bore on his shield at a tournament at Canterbury in 1349 :

" Hay ! Hay ! the wythe swan !
By Godes soul I am thy man !"

and expressions of his such as "It is as it is!" and "Ha! St. Edward! Ha! St. George!"

And the outcome of this development of a national tongue was naturally a national literature. The first poet worthy of the name since the Conquest was Laurence Minot, who, between the years 1333 and 1352 celebrated the victories of Edward III. in ten poems. The Vision of Piers Plowman, probably by William Langland, an allegory of life in the style of Bunyan's Pilgrim's Progress, of about 14,700 verses, came forth in 1362, and was followed some twenty years later by the still more famous Piers Plowman's Creed, a diatribe of the English peasant against the clergy.

Gower was of a Kentish family, but of his three poems only one, the *Confessio Amantis*, is written in English. Finally we have Chaucer who, although London born, probably resided in Kent, was a Kentish knight of the shire in 1381, and is best known by his Kentish Pilgrimage. "Certes" says he in 1392, "there be some that speke theyr poysy matter in Frenche, of whyche speche the French mennes have as good a fantasye (i.e., get as much fun out of) as we here in hearing French mennes Englyshe"—quite sufficient evidence that French had ceased to be the native tongue of Englishmen and was only known to those to whom it had been taught by a master.

As for our Kentish dialect, the best contemporary specimen extant is the *Ayenbite of Inwyt*, or the Remorse of Conscience, a literal translation of a French treatise by Dan Michel of Northgate, Canterbury, a brother of St. Augustine's monastery.

Although with no title to be placed under this particular period of history, we may append a few of the most striking features of the old Kentish dialect.

1.—Using ch instead of k.   Ex. : cherl for carl.
2.—   „   v for f.   „   vinger for finger.
3.—   „   z for s   „   zour for sour.
4.—Metathesis :   hirch for rich, gurt for great. (This peculiarity is also remarkable in Somersetshire, where the name Richard becomes Hurchard, 'red' becomes 'hurd,' and so on).
5.—Using ps for sp.   Ex. : waps for wasp.
6.—   „   g for y.
7.—   „   o for a.
8.—   „   e for a.   Ex. : epple for apple ; gled for glad.
9.—   „   e for i.   „   melk for milk.
10.—   „   y for ey.   „   gryhound for greyhound.
11.—   „   Reduplication of vowels.   Ex's. : bryead bread, che-ap for cheap.

PART III.—THE REIGNS OF HENRY IV., V., VI.; EDWARD IV. AND V.; AND RICHARD III.

HENRY IV. 1399-1413.

Henry, eldest son of Edward III.'s third son, John of Gaunt, practically elected himself King of England, with, of course, the assent of Parliament, although Edmund Mortimer, Earl of March, great grandson of Lionel, Duke of Clarence, second son of Edward III., really had a prior claim. He was, however, but a boy six years old, and was easily set aside. Under Richard II., as we have seen, Lollardry was connived at, but at the accession of the new King a general rectification of wrongs was looked for, and the tide turned strongly against the Wycliffites.

So in the second year of this reign was passed the Statute *De Heretico Comburendo*, which enacted that any heretic who relapsed or refused to abjure his opinions should be delivered over to the secular arm by the church and publicly burned. This is notable as the first penal religious Act in our history, by which is not to be understood that heretics were never burned before this date. On the contrary, they frequently were. This Act simply facilitated the process.

The danger apprehended from Lollardism was the close connection between it and the cause of popular liberty. What Piers Plowman's Creed did for the people as members of a body politic, as would-be free Englishmen, Wycliffe's Bible, Wycliffe's tracts against Romanism, and the plain, popular language in which his heterodoxy was set forth, supplemented and accentuated. So great had been this influence too, that, although the bulk of the Lollards were to be found among the people, sympathy with the teaching, if not actual conversion to it, had spread from the people up to the merchants, and even to the Knights.

During the reign of Henry IV. Lollardry spread so rapidly that the majority of the House of Commons were inclined to it, and they passed two petitions, one against the clergy, and one in favour of the Lollards, complaining of the excessive wealth and extravagance of the former, and praying for a repeal of the Act *De Heretico*.

In Kent the Lollards were very strong, and there is no doubt that in our county, although the above Act was a severe check, the new creed was cherished secretly by thousands up to the date of the Reformation.

In 1395 Sir John Oldcastle, of Cooling Castle, first appeared as a public Lollard agitator, openly championing the opinion that the Pope's power of excommunication should be limited. In 1409 the Archbishop of Canterbury complained that Oldcastle gave refuge to a man who did not fear to preach "contrary to our constitution and without asking either our leave or that of the diocesan of the place in the churches of St. Mary and St. Werburg in Hoo, Halstow, and Coulyng, and to blaspheme and mock at evangelical decrees and sanctions of the holy fathers, sowing damnably weeds and tares and heresies and errors." The chaplain was ordered to be arrested, Cooling church was interdicted, but this was taken off through the influence of Lady Oldcastle of Cobham. In 1413 Oldcastle was brought up before Archbishop Arundel, and gave his very unvarnished opinion about relics and images.

The rest of his career comes under the next reign.

Oldcastle's association with Kent does not end with his share in the Lollard movement. Mr. Halliwell, the Shakesperian commentator, considers that Sir John Oldcastle was the prototype of Sir John Falstaff. At any rate, the name of Sir John Oldcastle stood in the place of Sir John Falstaff until the time of printing the play of King Henry the Fourth ; and Mr. Payne Collier in support of Mr. Halliwell's theory quotes from a play by Field in 1618, entitled " Amends for Ladies :"—

> " Did you never see
> The play where the fat knight, hight Oldcastle,
> Did tell you truly what this honour was ?"

This can only apply to Falstaff's famous soliloquy in Henry IV.: Part I., Act 5, Scene 1.

Again, in the course of the play Prince Henry calls Falstaff, "My old lad of the Castle."

As we are on Shakesperian ground, we are reminded that the inimitable exploits of the Prince and his companions on Gads Hill took place in this reign.

In 1402 Henry married Joan of Navarre *by proxy* at Eltham, which became a favourite resort of the King and Queen. In 1406 Joan spent the summer at Leeds to avoid the plague which raged in London and the neighbourhood. In 1409 Christmas was spent in great state at Eltham.

Henry IV. lies in a splendid tomb of contemporary Decorated work in Canterbury Cathedral, and when his Queen died in 1437 she was laid beside him. There long obtained a tradition that the King's body was not there at all, based upon the assertion of one Clement Maydestone that he had helped to throw the Royal corpse overboard during a storm which arose as it was being conveyed from Westminster to Gravesend, and that the Royal coffin alone was placed in the tomb. An examination was made of the tomb in 1832, and the King's body is said to have been revealed, but the absence of such insignia as were always buried with a Royal body, and the presence of hay-bands and of a rude cross of wych-elm, such as a superstitious man would probably have put in after the commission of such sacrilege, would seem to corroborate tradition.

HENRY V. 1413-1422.

Shakespeare says that it was from Hampton that Henry V. sailed with the army which was to win Agincourt, but all older authorities say that Dover was the port of embarcation.

At any rate, it was at Dover that he landed after the victory, and Lingard describes how "the crowd plunged into the waves to meet him, and the Conquerer was carried in their arms from his vessel to the beach." His course towards London was one long triumphal procession, and on Blackheath the Lord Mayor and Aldermen of London and four hundred citizens clothed in scarlet met him.

Holinshed, however, remarks:

" The King, like a grave and sober personnage, and as one remembering from whom all victories are sent, seemed little to regard such vaine pompe and shews as were in triumphant sort devised for his welcoming home from so prosperous a journie; insomuch that he would not suffer his helmet to be carried before him, whereby might have appeared to the people the blowes and dints that were to be seene in the same; neither would he suffer any ditties to be made and sung by minstrels of his glorious victorie, for that he would have the praise and thanks altogether given to God."

Mr. Outram Tristram's remark upon which we entirely endorse: " A pious decision, but one which must have been extremely unsatisfactory to town councillors who had launched forth in the way of dress and decorations, and to the thousands of Londoners who had flocked out to Blackheath to see the show."

At Agincourt Sir Thomas Erpingham led a body of 300 Kentish bowmen, whose skilful disposition so as to catch the heavily mailed French cavalry in an ambush contributed in no small degree to the victory. Their banners are said to have been emblazoned with the device of a tree, representing Swanscombe Wood, with an arm holding a sword above the motto "Invicta."

In 1421 the King with his bride, Catharine of Valois, landed at Dover, where, says Monstrelet, she was received as if she were an angel of God.

In the meanwhile Lollardism was about to receive its last blow. Every effort to turn Oldcastle orthodox failed, and he, alarmed, shut himself up in Cooling Castle, and refused to come out. Whereupon he was arrested, tried, excommunicated, and imprisoned in the Tower. Thence he contrived to escape, probably with the aid of the

London 'prentices, who, like the Kent men, were at any rate strongly anti-clerical, if not Lollard.

In 1417 he was discovered in Wales, brought to London, and burned alive in 1418.

Thus came to an end as a movement in open operation what has been termed the Pre-Reformation. Lollardism was a child of untimely birth ; the times were not ripe for so sweeping a change ; men's minds were not made up, and when Wycliffe's influence failed, as it did when he strayed beyond the main objects of his attack, its backbone was broken. Englishmen were never fond of fanatics, and the later Lollards were certainly fanatics.

What is still called the Lollards Hole in the little town of Wye is a relic of these days—a subterranean chamber of massive masonry opposite the end of Church Street, and from its appearance evidently once connected by a passage with the old Manor House close to the church.

HENRY VI. 1422-1461.

The young King being but nine months old the government was placed in the hands of the Duke of Bedford as Protector, and, during his absence, of his brother Gloucester, whilst the person of the infant was confided to Henry Beaufort, bishop of Chichester, a legitimised son of John of Gaunt by Catharine Swynford.

In 1445 Henry arrived with his bride, Margaret of Anjou, at Dover. On Blackheath, which seems to have been from time immemorial the precise spot at which the welcome of the great City of London should be displayed to distinguished strangers, the Duke of Gloucester met her, accompanied by five hundred men wearing a daisy badge, and escorted her to Greenwich Palace. From there the Royal party returned to Blackheath, whereon the Lord Mayor, Sheriffs, and Aldermen met them attired in blue gowns, with embroidered sleeves and red hoods.

In honour of the new Queen Eltham Palace was magnificently renovated.

But the miseries of this reign were not long in showing

themselves. After the brilliant illumination of Agincourt dark indeed were the days of war for our armies in France. Between 1421 and 1453 we were defeated in half-a-dozen pitched battles, prominent amongst which were Beaugé, Montargis, Rocroy, Fourmigni and Castillon; we were driven from fortress after fortress; Orleans fell, and even Guienne, which had been English since the reign of Henry II., and, under the inspiration of Joan of Arc—a heroine whose fair fame not even the acutest of modern idol breakers has been able to tarnish--France exhibited those marvellous powers of recuperation which have so often been the admiration and envy of other States.

The ill success of the war corresponding so miserably with the exactions and taxes levied for its maintenance a loud and fierce cry for reform broke forth in the shape of the "Complaint of the Commons of Kent," in 1450.

This set forth;

1.—A demand of the truth of rumours that Kent was to be turned into a deer forest as punishment for the killing of William de la Pole, Earl of Suffolk, who, accused of selling Anjou and Maine to France, of being the cause of the loss of Normandy and Picardy, and of the movements of the House of York, in attempting to fly to France had been captured by Kentish ships, and after a mock trial by the sailors on the beach at Dover had his head knocked off on the gunwale of a boat.

2.—The frequent violation of laws which exempted the Cinque Port barons from subsidies.

3.—The tyranny of the King's officers at Dover.

4.—That "the people are not allowed to have their free election in the choosing of knights for the shire, but letters have been sent from divers estates to the great rulers of all the county, the which enforceth their tenants and other people to choose other persons than the common will is."

5.—Peculation in the distribution of collectorships.

6.—Annoyance, trouble and expense caused to litigants by the Assizes being held in one place only, both for East and West Kent, instead of two.

This was presented and refused. So on June 1st, 1450, the Kent men, said to have been provided with funds by London merchants, assembled on Blackheath to the number of twenty thousand, under the command of Jack Cade of Ashford. On June 7th the King hurried up to London, and on the 11th he marched against the rebels, who took up a position at Sevenoaks, awaited the Royal troops and beat them ; and, by the end of June, a reinforcement of Sussex men coming in, the whole array marched back to Blackheath. On July 3rd the Kentish rebels, encouraged by the news that the Essex men were mustering in great numbers at Mile End, marched on London, and, after some parleys, were admitted over London Bridge.

Cade made his head quarters at the *Hart* Inn, which, by the way, was not even the immediate predecessor of the fine old *White Hart* which was pulled down a few years ago, and which was famous as the spot where Mr. Pickwick engaged the services of Mr. Samuel Weller, for the back part of this latter inn was burned in 1669, and the whole of it in the great Southwark fire of 1676.

The proceedings of the night of Sunday, July 5th, are best described in the words of Hall the chronicler :

" The rebels, who never soundly slept for fear of sudden chances, hearing the bridge to be kept and manned (they were in Southwark) ran with great haste to open the passage, where between both parties was a fierce and cruel encounter. Matthew Gough, more expert in martial feats than the other captains of the city, perceiving the Kentish men better to stand to their tackling than his imagination expected, advised his company no farther to proceed towards Southwark till the day appeared, to the intent that the citizens hearing where the place of jeopardy rested, might secure their enemies and relieve their friends and companions. But this counsel came to small effect, for the multitude of the rebels drove the citizens from the wooden piles at the bridge fort to the drawbridge, and began to set fire in divers houses.

"Alas! What sorrow it was to behold that miserable chance ! For some desiring to eschew the fire leapt on his enemy's weapon, and so died ; fearful women with children in their arms, amazed and appalled, leapt into the river ; others, doubting how to save themselves between fire, water and sword, were in their houses suffocated and smouldered ; yet the captains, nothing regarding these chances, fought on this drawbridge all the night valiantly, but in conclusion the rebels got the drawbridge, and slew John Sutton, alderman, and Robert Heysand, a hardy citizen, with many other, beside Matthew Gough, a man of great wit, much experienced in feats of chivalry. . , . This hard and sore conflict endured on the bridge until 9 o'clock in the morning in doubtful chance and fortune's balance : for some time the Londoners were beat back to the piles at St. Magnus Corner, and suddenly again the rebels were repulsed and driven back to the piles in Southwark, so that both parties being faint, weary and fatigued, agreed to desist from fight and to leave battle to the next day on the condition that neither Londoners should pass into Southwark nor the Kentish men into London."

Shakespeare places the fighting and the death of Matthew Gough at Smithfield, but the old accounts agree with Hall. The rebels at any rate seem to have won the bridge, marched through London by Cannon Street, where Cade struck London Stone with his sword and boasted of his mastery of the capital, to Smithfield.

Here took place the murder by the rebels of Lord Say and Seal, who in Shakespeare it will be remembered describes Kent in Latin as a good country inhabited by bad people, but, being asked to explain himself, tries to save his head by the oft-quoted flattery :

"Kent in the Commentaries Cæsar writ,
Is term'd the civil'st place of all this isle ;
Sweet is the country, because full of riches,
The people liberal, valiant, active, wealthy ;"

But he merely wasted breath and was executed.

Cade then negotiated, repeated the demands made in the complaint, with the addition of a general pardon. This was all granted and the Commons of Kent dispersed, but Cade, like Tyler, was not satisfied about the integrity of the Royal word, remained under arms, and with a few hundreds of followers marched to Rochester for the sake of plunder, whence they proceeded to Queenborough, made an unsuccessful attack on the castle, and as they now began to quarrel among themselves over their plunder Cade left them, fled inland, was killed by Alexander Iden, a gentleman of Kent, and his head fixed on the South Gate of London Bridge.

Whether Cade was killed at Cade Street, near Heathfield in Sussex, as the monument there erected states, or near Hothfield in Kent, is a question not likely ever to be settled to the satisfaction of everybody. The opinions on each side are pretty equally divided.

Philipot and Kilburne writing in 1659, Harris, Seymour, Hasted, Speed, and the Grey Friars' Chronicle, say that Iden, a gentleman of, if not sheriff of, Kent, killed him at Ripley Court, between Westwell and Hothfield in Kent. Shakespeare lays the scene of Act IV., Second Part of King Henry the Sixth, in "Kent: Iden's Garden." Hasted speaks of a field at Hothfield known in his time as "Jack Cade's Field," and Mr. Furley says that a field in Westwell, belonging to the Tufton family, part of the Park Farm, is still called "King Henry's Meadow," and suggests that it was purchased with the reward money paid to Iden.

Horsfield, Durrant-Cooper, Hume, Skinner, Fabyan, Holinshed, Creasy, and the English, Grafton, Hall's, and Baker's Chronicles, and, above all, Mr. Lower, decide for Heathfield in Sussex.

Holloway, in his History of Rye, alludes to the Issue Rolls of the Exchequer in which appears a reward paid to John Davy for help in capturing Cade at Heathfield in Sussex. Mr. Lower argues for Sussex by saying that Cade

is an old Sussex name about Heathfield, and points to place
names like Cade's Castle, Iden's Gate, Cade Street, and so
forth, but Mr. Furley rejoins that Cade is quite as common
a name in Kent as in Sussex, and fails to see why Cade
should have gone so far out of his way. At the same
time he concedes that the concensus of opinion is in
favour of Sussex.

For ourselves we believe that Cade, being an Ashford
man, would naturally, when hard pushed, make for a district where he had friends to hide and protect him, and we
cannot help believing that near Hothfield is to be distinguished as the scene of his capture and death. *(See
Note E at end of Chapter).*

So far from being "the scum of Kent" the followers of
Cade numbered amongst them one knight, eighteen
esquires, seventy-four gentlemen, and five clergymen, and
the wide-spread sympathy with the rebellion is perhaps
testified by the fact that the quarters of the twenty-six
leaders executed after the King's Commission of Enquiry
at Canterbury were sent to such distant places as Norwich,
Salisbury, Gloucester, Chichester, Portsmouth, Colchester,
Stamford, Coventry, Newbury, and Winchester.

Even after this signal punishment disturbances occurred.
One Poynings got up an agitation at Westerham in 1453,
and there were riots at North Cray and Farningham in
1454, but the spirit of the rebels was crushed, and the
Kent men were glad to ask their sovereign's pardon on
Blackheath, clad in their shirts, with halters round their
necks.

We now come to one of the most momentous and
miserable periods of our History, that of the Wars of the
Roses. Moreover, although it is an historical period, as
distinguished from a semi-mythical period, it is more
difficult to examine than any other, even of earlier date,
for so torn and convulsed were the districts over which the
war was carried, that old records perished, no new records
were made, many of the oldest families disappeared never
to rise again, and the only employment was that of arms.

In the fourteen pitched battles fought between the years 1455 and 1485 it has been calculated that more Englishmen lost their lives than during the Hundred Years' war with France.

And yet we are told that in the districts not immediately affected by the war, our own county amongst them, not only did life go on much as usual as regards business, but that the Courts of Justice never interrupted their sittings.

In reality it was an aristocratic war, a struggle between rival nobles, the result of an utter breakdown of government, of debt, anarchy, and the independence of the great lords. Its chief result was that final shattering of the feudal system, till now the great check upon unlimited monarchy, which paved the way for the despotism of our Tudor monarchs.

Ostensibly the rival claims of the York and Lancaster factions were these :—

Richard Duke of York was descended from Lionel Duke of Clarence, third son of Edward III.

Henry VI. was the great grandson of John of Gaunt, the fourth son of Edward III.

York's claim was based upon the seniority of his ancestor ; Henry's upon the right of hereditary succession.

Henry IV., son of John of Gaunt, had ousted Richard II. and had been duly elected King, and the Lancastrians rationally argued that this could not be upset by any claim based upon the seniority of Clarence.

The act which immediately led to war was this :—

Henry VI. was mentally afflicted, so Richard Duke of York was made Protector. But Henry recovered, and the Duke of Somerset, York's rival, who had been impeached and imprisoned in the Tower by York, was restored to favour by the influence of the Queen. York, thereupon, backed up by the nobles and by the County of Kent, took up arms. This was in 1455.

In 1459, to come at length to matters of county interest, after the defeat of the Yorkists at Bloreheath, the Earl

K

of Warwick and his father, Salisbury, fled to France. Warwick—afterwards famous as the King Maker—tried to get the governorship of Calais, but Somerset kept it from him, so Warwick landed at Sandwich, where he found Lord Cobham with 4,000 men awaiting him, and marched on London, being joined on the way by Kent people until it is said the Yorkist army numbered 40,000. This must be an exaggeration, for the population of the county at that time would hardly permit of the enrolling of 36,000 men during the short course of a march from Sandwich to London.

However, this was no doubt the army which won the battle of Northampton in 1460, in which the King was taken prisoner and brought to Eltham, where he passed his time in hunting.

After this battle a "Parliament" so-called was held, and York came over from Ireland to assert his claim. He, however, consented to the decision that Henry should continue to reign during his life, and that he should succeed him. But Queen Margaret of Anjou was not the woman to acquiesce in an arrangement by which her son would be kept from the throne, she collected an army in the North, and utterly defeated York at the battle of Wakefield, in 1460.

It was to block her progress on to London that Warwick's Kentish army marched Northward. At St. Albans the Queen defeated Warwick in 1461, and had she marched at once on London she might have seized the capital unopposed, but instead of doing so she wasted time in executing prisoners, and, moreover, young Edward Duke of York had beaten the other division of her army under Jaspar Tudor at Mortimer's Cross, so she had to retreat.

After her went the Kentish army and took part in the great victory at Towton in 1461, which has been called the Pharsalia of England on account of its momentous consequences, Prince Edward being crowned Edward IV. of England.

By the will of Sir John Fogge masses were ordered to

be said in Ashford Church for the souls of the Kent men who were killed at Towton, in which battle, says Drayton, Lord Cobham's bowmen did wonders against the Lancastrians. The commander of the Yorkist van, Robert Horne of Appledore, was killed at Towton.

EDWARD IV. 1461-1484.

In 1462 the King levied what is believed to be the first so-called *Benevolence* in our history, addressing the Mayor of Fordwich and asking "voluntary contributions to resist Henry and Margaret and the Duke of Valois, calling himself King of France."

In 1464 the King married Elizabeth Woodville, or, to be correct, Elizabeth Gray, and the pair remained at Eltham Palace until the coronation. On their way from Eltham to London for this ceremony the Lord Mayor and Aldermen met them at the foot of Shooters Hill. The existing portions of Eltham Palace, we may remark *en passant*, were built during this reign.

"In 1470," Holinshed says, "The Kent men whose minds be ever movable at the change of princes, go to London, rob, kill, and release prisoners from the King's Bench, and would have gone farther had not Warwick crushed them."

This was on account of Warwick the King Maker's change of front. From being a supporter of Edward and an enemy of Margaret, he turned to her side and promised to place Henry VI. again on the throne. Why he did this we cannot learn from the confused history of the times, perhaps he was offended at the secrecy of Edward's marriage with Elizabeth Gray.

Warwick kept his word; Edward was defeated near Doncaster and fled, Henry was re-enthroned, but in 1471 Edward landed at Ravenspur, gained London, where he was popular, at the battle of Barnet defeated and killed Warwick, and in turn re-ascended the throne.

In 1471 took place Falconbridge's Lancastrian rising in Kent. This seems to have been a regular County affair, although the accounts of it are most meagre. At any rate, the fact that a rising in such a cause should even receive encouragement in a County which had hitherto shown itself so thoroughly Yorkist would seem to bear out the character borne by the Kent men of the day, as given by Polydore Vergil, who says, " Civil dissensions, whereunto the Kentish people are most prone, as well for that they can hardly beare injuries as for that they are *desirous of novelties.*"

The people seem to have gone in for the very fun of fighting and excitement, for Falconbridge landed without opposition, " and finding " says the old chronicler, " many of the countrye of Kent were assentynge and cam with theyr good wills, as people redy to be appliable to such seditious comocions," besides many who had no stomach for fighting, and " would righte faine have sytten still at home," were compelled to join, or to send substitutes, with the result of an army of 17,000 men.

From Sittingbourne, Falconbridge addressed the Mayor, Aldermen and Commonalty of London for the release of the wretched Henry VI. But their reply was to the effect that as Edward IV. had commanded them on their allegiance to keep London, they will oppose his coming.

Falconbridge sailed up the Thames and made his head quarters at Southwark, giving out that he had come to free Henry VI., then burned part of the bridge and some of the houses in Southwark, when he found that the Mayor and Aldermen intended to be as good as their word and from Baynard Castle to the Tower were at their guns. He then turned Eastward, attacked Aldgate with 5,000 men, but the portcullis was dropped and a number were entrapped ; it was pulled up again, Robert Bassett, Alderman of Aldgate, made a sortie, drove the rebels as far as St. Botolph's, where other forces joined in against them, and drove them to Mile End and Stratford, where they scattered and fled.

Edward now came up to London, whereupon Falconbridge retreated to Blackheath, thence to Sandwich, where he was captured, pardoned, but beheaded all the same.

Edward held a Court of Enquiry at Canterbury into the conduct of Kent, and heavily fined the County, so that " the Kynge made out of Kent myche goode and lytelle luff." This was followed by merciless executions, especially at Canterbury and Rochester and Blackheath.

Edward IV. amidst the turmoil of his surroundings seems to have shown that under more favourable circumstances he might have been a good, if not a great, King, although inclined to abandon himself to pleasure.

The woollen industry of Kent was the subject of many protective statutes in this reign, amongst which was the quaint one for the regulating of burials in wool, a frequent remark appended to the entries in our burial registers even so late as the beginning of the present century being " buried in wool." Indeed it is very remarkable that although the adage " *inter arma leges silent* " holds perfectly good with regard to the reign of Edward IV., inasmuch as this was the first reign during which no statute was passed for the redress of grievances, or maintenance of the subject's liberty, our trade attained a pitch of unexampled prosperity, and the evil effects of the terrible war were local and rapidly effaced. It was in this reign, in 1462, that the famous charter was granted to Romney Marsh by which the government of the district, not merely as regards internal affairs, but for the purposes of defence, was settled upon a Bailiff, twenty-four jurats, and the Commonalty, a form of government which exists to this day, excepting that the twenty-four jurats have dwindled to five. The " Grand Lath " or meeting is still held at Dymchurch on the Thursday in Whitsun week and four " Petty Laths " are held in the year. At these Laths, in a quaint old house called New Hall, all the business of the Marsh—of its drainage, of the all important maintenance of the sea wall, its groynes and its sluices, the levying of " scots " or rates, is transacted.

It is to this reign that we owe most of the semi-military, moated houses of which so many still exist in Kent. Where the houses have disappeared the moats often remain, of which very good specimens may be seen at Sevington, near Ashford, and close to Wilmington Farm, near Kennington. Statelier buildings of the type of parts of Knole and Hever exhibit very fairly the change wrought in the condition of society by the shattering of the baronage.

William Caxton is the chief Kentish figure of this reign. Born in the Weald, " where I doubt not is spoken as broad and rude English as in any place of England," he started in business in the Almonry at Westminster, whence from his press he issued the Canterbury Tales of Chaucer, for whom he had a reverence amounting to worship, the poems of Lydgate and Gower, the Chronicle of the Brut, translations innumerable, service books, sermons, chivalrous tales and ballads. His first work was the moral treatise entitled The Game and the Playe of the Chesse, dated 1474 ; his last was the Golden Legend, 1490.

RICHARD III.   1483-1485.

Kent was, of course, concerned in the premature attempt of Henry of Richmond to oust the usurper Richard from the throne. There was an assembly at Maidstone under Richard Guildford, and Richmond was proclaimed, but the times were not ripe and Richard was too firmly seated yet to be shaken. There was also attempted a rising at Gravesend of some five thousand men in connection with the Duke of Buckingham's plot, but upon his betrayal and execution it evaporated.

In 1720 Dr. Thomas Brett showed the Earl of Winchilsea at Eastwell an entry he had found in the church registers under the year 1550, as follows :—

> " Richard Plantagenet was buryed the 22nd daye of December."

The legend was then still extant about the bricklayer employed at Eastwell when Sir Thomas Moyle built the house in 1544, who attracted his attention by reading from a Latin book at every spare moment, and who, when questioned, spoke about having been summoned as a boy to Bosworth Field to see his father. The entry more than probably records the death of this old man, whom Moyle pensioned and settled in a cottage, which was standing at the beginning of this century not far from where the lane turns off from the Westwell road to Eastwell church, and who was either a real or natural son of Richard III.

A plain, uninscribed tomb in the chancel of Eastwell church is pointed out as that of the Plantagenet.

Perpendicular was the prevalent architecture of the 15th century, and in Kent we have many notable examples of it, especially in the church towers. Ashford, Lydd, Cranbrook, Westerham, Goudhurst, Lenham, Charing, Chartham, Lyminge, Wingham, Tenterden, Rolvenden and Headcorn may be chosen as specimens of Kent churches in which Perpendicular work, either in towers, or windows, or doors is to be remarked.

In Canterbury Cathedral we get all Chillenden's work of this period—the screens of the cloisters, the Baptistry, and the Warriors' Chapel; also the tombs of Henry IV. and of Chichely, the Chantry of Henry IV., the Oxford or Dunstan's steeple, and the Dean's or St. Mary's Chapel. The glass in the great North window of the West transept and Bourchier's tomb are of this period, and in 1495 Bell Harry Tower was raised to its present height.

The decline of the Cinque Ports during the 15th century is very notable, although some exploits are to be recorded.

In 1405 their squadron captured off Milford Haven the French fleet sent to assist Owen Glendower, and in 1407, under Henry Page, it surprised and took 120 French merchant ships " Laden with salt, iron, oyle, and no worse merchandise."

It was for the coronation of Henry IV. that the Ports claimed and won, even from so powerful a rival as the Abbot of Westminster, the right that their barons should bear the royal canopy, four to each of the four staves, and of sitting at the right hand table next the King at the Coronation banquet.

Sandwich was fast ceasing to be a principal port of communication with the Continent, owing to the silting up of the harbour, although it was not to lose its commercial importance for some time yet. Romney, despite the determined efforts of its burghers, had practically given way as a port to Hythe, and Hythe was already on its downward course. Winchelsea had never recovered the French visitation in Edward III.'s reign. Dover and Hastings alone were in a prosperous condition.

A Kentish apprentice's indenture of Edward IV.'s time may be interesting.

"Between John Gare of St. Mary Cray, cordwainer, and Walter Byse of Wimelton in the same county.

Witnesseth that said Walter hath covenanted with said John Gare for the time of eight years, that John Gare will find Walter Byse meet, drink, and clothing, and teach him his craft, and John Gare shall give him first year three pence in money, and add three pence a year, to the last year when he shall give him ten shillings. And Walter Byse shall truly keep his occupation, and do as John Gare bids him, and shall go neither to "rebeld" or sport during the said eight years without leave of John Gare."

NOTES ON PLANTAGENET KENT.

A.

The appearance of Otford Castle, like that of another archiepiscopal residence, Charing, is a pathetic sermon on the mutability of human grandeur. After it passed into the hands of Henry VIII. it seems to have been utterly dishonoured and neglected. In 1570 Lombarde writes that nothing was left but the hall and the chapel. Hasted at the end of the last century saw but two towers, a wall, and part of the outer court. Until quite recently the tower was used as a smithy. The stones were carried away for buildings in the neighbourhood ; carved oak panels and quaint old woodwork are still to be found put to base uses, and at the Bull Inn is still a carved chimney piece with figures said to represent Henry and Catharine of Arragon. It is said that George IV. once came to Sevenoaks for a review, but not having time to come to Otford the local enthusiasts stripped the tower of its ivy and whitewashed it so that the King might see it from Knowle.

B.

Wye, it may be remembered, was the manor first given as a reward for services performed at the Conquest, and was bestowed on the Abbey of Battle. In Anglo-Saxon times it was a Royal Vill, and it was the privilege of the men of the lands in Wye to guard the King at Canterbury and at Sandwich for three days if he came there.

C.

" All the brothers," said St. Francis in his Rule, " are to be clad in mean habits, and may blessedly mend them with sacks and other pieces . . . . they must be meek, peaceable, modest, mild and humble . . . . they are not to ride unless some manifest necessity or infirmity oblige them . . . . they must beg in order to get necessaries of life, but they must receive them in kind, never in money. The brothers shall not make anything their own, neither house, nor place, nor any other thing ; and they shall go confidently to beg alms like pilgrims and strangers in this world serving our Lord in poverty and humility."

Yet thirty-two years after they appeared in England they already possessed forty-nine convents ; in the magnificent church of the Franciscans on the site of Christ's Hospital—" three hundred feet long, ninety-five wide, and sixty-four high, with columns and pavement of marble,"—were buried the hearts of Isabella, wife of Edward III., and of Queen Eleanor, and Kings and Princes vied in enriching the building ; and the no less magnificent church of Black Friars was especially favoured by Edward I. A minute description of one of the splendid Dominican Convents is given in Piers Plowman's Creed, written at the end of the 14th century.

Gradually not only reformers like Wycliffe, but the old-established monks, began to hate the friars. Thomas Walsingham, a monkish contemporary of Chaucer, after a violent tirade against the friars, adds that a popular saying in his time was : " He is a friar, therefore a liar."

D.

With reference to the locality of the Black Prince's death, Mr. Furley, who is almost invariably accurate, says : " Lingard is in error in stating that his death took place in Canterbury ; and Hasted, on the authority of Stow and others, makes the same mistake. He died in the Palace of Westminster, whither, in order to be nearer Parliament, he had removed, either from his house in Fish Street Hill or from his Castle in Berkhampstead. He was buried by his own directions in Canterbury Cathedral."

E.

Since writing the above I have renewed my search for evidence in support of the theory that Cade was killed at Hothfield and not at Heathfield.

I can find no trace of a "Cade's Field" at or near Hothfield, or of a "King Henry's Meadow" at Westwell, and no such names appear on any maps that I have consulted.

At Ripple Court Farm, near Hothfield railway station, known to have been the property of the Idens at the time of Cade's rebellion, the tradition is of course firmly adhered to that Cade was killed in the garden, and, as I have already said more than once, it is unjust to reject tradition as worthless because nothing tangible exists to give it colour. At the same time it must be conceded that if there is no historical evidence to establish the fact that Cade was killed at Hothfield there is no more to strike the balance in favour of Heathfield.

VI.—TUDOR KENT.

Part I.—Henry VII. and Henry VIII.

Henry VII.   1485-1509.

IN 1495 Perkin Warbeck, a creature of Edward IV.'s sister, the Duchess of Burgundy, pretending to be Prince Edward, one of the young princes said to have been, and now known to have been, murdered by Richard III. in the Tower, tried to effect a landing in Kent. He arrived in Pegwell Bay and sent one hundred and twenty of his followers ashore to ascertain the feeling of the country people. The Kent people, however, were too well inured to alarms and excursions not to be on their guard against surprise and treachery, and the Gentlemen of Kent inland were ever ready at the first flicker of a beacon, or the first boom of an alarm bell, to buckle on their harness and present themselves at the meeting point ready and equipped. And so in this case, Perkin Warbeck's men landed in Kent, but never got out of it again, for they were seized, chained in couples, and sent up to London, where they were executed.

Henry was very pleased at this, and thanked the County.

Strutt's account of a May festival held at Greenwich, from a manuscript of this reign, may be interesting to some. A number of gentlemen, professing themselves to be the servants of the Lady May, promise to be in the

Royal Park at Greenwich, day after day, from two o'clock
in the afternoon till five, in order to perform the following
sports :—

On May 14th they meet at a place appointed by the
King, armed, to keep the field, and to run with every
comer eight courses.

On the 15th the archers took the field to shoot "at the
standard with flight arrows."

On the 16th they held a tournament with "swords
rebated to strike with every comer eight strokes."

On the 18th they were ready to wrestle with all comers
in all manners of ways.

On the 19th they were to enter the field, to fight on foot
at the barriers, with spears in their hands and swords
rebated by their sides, and with spear and sword to defend
their barriers ; there were to be eight strokes with the
spear, two of them " with the foyne " or short thrust, and
eight strokes with the sword, every man to take his best
advantage with gript or otherwise.

On the 20th they were to cast the bar.

And this went on through May and a fortnight into
June.

(These extracts which we shall give from time to time,
as we survey the festive and dramatic period of our history,
may not be severe history, but are assuredly quite as
illustrative of history as columns of facts and figures.)

In 1497 the King required a loan for the war in
Scotland.   Cornwall was asked, that is, ordered, to
contribute, and the people of Cornwall, who, like our
Kentish folk, were ever ready in sturdy resistance to
attacks on popular rights and liberties, resented being
asked to contribute to a cause with which they in their
remote corner of our isle had so little concern.

Flammock, a lawyer, argued that the Border counties
should defend the Border, and that counties hundreds of
miles away should no more be expected to pay for war
against the Scots, than the Border Counties should be
taxed to pay for the defence of the Southern Coast.

The Cornishmen asked to be led into Kent " as the people there were the freest in England," and would certainly help them. But Henry had so graciously rewarded the Kent men for their part in the affair of Perkin Warbeck that they remained loyal and would not stir to help the Cornishmen.

The Cornishmen, however, came eastward and encamped on Blackheath. The King recalled the troops destined for Scotland, and collected a large army in London. One portion remained in St. Giles's Fields, another, under the Earls of Oxford and Suffolk, made a circuit of the plateau of Blackheath and got to the rebels' rear. A third force under Lord Daubeny attacked in front; two thousand of the dispirited and ill-armed rebels were killed, and the rest fled. Lord Audley, Flammock and Michael Joseph were taken and executed, but the usual stern justice of the times was not meted to the poor rabble.

In 1489 the great event of the next reign was foreshadowed by a cursory visitation of monasteries, which revealed the existence of great evils.

Henry VII. preferred Greenwich as a palace, but at Eltham his children were educated, and he built a handsome front to the Palace. He also greatly embellished the Archbishop's Palace at Canterbury, and here made his will.

It is interesting to note that during this reign hops were first introduced into Kent from Flanders.

Sir Edward Poynings, the author of the important law bearing his name, by which it was enacted that no law was to be passed in Ireland without the consent of the English House of Commons, was a Kent man by birth, says Fuller ; " he was a great favourite of Henry VII., who made him Knight of the Garter, Constable of Dover Castle, and Lord Warden of the Cinque Ports."

HENRY VIII. 1509-1547.

The young King who now ascended the throne was hailed by such a burst of general enthusiasm as had not

been accorded to any of his predecessors, and nowhere
more cordially than in the County of Kent, of which he
was a man born and bred. It was a manly age, and the
good people of Greenwich loved to hail as their lord and
master a man who topped most of them in inches, who
could wrestle with the burliest, heave the bar with the
strongest, and draw a bow which taxed the muscle of all
but picked archers. Nor was Henry a mere magnificent
animal : he was a linguist, a skilled musician, more than a
dabbler in metaphysics, and a pretty rhymster, and, above
all, he very soon showed that he was an Englishman to the
backbone. The chief events of Henry's reign are the
Suppression of the Monasteries and the Reformation, and,
for the convenience of readers, we shall proceed at once to
describe the first, especially in its relation to our county,
and continue to its end without turning aside here and
there to deal with contemporary events, which in due
course shall likewise have undivided attention.

In the year 1511 the shadow of the most tremendous event
of this reign was cast by the visitation of certain religious
houses suspected of not being satisfactorily managed.
Archbishop Warham instituted this visitation, and in
Kent he visited in Canterbury, Christ Church, St. Gregory's,
St. Sepulchre's, and St. James's. He was also at Wingham
College, St. Martin's, Dover, the Maison Dieu at the same
place, Folkestone, Wye College, Davington, Ospringe,
Faversham, Leeds, Minster in Sheppey, Maidstone, and
Combwell.

The summary of his report was that, although no grave
charges of immorality had been established, there were
constant complaints about the alienation of funds, badness
of food, general laxity of management, and altogether
evidences of a progressive decay in the monastic spirit.

In April, 1524, Wolsey, bearing this report in mind, and
wishing to found colleges at Oxford and Ipswich, got a
bull from the Pope to suppress such houses as failed to
come up to a certain standard, and in June, 1525, the
Royal consent was given to the Act, but affairs of state

MONKS HORTON.

delayed its being put into operation. A tremor of alarm ran through the entire ecclesiastical community, and every device was compassed, if not to stave off the disaster, at any rate to minimize its effects. The first result of this was no doubt the affair of the Maid of Kent.

In the year 1525—we abridge from Cranmer—Elizabeth Barton, a girl of humble parentage living at Aldington, had a severe illness, during which she declared she had trances and revelations of Heaven, Hell, Purgatory, and the state of souls departed. In one of these she was warned to go to Our Lady of Court-at-Street, or, as it was sometimes written, Courthope Street (the next village to Aldington towards Lympne, where the walls of the chapel still remain); and when she was brought thither and laid before the image of Our Lady her face was wonderfully disfigured, her tongue hanging out, and her eyes being in a manner plucked out and laid upon her cheeks, and so, greatly disordered. Then there was heard a voice speaking in her belly as it were in a tun. This continued three hours, the voice speaking sweetly of Heaven and terribly of Hell. She then had a command from God in a vision to become a nun. These trances always happened on the anniversary of the Conception of the Blessed Virgin.

Masters, the successor of the great Erasmus at Aldington, saw that in this girl might be found a powerful weapon to aid the threatened Church. Great multitudes of people of every condition came from all parts to Court-at-Street, and she was generally believed to be a divine prophetess against the prevalent apostasy.

With the aid of Edward Bocking, a monk of Christ Church, Masters obtained her removal to the Nunnery of St. Sepulchre's in Canterbury.

Cranmer continues, "That having trances every week or fortnight she was visited by great numbers of people, chiefly clerical, who communed with her concerning *the King's marriage.*" (The italics are ours, for herein lies the occasion of her downfall, it being remembered that Henry

was at this time striving with might and main to obtain a
divorce from Catharine of Arragon so that he might marry
Anne Boleyn). "And the heresies and schisms of the
realm.   Of divers matters she had secret knowledge
which she pretended came from Heaven, and even wrote
letters purporting to come from Heaven to earthly
creatures."

Elizabeth Barton was backed up by such men as
Warham, Fisher, and Sir Thomas More. She told Wolsey
that if he sanctioned the King's divorce from Catharine,
and the marriage with Anne Boleyn, God would punish
him, that the King would not continue King a month
after his marriage, but would be destroyed in six months
by a plague of unheard of severity.

The King at first paid no attention to what he deemed
but the incoherent babblings of a mind bereft of reason,
but at last it was time to curb the strong feeling which
was being excited against the marriage.

Cranmer says in 1534 :—

"I sent for this maid to examine her, and afterwards
she went before Mr. Cromwell. And now she has confessed that she never had a vision in her life, but feigned
them all, and that a letter purporting to have been written
by Mary Magdalen in Heaven and sent to a widow in
London was really written by Hawkehirst, a monk of St.
Augustine's.

She was executed at Tyburn in 1534, and with her
two Friars observant, two monks, and one secular
priest. Sir Thomas More and Bishop Fisher, who had
been strongly influenced against the King's marriage by
the maid, were committed to the Tower about the time of
her execution. Edward Bocking, John Dering, Richard
Master, and Thomas Abell, the chaplain and intimate
friend of the Queen, were all involved in the affair. Dering
had written a book against the marriage, but burned it.
Abell's book, a violent diatribe under the motto of
"Invicta Veritas," procured his committal to the Tower,
wherein may still be seen his rebus deeply carved in the

wall of the White Tower, and he was afterwards burned at Smithfield. The Charterhouse in London, and the Houses at Richmond, Sion, and Greenwich were also implicated, and were amongst the first to be visited in 1534. The Greenwich friars in particular are described as being "very stiffe." In 1534, when Henry was disappointed of getting Papal consent to his divorce from Catharine, he determined to separate from the Papacy altogether and become Supreme Head of the Church, and this momentous decision was put into effect by the Act of Supremacy. The monastic orders had naturally always been the strongest supporters of the Papal authority, and no doubt at this great crisis employed all their great influence in promoting discontent at the new order of things. Henry therefore resolved to deprive them of their means of opposing him and to use their wealth for the defence of the country.

Cromwell was made the King's vicar general, and the visitation of the monasteries was resolved upon. Eighty-six questions were drawn up by Leyton, who was one of the commissioners for Kent, of which the following were the principal:

1.—Had the houses their full numbers according to their foundation?

2.—Did they perform Divine worship at the appointed times?

3.—Were their vows observed?

4.—Did they live according to the severities of their Orders?

5.—Did nuns go abroad, or were men allowed to enter nunneries?

6.—What priests did they use for confessors?

7.—How were their lands and revenues managed?

The visitors drew up and presented a report to Parliament asserting that property was misapplied, rules systematically violated, gross immorality indulged in, and disgraceful impostures, such as the Rood of Grace at Boxley, practised by the monks to draw money from the purses of the pious.

L

A beginning was made with the smaller monasteries, which, without wealth or influence, could be easily dealt with, and in 1536 an Act was passed for the suppression of 376 monasteries having incomes of less than £200 per annum. This meant spoil to the amount of £30,000, besides £100,000 in plate.

In Kent this affected the following houses :

St. Radegunds, Bradsole, Premonstratensian Abbey.
Combwell - - - Augustine Priory.
Bilsington - - - Augustine Priory.
Horton - - - Benedictine.
Mottenden - - - Trinitarian.
Wingham, Langdon, and St. Gregory's, Canterbury.

By this step a large number of persons who could not, or would not, be transferred to the larger monasteries became beggars, and went about the kingdom exciting discontent and sympathy by the story of their sufferings. This culminated in the great Lincolnshire and Yorkshire insurrection known as the Pilgrimage of Grace, to help in the suppression of which Kent sent 2,500 men.

Although the Act for the suppression of the smaller monasteries was passed in 1536, visitations of a preparatory nature had already been made. Thus, under date of October 22nd, 1535, Layton, one of the commissioners for Kent, writes :

" I rode back to take an inventory of Folkestone, and thence back to Langdon, where I sent Bartlett, your servant, with my servants to circumcept the abbey, and keep all starting holes. I went alone to the Abbot's lodging joining upon the fields and wood, even like a cony clapper full of starting holes, and was a good space knocking at the door. I found a short pole axe and dashed the door in pieces, and went about the house with the pole axe, for the Abbot is a dangerous, desperate knave and hardy. Finally, the Abbot's ' gentlewoman ' bestirred her stumps towards her starting holes where Bartlett took the tender damoisell."

The house is described as decayed, with no grain or

victual; the Abbot as unthrifty, an "evil husband" and of ill rule. He continues:

"The Prior of Dover and his monks are as bad as the others. The Abbot of Langdon is worse than all the rest, the drunkennest knave living. His canons are as bad as he, without a spark of virtue." Dover is described as a goodly house.

"Another priory called Fowlstone, ten or twelve miles from Canterbury . . . . . . house in utter decay . . . . Prior an apostate and runagate. Prior of Dover excused himself, saying he had spent much money on the place."

This must not be confused with Folkestone, which is described as "well repaired, Prior a very honest person and a good husband."

About this time was exposed that famous piece of clerical humbug known as the Boxley Rood. This was an image of the Virgin, of which the body bowed, the forehead frowned, and the lower lip dropped to the amazement of the credulous bumpkins, and probably of a great many who were not bumpkins.

It was shown at Maidstone and is described as made of "certain engines and old wire, with old rotten sticks at the back of same which caused the eyes to move and stir in the head thereof like unto a lively thing, and also the nether lip in likewise to move as though it should speak, which was not a little strange."

"A brave fellow smelt the deceit, loosened it from the wall, and exposed the trick—the juggler was caught." It was taken up to London, made to go through its performance at Whitehall, and at Paul's Cross dashed to pieces and burned.

About this a Maidstone man (probably a Lollard), writes:

"Dagon was everywhere falling in England. Bel of Babylon had been broken in pieces. A wooden god of the Kentishmen had been discovered, a hanging Christ who might have vied with Proteus, for he nodded his head, winked his eye, wagged his beard, and bent his body to reject and to receive the prayers of those who came to him."

Besides the Rood, there was at Boxley a piece of St. Andrew's finger set in silver, but at the Dissolution *it was in pawn !*

At Otford there was a miraculous image of St. Bartholomew, efficacious it was believed for the propagation of the species. If a woman wanted a son she offered a cockerel, if a daughter a pullet. "Thus," says Lambarde, "the priest of Otford managed to purvey to himself all the poultry in the neighbourhood, the country women being as stupid as the capons they brought."

This was exhibited before the King, who ordered it to be removed.

The parson of Kemsing, too, drove a good trade upon much the same lines. St. Edith, the local patroness, whose name still clings to the quaint old well on the village green, was reputed to have the power of protecting crops from disaster if she was properly approached. People offered corn at her shrine, the priest took it, "hallowed" a small—very small—portion, which he returned to the votary with the assurance that if it was mixed with new seed all would be well, and kept the rest for himself.

In fact, the whole country swarmed with lazy ecclesiastics who throve and fattened upon the credulity of the bumpkin, and in 1538 there was presented to the King a petition against popery by the beggars of England, which enumerated the vices and tyranny of the " bishops, abbots, friars, deacons, archdeacons, suffragans, priests, monks, canons, pardoners and somners."

In 1537 Cranmer reported that the Kent people were very obstinate in keeping their old holidays which had been forbidden by the new laws for the redress of the Church of England.

In 1538 it was determined that the name of Thomas à

ST. EDITH'S WELL,
KEMSING.

Becket, who had become a positive object of idolatry, should be removed from the list of holy people. So he was formally cited to appear in Court and answer to the charges brought against him. Thirty days were allowed for his appearance, but as not even the age of a Boxley Rood could produce Thomas from his four hundred year old resting place, he was found guilty of rebellion, contumacy and treason, his bones were ordered to be publicly burned and all offerings at his shrine were forfeited to the Crown. To this sentence a rider was appended to the effect that as he had been killed in a riot excited by his own obstinacy and intemperate language, he was declared no saint, but rather a rebel and traitor to the prince, and all pictures and images of him were to be destroyed, all festivals in his honour abolished, and his name erased from all service books.

This was carried into effect. After the mock trial the clearance of the shrine began : the offerings and silver filled twenty-six waggons, the jewels and the gold were carried away in two strong coffers. So thoroughly was the work of expurgation carried out that it is hard to find Becket's name on any contemporary bull or document; his figure was erased from every window and picture and even the arms of the city and cathedral were altered. *(See Note A at the end of Tudor Kent).*

In Canterbury Cathedral the only trace of a portraiture which must have been well nigh ubiquitous is to be found upon some fragments of painted glass, and in the half-defaced fresco upon the canopy of Henry IV.'s tomb. *(See Note B at the end of Tudor Kent).*

The description given by Erasmus of the shrine as it appeared not very long before its demolition may be of interest :—

" Iron screens prevent ingress, but allow a view of the space between the extreme end of the church and the place which they call the choir. Thither you ascend by many steps, under which a vault opens entry to the north side. There is shown a wooden altar dedicated to the Blessed

Virgin, but not remarkable for anything save as a monument of antiquity, putting to shame the extravagance of these times. Here the saint is said to have made his last farewell to the Virgin when his death was at hand. On the altar is the point of the sword by which the head of the most excellent prelate was cleft. Descending to the crypt, which has its own mystagogues, we are shown the perforated skull of the martyr.

" ' Did you see the bones ? ' " asks the inquirer.

" ' That is not allowed. But a wooden shrine covers the golden shrine, and when that is drawn up with ropes it shows inestimable treasures. The meanest part was gold ; every part glistened, shone and sparkled with rare and very large jewels, some of them exceeding the size of a goose's egg. The Prior with a rod pointed out each jewel.' "

The lower part of the shrine was of stone in arches, and between these arches sick and lame folk pushed and rubbed themselves in the sure hope of being cured.

The year of spoliation happened to be one of the best in the receipt books of the shrine. There were, for instance, no offerings at God's altar, only £4 1s. 8d. at the Virgin Mary's, but £954 6s. 3d., or more than £12,000 of our money, at the altar of St. Thomas.

In September, 1538, Becket's bones and relics were shown for the last time to a party of French ladies. In 1888 the skeleton of a large man with a deep incision in his skull was found beneath the floor of the crypt, and it is supposed that this may be the skeleton of the great archbishop, which had been secretly removed by devout persons at the first hint that the shrine was to be destroyed.

In 1539 all the greater monasteries were suppressed. The heads of Glastonbury, Colchester and Reading refused to submit, whereupon they were promptly arrested, tried and executed.

In Kent this sweeping edict affected the following houses :

Christ Church, Canterbury - Benedictine Mitred Priory.

St. Augustine's, Canterbury - Benedictine Mitred Abbey.
(The site was turned into a deer park).

Faversham	-	-	- Benedictine Abbey.
Dover	-	-	- Benedictine Priory.
Dartford	-	-	- Augustinian Nunnery.
Malling	-	-	- Benedictine Nunnery.
Leeds	-	-	Augustinian Priory.
Rochester	-	-	- Benedictine Priory.
Dover	-	-	- The Maison Dieu.
Boxley	-	-	- Cistercian Abbey.
Maidstone	-	-	- College.
Tunbridge	-	-	- Black Canons.
Bayham	-	-	- Premonstratensian Abbey.
Losenham	-	-	- Carmelite Friars.
Canterbury	-	-	- Grey Friars : turned into a cloth factory.
Minster in Sheppey		-	Nunnery.

It must not be understood that all this ejectment and spoliation meant the reduction of hundreds and thousands of men and women to beggary. Where the visitors' reports were favourable the ecclesiastics were pensioned for their lives, the amount thus paid in Kent alone amounting to £1,263 16s. 5d., that is, not far short of £20,000 modern money. Moreover, the politic amongst the great houses "surrendered" in time, and were for so doing let off comparatively easily.

At the same time the blow fell very hardly on the poorer classes. The monasteries had been their almshouses, their poor houses, their hospitals and dispensaries, and in many cases their schools. Their discontent was increased by the new landlords spending their revenues at Court instead of at the place where they were gathered, and by the enclosure of common lands which ensued, and this caused Ket's Norfolk rebellion in the next reign, whilst the severe laws passed against beggars and vagabonds, then for the first time necessary, testified to the distress which existed.

Altogether it is estimated that between fourteen and

fifteen millions sterling, modern money, besides jewels and
vestments, were netted by this move. The time for some
reform had evidently come, for during 100 years only eight
religious houses and seventy for purposes of teaching and
charity had been founded, whilst some 780 foundations
had decayed.

Thus was shattered the mighty monastic system of
England. Swift, however, and sudden as was the blow,
the traces of the monks footsteps remain indelible to this
day. Go where we will we strike them—here in the
tangible shape of some majestic ruin, so beautiful in its
forlornness that we forget the wantonness and wickedness of which it was too often the mask; here, there,
and everywhere in place-names which no waves of change-
ful times have ever been able to efface; here in the quaint
nomenclature of cottage flowers; here in the lingering
belief in homely simples and cures; in tradition, in
legend, in song, in proverbial expression; in holy wells
and holy trees and holy hills, and in a hundred other
shapes which bring a mighty past forcibly before the most
unimaginative of minds.

Meanwhile the Reformation was proceeding. It is
foreign to the particular object of this work to deal in
detail with this tremendous event, but we can hardly pass
it by unnoticed. Briefly, therefore, its causes were :

1.—The revival of learning caused by the invention of
    printing.
2.—The sale of indulgences by the Papacy, against
    which Luther so particularly set himself.

Its progress may be summed up :—

1.—The Pope by thwarting Henry in the matter of
    the divorce of Catharine of Arragon drove the
    King to be a Protestant, although he was
    essentially a Romanist.
2.—The Act of Supremacy, 1534, which transferred
    the headship of the church from the Pope to
    the King.
3.—The dissolution of the monasteries.

4.—The temporary check given to its progress by the Law of the Six Articles, which were distinctly un-Protestant.

5.—The Reformation emphasised by the Act of Uniformity.

We are now at liberty to turn to the general history of this reign in its particular association with the county of Kent.

Henry was particularly partial to Greenwich Palace, and a few descriptions of the magnificent festivities there may be interesting.

The Christmas of 1513 was kept at Greenwich, and Hall thus describes the Twelfth Night festivities :

"According to olde custom there came into the greate hall a mount called the riche mount. This mount was set full of riche flowers of silk, and especially of brome slippes full of poddes, the branches were greene satin, and the flowers flat gold of damaske, which signified Plantagenet; on the top stood a goodly bekon giving light, rounde above the bekon sat the King and five other, al in coates and cappes of right crimosin velvet, embroidered with flat gold of damaske, their coats set full of spangells of gold; and foure woodhouses drew the mount till it came before the Queen, and then the King and his compaigne descended and daunced; then suddainly the mount opened and out came six ladies all in crimosin sattin and plunket, embroudered with golde and perle, with French hoodes on their heddes, and they daunced alone. Then the lordes of the mount took the ladies and daunced together, and the ladies re-entered, and the mount closed, and so was conveyed out of the hall."

In 1515 there was a picturesque observance of the old English May Day festival on Shooter's Hill.

Miss Strickland thus describes it :

"Catharine and the royal bride (Mary, Henry's sister, who had married Louis XII. of France) rode a maying with the King from the Palace of Greenwich to Shooter's Hill. Here the archers of the King's guard met them

dressed like Robin Hood and his outlaws, and begged that
the royal party would enter the good green wood and see
how outlaws lived.

"On this Henry, turning to the Queen, asked her if she
and her damsels would venture into the thicket with so
many outlaws.

"Catharine replied that where he went she was content
to go.   The King then handed her to a sylvan bower, formed
of hawthorn boughs, spring flowers and moss, with apartments joining, where was laid out a breakfast of venison.
The Queen partook of the feast and was greatly delighted
with this lodge in the wilderness.   When she returned
towards Greenwich with the King they met on the road
a flowery car, drawn by five horses ; each was ridden by
a fair damsel.   The ladies and their steeds personated the
attributes of the Spring.   The horses had their names
lettered on their head gear, and the damsels had theirs on
their dresses.   The first steed was Caude, or Heat, on
him sat the lady Humid ; the second was Memeon, on
which rode the lady Vert or Verdure ; on the third,
Phæton, was the lady Vegitive ; on the steed, Rimphon,
sat the lady Plesaunce ; on the fifth, Lampace, sat lady
Sweet Odour.   In the car was the Lady May, attended by
Flora.   All these damsels burst into sweet song when they
met the Queen at the foot of Shooter's Hill, and preceded
the royal party carolling hymns to the May, till they
reached Greenwich Palace."

The amusements of the day concluded with the King and
the Duke of Suffolk riding races on great Flemish
coursers—said to be the first mention of horse racing in
English history.

In 1518 a play was exhibited in the great hall at Greenwich.

"A rock ful of al maner of stones very artificially
made, and on the top stood five trees : the first was an
olive tree, on which hung a shielde of the armes of Rome ;
the second was a pyneaple tree, with the armes of the
Emperor ; the third was a rosyer, with the armes of

England ; the fourthe a braunche of lylies, bearing the armes of France ; and the fifth a pomegranet tree, bearing the armes of Spain ; in token that all these five potentates were joined together in one league against the enemies of Christ's fayth : in and upon the middles of the rock satte a fayre lady, richly appareyled, with a dolphin in her lap. In this rock were ladies and gentlemen appareyled in crimosyn sattin, covered over with floures of purple sattin, embroidered with wrethes of gold knit together with golden laces, and on every floure a hart of gold moving. The ladies tyer (head dress) was after the fashion of Inde, with kerchiefs of pleasaunce hacked with fine gold, and sett with letters of Greeke in gold of bullion, and the edges of their kerchiefs were garnished with hanging perle.   These gentlemen and ladyes sate on the neyther part of the rock, and out of a cave in the same rock came ten knightes armed at all poyntes, and faughte together a fayre tournay.   And when they were severed and departed, the disguysers dissended from the rock and daunced a great space, and sodeynly the rock moved and receaved the disguysers and immediately closed agayn. Then entred a person called Report, appareled in crymosyn sattin, full of tongues, sitting on a flying horse with wynges and feete of gold called Pegasus ; this person in Frenche declared the meaning of the rock, the trees and the tournay."

In 1520 was enacted the famous pageant of the Field of the Cloth of Gold.   Henry travelled from Greenwich to Otford, Leeds, Charing and Canterbury, stopping at the Archbishop's manor houses in these places at a tremendous cost to their owners.   From Canterbury the King rode towards Dover to meet his nephew, afterwards the Emperor Charles V., but the latter had had a bad Channel crossing and was lying prostrate in Dover Castle.

The King's suite on this occasion consisted of over 4,000 people and 1,700 horses, and he travelled very heavily.   With him he took a "house" of timber in fourteen waggons, a tent of cloth of gold, besides others;

an army of cooks and attendants, an enormous wardrobe, and the complete choir of his Chapel Royal, 115 in number.

The uniform of English troops seems to have been first settled on this occasion. It consisted of a blue coat picked out with red, one stocking red, the other blue, and the latter with a three-inch red stripe along the seam.

In 1525 the King, or rather Wolsey, in order to meet the cost of a war in alliance with Charles V. against France, attempted to demand a levy of a sixth of every man's substance, payable in money, plate, or jewels, according to the last valuation. The Commissioners appointed to collect it were driven out of Kent, and the people absolutely refused to pay, declaring that the taxes of England were becoming worse than those of France, and that the last loan they granted had never been repaid.

Moreover they pleaded poverty; the clothiers of Romney Marsh complained bitterly of business, and Warham was much ridiculed for urging that Kent should meet the demand willingly inasmuch as the King was a Kent man. So strong indeed was the feeling amongst the clothiers of the Cranbrook and Goudhurst districts that at one time affairs seemed to point to a rising. At any rate it was probably the determined resistance of the loan in Kent, coupled with the issue of the battle of Pavia, by which the power of France was crushed, that it failed.

In 1527, on the occasion of the reception of the French ambassadors, a play was acted before them by the boys of St. Paul's School at Greenwich. Hall describes the play, but on the chance that a repetition of such ceremonies may prove wearisome, we omit it. Mr. Froude's addendum, however, in the shape of a list of the costumes is too characteristic not to be given. The characters were:

An orator in apparel of cloth of gold.

Religio, Ecclesia, Veritas, like three widows, in garments of silk, and suits of lawn and cypress.

Heresy and False Interpretation, like sisters of Bohemia, apparelled in silk of divers colours.

The heretic Luther, like a party friar, in russet
damask and black taffety.

Luther's wife, like a frow of Spiers in Almayn, in red
silk.

Peter, Paul, and James, in habits of white sarsnet,
and three red mantles, and lace of silver and
damask, and pelisses of scarlet.

A cardinal in his apparel.

Two sergeants in rich apparel.

The Dolphin and his brother in coats of velvet embroidered with gold, and capes of satin bound
with velvet.

A messenger in tinsel satin.

Six men in gowns of grey sarsnet.

Six women in gowns of crimson velvet.

War, in rich cloth of gold and feathers, armed.

Three Almeyns in apparel all cut and holed in silk.

Lady Peace in lady's apparel white and rich.

Lady Quietness and Dame Tranquility richly beseen
in lady's apparel.

It was at this entertainment that the little Princess
Mary, afterwards Queen, danced with five of her companions dressed as Icelanders with six similarly clad
gentlemen.

About this time Henry first cast eyes on Anne Boleyn,
who was a lady-in-waiting to Queen Catharine, and,
hearing that young lord Percy, also in the Household,
was a suitor for her hand, he caused her to be removed,
and she returned to her father's house at Hever.

For this she blamed Wolsey, nor did she ever after cease
to work against him.

Sir Thomas Wyatt of Allington was another of her
admirers, but prudently he kept quiet when he saw that the
king was on the path, and consoled himself with these lines:

" Who list to hunt, I put him out of doubt,
As well as I, may spend his time in vain !
Graven with diamonds in letters plain,
There is written her fair neck about,
Noli me tangere ! For Cæsar's I am,
And wild for to hold, though I seem tame."

The Christmas of 1527 was celebrated with much pomp at Greenwich. The "sweating sickness" was raging now virulently about the Court and neighbouring county, and Anne was seized with it. Henry paid her marked attentions at Hever, riding over from Greenwich almost daily, and is said to have given notice of his approach by sounding a horn from "King Harry's Hill." There is a "Mount Harry" at Sevenoaks, but no Elizabethan horn blown into even by the robust lungs of a Bluff King Hal could possibly have been heard from here at Hever. (*See Note C at the end of Tudor Kent*).

In 1528 Anne Boleyn was with the King at Greenwich for Christmas, although Queen Catharine was still at Court, and much comment was provoked thereby. Feeling her power, Anne began to use it. She interceded for Sir Thomas Cheney, Lord Warden, whom Wolsey had driven from Court, and devoted herself to schemes against the Cardinal with such success that it was considered his fall was greatly due to her. In 1529 Anne Boleyn kept a rival Court at Christmas to the Queen. Then came the separation from the Papacy—Cromwell's work; the King sends an ultimatum to the Queen, which she rejects and quits Greenwich accompanied by Thomas Abell, her chaplain and confessor, who, however, to her great sorrow was shortly removed from her.

Anne Boleyn was now continually in the King's company. In 1532 she was made Marchioness of Pembroke, and was virtually Mistress of the Court: she accompanied the King to Canterbury, Dover, and Calais, and was present at his interview with Francis I.

She was about this time secretly married to Henry, whether at Blickling in Norfolk, or at Dover, or at Whitehall, is not certain. In 1533 the ceremony was openly solemnised, and the next year she was crowned Queen, at which ceremony her quondam lover Sir Thomas Wyatt, holding the position of Chief Ewerer, had to perform the duty of pouring scented water over her hands.

In 1533, to the immeasurable disgust of the King, a

HEVER CASTLE

daughter, afterwards the renowned Queen Elizabeth, was born at Greenwich. Henry never got over this disappointment, and three years later his susceptible heart was smitten by the charms of Jane Seymour, and in consequence of this semi-detached state of affairs Anne led a sad, neglected life at Greenwich, finding her pastime in laying out the Park after the model of her beloved Blickling, operations still visible in the stately avenues of Spanish chestnuts.

Henry was now keenly on the watch for a valid excuse to get rid of Anne, and the opportunity occurred at a tournament held at Greenwich where Anne coquetted with Norris. The trial and execution of Anne followed in due . course, and on the morning after, Henry became the husband of Jane Seymour. This was in 1536.

The winter of 1536-7 was so severe that the Thames at Greenwich was frozen sufficiently thick to be crossed on horseback.

In the spring of 1537 the King went to Canterbury to see that the destruction of Becket's shrine had been thoroughly effected, and possessed himself of the famous ring offered by Louis IX. called the Regale of France.

In 1539 the threatening aspect of the Continental sovereigns consequent upon Henry's defiance of the Papal power compelled him to put the southern counties in a thorough state of defence, and he personally made a tour of inspection of the musters and beacons of the county of Kent.

Lambarde says :

"Of this I hold me well assured that King Henry viii, having shaken off the intolerable yoke of the Papal tyranny, and espying that the Emperor was offended by the divorce of Catharine his wife, and that the French King had coupled the Dolphine, his son, to the Pope's niece, and married his daughter to the King of Scots, determined to stand upon his own guard and defence, and without sparing any cost he builded castles, platforms, and block houses in all needful parts of the Kindgom, and erected near together three fortifications which might at all times keep and beat the landing place, viz : Sandown, Deal, and Walmer."

Marillac, the French Ambassador, in passing Dover saw new ramparts and bulwarks on the rock where the sea beats, and well pierced with great and small artillery. At Canterbury and other places he saw them making musters of all subjects who can bear arms, enrolling all over seventeen or eighteen years of age, without excepting the aged. He met on the road a band of men going into garrison upon the Dane, who said they would be from five to six thousand men, " in short, they have gone so far that whatever hurt come they could not be taken unprepared."

In 1539 Jane Seymour died, and Thomas Culpeper, one of the King's train, went over to Calais to meet Anne of Cleves, who, on the strength of flattering portraiture, had been recommended to Henry as a successor.

Anne arrived at Deal on December 27th, and was lodged in the new Walmer Castle, whence the gentry of Kent escorted her to Dover Castle. From Dover she went to Canterbury, being met on Barham Downs by Cranmer, five bishops, and the local clergy and gentry, who accompanied her to St. Augustine's. It was very foul weather when Anne arrived at Canterbury. She was received by torchlight with a great peal of bells, and was presented by Cromwell with fifty " sufferans," to which the City of Canterbury added fifty angels. The next day she went to Ospringe, where she slept at Maison Dieu, then to Rainham, where she was met by the gentry of Norfolk and Suffolk, and then to Rochester, where she stayed at the Bishop's Palace until New Year's Day.

On New Year's Eve, Henry, who lodged at the Crown Inn at Rochester (where part of the original stable in which took place the Carrier's Scene in Shakespeare's Henry the Fourth stood until quite recently), came to have a peep incognito at his intended bride, together with eight gentlemen of his Privy Chamber "all dressed alike in coats of marble colour."

Sir Antony Browne, who brought Anne a New Year's gift, says he was struck with consternation when he was shown the Queen, and was never so dismayed in his life as to see a lady so far unlike what was represented. The King "recoiled in bitter disappointment," called her "a Flanders mare," and Lord Russell says "That he never saw his Royal Highness so marvellously astonished and abashed as on that occasion."

She too was not more charmed at the great, bloated being who was to be her lord and master, but there was nothing to be done on either side but to grin and bear, and so the King dissembled admirably and received her graciously. But he returned to Greenwich in a very melancholy mood and began to revolve schemes by which he could get out of his engagement. Anne went on to Dartford.

The first public meeting of the King and Anne of Cleves took place on Blackheath. It was a gorgeous pageant, for details of which we may refer the reader to Hall's Chronicle, but it is interesting to note that the exact meeting place of the King and his bride was at that tumulus known as "Jack Cade's Mound," but formerly called after the cross which stood there until the time of Charles II.

The pageant passed across the Heath and through the Park to the Palace, and here on Twelfth Night the marriage was celebrated.

Henry never conquered his repugnance to Anne, and pretty severely he made those suffer who had so misrepresented her as to induce him to betroth himself to her, the fall of Cromwell in particular being directly attributable to the part he had taken.

After a great deal of consultation and legal hair-splitting the following grounds were considered valid enough for a divorce :

1.—Anne was pre-contracted to the Prince of Lorraine.

2.—In marrying her against his will Henry could not be considered as having consented.

M

In July, 1540, the divorce was pronounced; Cromwell and Barnes, the chief agents in the marriage negotiations, were executed, and Anne was sent off to Place House, Dartford, a remnant of the once famous Augustinian nunnery for noble Kentish ladies, remains of which still exist.

Very shortly afterwards the King married Catherine Howard, who on her mother's side was a Culpeper of Hollingbourne, and had been a maid of honour to Anne of Cleves.

The Royal pair spent much of their time at Greenwich and Eltham, but Catherine was a flighty lady, and being suspected of undue intimacy with her cousin, Sir John Culpeper, he was executed first and in 1542 she shared the same fate.

In 1544 Henry was present at the siege of Boulogne, and on his return stayed at Upper Hardres, the residence of Sir Thomas Hardres, who had accompanied his royal master to the picnic, and in token thereof was presented by Henry with the gates of the captured town and with his own dagger.

Both of these curiosities were shown for a long time after, but at the beginning of the present century the gates were actually sold for the price of the iron in them.

In 1545 England, which had made no progress in the science of war since the accession of Henry VII., who was essentially a pacific monarch, was thoroughly alarmed and awakened by fears of foreign invasion, and even the Archbishop of Canterbury asked for artillery for the cliffs. The days of archery were past, and our fleet at the accession of Henry VIII. consisted of 30 men-of-war, averaging 150 tons, and one of 1,000 tons. For the first time in our history the nation was provided with a navy worthy of the name, and an origin of our national anthem words may perhaps be found in the challenge and answer of this time, the former being " God save the King " and the latter, " Long to reign over us."

At this time the population of England was about

4,000,000, whilst that of France was 14,000,000, and of the Spanish Empire 16,000,000. The population of London and its suburbs was about 130,000, whilst Paris numbered more than 400,000, and even Milan and Ghent 250,000. Our trade was chiefly in the hands of foreigners, and the commerce of the world was carried in Hanseatic, Venetian, Spanish, Flemish and French ships. The revenue of Venice was even greater than that of England, which was about £125,000, whilst that of France was £800,000, and of Spain £1,100,000. We give these details in order to accentuate the boldness of the step taken by Henry in practically defying Christendom by his throwing off the Papal supremacy, and to afford some estimate of the tremendous odds against England in the event of an European combination to crush her.

The French were very lively in their aggression. They landed on the Isle of Wight, but were handsomely repulsed, and repeating the experiment at Seaford met with the same fate. It was during this scare that the *Mary Rose* went down in Portsmouth Harbour with three hundred men.

A "benevolence" was levied in this year, but no one was called upon to contribute whose lands were of less value than forty shillings, or whose chattels were less than fifteen pounds. Perhaps we may get an idea of the comparative standings of the counties by the results of this levy, although we must remember that the Cinque Ports, their limbs and members, were absolved by the character of their peculiar services from being called upon. Thus we find Kent returned for £6,471, Suffolk £4,512, Norfolk £4,046, Somerset £6,800 and Lancashire only £660.

PART II.—EDWARD VI; MARY; ELIZABETH.

———

EDWARD VI. 1547-1553.

There is not much connected with Kent to detain us during this reign.

The Kent men showed themselves no more disposed than did the Londoners to back up Northumberland in his violent scheme of placing the innocent Lady Jane Grey—of whom it was written:

" Girl never breathed to rival such a rose,
Rose never blew that equall'd such a bud :—"

great grand-daughter of Henry VII., who had married Northumberland's son, Lord Guldeford Dudley of Halden, on the throne upon the death of the King to the exclusion of the Princesses Mary and Elizabeth, although Northumberland, with the history of the past before him, had no doubt counted upon the county.

The murder of Arden of Faversham—or Feversham as it was called and is still written on some mile stones—which occurred in this reign, is interesting as being the theme of one of the earliest examples of English domestic drama in blank verse. So late as 1770 the Tragedy of Arden of Feversham, or to give it the full title : "The Lamentable and True Tragedy of Mr. Arden of Feversham who was most wickedly murdered by the means of his wanton and disloyal wife, who, for the love she bore to one Mosbie, hired two desperate ruffians, Black Will and Shagbag, to kill him," was attributed to Shakespeare, the grounds of supposition being that the story is fully told by Holinshed upon whom Shakespeare drew largely for his facts, that Arden was the name of Shakespeare's mother, and that, shortly after the murder, the Earl of Leicester's players, whose London home was the Blackfriars theatre, happened to be at Faversham.

Edward lived much of his short, sickly life at Greenwich. Early in 1552 he was stricken here with measles and small-pox, and records "I was sick, and not able to go abroad; so I signed a bill containing the names of the Acts I would have passed."

At Greenwich he was visited by a celebrated Milanese doctor, Cardonao, who speaks of him thus highly :

"You may know the lion by his paw. His ingenuous nature and sweet conditions rendered him great in the expectations of all, whether good or learned men. He began to favour learning before he could know it, and he knew it before he knew what use to make of it. Oh, how true is the saying, 'Precocious growths are short-lived, and rarely arrive at maturity!' This prince could give you a taste of his virtues, not an example. He was stored with graces, for, being yet a child, he spake many languages, his native English, Latin, French, and Spanish. He wanted neither the rudiments of logic, the principles of philosophy, nor music. He was full of humanity, had the highest sense of morality, and displayed the gravity befitting royalty of hopes like his. A child of so great wit and promise could not be born without a kind of miracle of nature."

The story was long popular that after the young king's removal as an invalid from Whitehall, whither he had gone during a temporary rally, to Greenwich, his medical attendants were sent away and a quack nurse substituted, who hastened his end. It was also said that his body lay unburied at Greenwich during the short reign of Lady Jane Grey, and quite recently the discovery at Windsor of a coffin enclosing the remains of a youth evidently of distinction has re-awakened the belief that by the machinations of his sister Mary he had been poisoned, and hastily and secretly buried. But the detailed accounts extant of his last illness and of his funeral in Westminster Abbey would seem to disprove these legends.

MARY. 1553-1558.

Mary Tudor, who was born at Greenwich, was hailed Queen by the almost universal suffrage of the nation, and it became very soon evident that she was bent upon the re-establishment of the old religion from which she had never recanted. Wholesale ejectments of bishops took place, and Cranmer, foreseeing the storm, sought to evade it by retiring first to Bekesbourne and then to Ford, but from here he was summoned to London and committed to the Tower.

Mary made no secret of her designs, which were indeed encouraged by almost the whole country except the City of London. For instance, although the funeral of Edward VI. was solemnized according to the ritual of the Church of England, the Queen at the same time held a Requiem Mass in the chapel of the Tower. Finally the question of her marriage with Philip the Second of Spain was brought forward. At once the scare of a Spanish Alliance filled the minds even of Roman Catholics with intense dread; and ominous murmurings were heard at the prospect of an union between two monarchs to whom, to quote Mr. Motley, " The maintenance of the supremacy of the church seemed the main object of existence; to execute unbelievers, the most sacred duty imposed by the Deity upon anointed princes; to convert their kingdoms into a hell, the surest means of winning Heaven for themselves."

The outcome of this feeling in our county was the rebellion of Sir Thomas Wyatt, son of the lover of Anne Boleyn.

He undertook to raise Kent, whilst the Midlands and the Western Counties were to act simultaneously, all the movements converging on London.

On January 22nd, 1554, fifteen hundred men assembled at Allington Castle, whilst five thousand more held themselves ready when called upon in their homes. Rochester Castle was fixed upon as the head quarters, Sir George Harper of Sutton Valence was elected joint commander, a squadron in the Thames promised support, Rochester Bridge was covered by artillery, and the armoury at Penshurst was rifled during the absence at Court of Sir Henry Sidney.

Wyatt caused the following proclamation to be published at Tunbridge, Sevenoaks, Ashford and Maidstone :—
" Forasmuche as it is now sprede abrode and certainly
pronounced by the Lorde Chancelour and other of the
Councel, of the Queene's determinate pleasure to marry
with a stranger. We therefore write unto you, because ye
be our neyghbours, because ye bee our frendes, and
because ye bee Englishmen, that ye wyll joyne with us as
we wil with you unto death in this behalfe, protesting
unto you before God that no other earthly cause could
move us unto this enterprise but this alone, wherein we
seeke no harme to the Queene but better counsel and
counselours, which also we would have foreborne in al
other matters, saving only in this. For herin lieth the
helth and welth of us al. For trial herof and manifest
proof of this intended purpose, lo now even at hand
Spaniards be nowe alreadye arrived at Dover at one
passage to the nombre of an hundreth passing upwarde to
London in companies of ten, foure, and VI., with harnes,
harquebuses, and morians, with match light, the foremoste
company whereof be alreadie at Rochester. We shall
therefore require you to repaire to such places as the
bearers hereof shall pronounce unto you, there to assemble
and determine what may be best for th advauncement of
libertie and commonwealth in this behalfe, and to bring
with you such ayde as you maye."

A most practical and common-place address compared
with that which Tennyson has put into the mouth of
Wyatt, in " Queen Mary," commencing " Men of Kent !
England of England ! "

Canterbury remained loyal, as did Lord Abergavenny
and Sir Robert Southwell, Sheriff of Kent, who were at
once proclaimed traitors by Wyatt, but the mass of Kent
men were for Wyatt.

The Sheriff and Lord Abergavenny assembled a force at
Malling, and at once marched on Rochester to intercept the
men of the Weald coming to reinforce Wyatt, and near
Wrotham Hill came up with them. On Blacksole Field

there was a fight, of which the rebels got the worst, but at
the moment of victory a large party of loyalists deserted
to Wyatt's standard.

The Commons of Kent, " the same violent and in-
flammable people whom John Cade had a century before
led to London," as Froude calls them, swarmed in to join
Wyatt from all sides, and for the moment things looked
black for the royal cause.

Mary, however, was equal to the occasion : she made an
impassioned harangue to the Londoners—to the people, be
it noted, of that city which was distinguished almost from
the rest of England by its sturdy Protestantism—obtained
the promise of 500 men, and as a preliminary sent an offer
of pardon to all rebels who should lay down their arms.
The offer was rejected, whereupon the Duke of Norfolk
advanced to attack Rochester.

The action was on the point of commencing when a shout
of " Treason " was heard, and the whole of the London
" whitecoats " crossed over and joined the ranks of
Wyatt.

This was a severe blow to the Royal cause at the very
onset, and, had not the Western rising under Carew failed
at this time, the course of history might have been
materially changed.

Wyatt now determined to march on London, but, to
secure Lord Cobham who was shut up in his castle at
Cowling, hesitating what course to adopt, he turned aside
aud stormed the castle with 2,000 men, whereupon Cobham
surrendered it, and Lord Abergavenny and the Sheriff,
whose men were deserting wholesale, fled to the Court.

London, however, remained true to the Queen, and
prepared to receive the rebels.

These marched by Gravesend and Dartford, numbering
about 12,000 men, and arrived in Southwark, February
3rd, 1554.

They found the drawbridge cut away, the gates of
London Bridge barred, and Lord Howard ready for them
with four guns.   The next night, however, the Lieutenant

of the Tower trained seven guns to bear upon the steeple of St. Mary Overies and St. Olave's, whereupon the people of Southwark beseeched Wyatt to withdraw, and he magnanimously agreed to. The rebels seem to have behaved very well during their sojourn in Southwark, the only act of violence recorded against them being the burning of Winchester House and the destruction of its contents.

Wyatt quitted Southwark with the object of crossing the river at Kingston Bridge, but already the heart of the insurgents seems to have been broken, for he marched with only 1,500 men.

At Kingston he found the bridge broken. The repair occasioned some delay, but the river was crossed and the march Londonwards along the other bank resumed on bad roads in bad weather. Wyatt's followers were becoming more and more dispirited; the Rochester men left him, and only the London men with Sir George Harper, Antony Knevett, and Lord Cobham's sons remained.

Wyatt's object was to enter the city by Ludgate, which was to be opened to him by friends within, but the scheme reached the ears of the Royal chiefs, and Ludgate was strongly manned.

At Knightsbridge, where was a stream and much marshy land which so seriously incommoded the rebels that they were dubbed "Draggletails," Wyatt halted his wearied men. The next morning he reached Hyde Park Corner, where he was fired on by a battery on Hay Hill, and further on a manœuvre of the Royal Cavalry cut him off from some 300 of his men. He pushed on, however, along Pall Mall, Charing Cross, and the Strand, fighting pretty stiffly all the way, descended Fleet Street, and arrived at Ludgate only to have it shut in his face. By this time he had but twenty-four men left, and, thoroughly sick at heart, he sat down at a stall opposite the *Belle Sauvage* Inn, and surrendered himself to Sir Maurice Berkeley, and the ill-timed attempt was at an end.

Then came the retribution. Fifty deserter citizens who

had fled were hung at their own doors. Stow gives the numbers executed at eighty men in London and twenty-two in Kent. The two Isleys were executed at Maidstone, the two Knevetts at Sevenoaks, Brett at Rochester, the Duke of Suffolk and his two brothers, whilst the Cobhams got off by laying their heads on the block. Lord Guldeford Dudley and Lady Jane Grey were executed on Tower Hill, and in April Wyatt suffered at the same place. Under examination, that is, the rack, it is probable that he said something to incriminate the Princess Elizabeth, but on the scaffold he stoutly denied that she had any hand in the matter.

Long after this event Kentish boys played at " Queen's Men " and " Wyatt's Men," just as Somersetshire boys more than a century later played at " Monmouth's Men " and " King's Men " after Sedgemoor.

Maidstone was disenfranchised for the share she had taken in Wyatt's rebellion. Kent indeed was hasty : if she had waited a little the South West, the Midland, and Wales would have joined cause with her, and the result might have been that the Princess Elizabeth would have ascended the throne.

The Marian persecution of the Protestants, which followed closely upon the Queen's marriage with the King of Spain, affected Kent more severely than any other part of England except the diocese of London.

Between January, 1554, and November, 1558, thirty-eight men and sixteen women were executed in the county, a goodly proportion of the estimated number of victims altogether, which is fixed at between three and four hundred. Canterbury was naturally the head centre of persecution, but Ashford and Wye each claimed two victims. (See Note D at the end of Tudor Kent). The first female martyr in England was Margaret Polley, who was burned at Tunbridge, and the last victims of the persecution were three men and two women who were burned at Canterbury, November, 1558.

It is difficult to arrive at a real estimate of Mary's share in these horrors. Had she been less devoted to her fanatic husband there is sufficient evidence in the character of the legislature of her reign to justify us that much of the reputation she enjoys is undeserved. Possibly she may be regarded as a scapegoat, the real offenders being Gardiner, Reginald Pole, Bonner, and the Parliament acting under the influence of the King.

During the period of the persecution she was in a miserable state of health, which prevented her from exercising her woman's prerogative of mercy. Her Court was pure and frugal. Many of her laws were manifestly ahead of her times, notably that which directed that judges should take the examination of felons in writing. The gaols were in a respectable state : the poor were bountifully relieved, as is shown by the absence of insurrections during a period when corn was at a famine price. Very few monasteries were re-established, and the " benefit of the clergy " was abolished, by which the ancient law that the Church could claim jurisdiction over all civil criminals who could read was rendered null and void. She kept her word that no alterations should be made in the national religion without general consent; she had no standing army to overawe Parliaments and no rich civil list to bribe them. On the whole, therefore, Mary's most virulent detractors are inclined to class the acts for which she was personally held responsible as those of a woman deranged in mind. The strange combination of characteristics in Mary's personality is thus set forth by Motley :

" Small, lean and sickly, painfully near-sighted, yet with an eye of fierceness and fire ; her face wrinkled by care and evil passion still more than by time ; with a big man's voice, whose harshness made those in the next room tremble ; yet feminine in her tastes, skilful with her needle, fond of embroidery work, striking the lute with a touch remarkable for its science and feeling; speaking many languages, including Latin, with fluency and grace ; most feminine, too, in her constitutional sufferings, hysterical of habit, shedding floods of tears daily at

Philip's coldness, undisguised infidelity, and frequent absences from England—she almost awakens compassion, and causes a momentary oblivion of her identity."

The last year of Mary's reign was a black one in the annals of England. The people were sickened with the persecutions, wearied by the continual wars with Scotland and France; the empty Treasury had to be filled by a forced loan, and, to cap all, Calais, "the brightest jewel in the English crown," the last remnant of our Plantagenet conquests, the sturdily held fortress over the gate of which was inscribed

"Then shall Frenchmen Calais win,
When iron and lead like cork shall swim;"

was torn from our grasp in fair fight by the French. It may be noted that Calais sent two representatives to Parliament.

This roused the nation to one of its feverish fits of warlike preparation. An ordinance was put forth by which every peer, knight, or gentleman with an income above £1,000 a year, was to furnish sixteen horses with steel harness, forty corslets, coats of mail, and morions, thirty long bows with arrows, and as many steel caps, halberds, black bills and haquebuts, and so on in a descending scale. All able-bodied men between the years of sixteen and sixty were to be held ready for service, and the muster roll of each county was to be presented.

It was, however, but a flash in the pan. The people were dispirited: in many counties, Kent amongst them, the ordinance was simply ignored, and no muster returns made, and then, happily for everybody, the unhappy Queen died, and the Princess Elizabeth ascended the throne.

ELIZABETH. 1558-1603.

On the accession of Elizabeth, as we have seen, England was in a bad condition, and the fate of the nation now depended, perhaps more than at any other period of its history, upon the personal character of its sovereign; and, as Elizabeth, despite occasional outbursts of Tudor self

will and imperiousness, had been little known to the
English people except as a scholarly and somewhat crushed
recluse, it may be imagined that at a crisis when strong,
vigorous action on the part of the Head of the State was
required some anxiety should be felt as to the issue of
events.

How the personal character of Elizabeth the Queen was
an important factor in the glory of her reign is, of course,
now a matter of history.

Elizabeth was born at Greenwich, in the room known
from its tapestry hangings as the Chamber of the Virgins,
she was christened at the Convent of the Grey Friars, and
throughout her reign preferred Greenwich to any other of
her palaces, not excepting Windsor, so that she was essentially more Kentish a Queen than even the wife of Ethelbert. As Miss Strickland says :

" Every dell and hill about Greenwich and Blackheath
is classic ground, trod by the footsteps of England's
Elizabeth—scenes where she walked, and meditated, and
resolved her great measures for the public weal, or
matured the little household plots which agitated the under
current of her domestic history." And again she quotes
from Rowland Whyte, " The queen at Greenwich uses to
walk much in the park, and takes great walks out of the
park, and round about the park."

Outside the grand old park, however, wholesale jerry-
building has knocked on the head all the Elizabethan
romance about Greenwich and Blackheath, and the most
vivid imagination requires painful stretching to picture
the neighbourhood as it was in the days of Gloriana. As
regards our county especially during this reign, the interest
centres around the development of her industries and the
part she played in the great Drama of the Armada.

In 1561, Sandwich, a fast decaying port owing to the
silting up of her harbour, was authorised to receive some
five-and-twenty master workers in baize and flannels from
the Netherlands, where the tyranny of Alva and his
lieutenants, and the operation of the Inquisition, were

sapping the very heart of national life. These immigrants also brought with them the knowledge of other useful arts, such as the manufacture of paper and the cultivation of flowers and vegetables, and their memory is still preserved in such names as Delf Street, and of the surrounding marshes, which are called " The Polders."

In 1567 Maidstone petitioned and was allowed to receive weavers of linen thread, whose peculiar work was long after known as " Dutch." In the same year French Protestant refugees settled in Canterbury and established there a silk weaving industry. For many years they set up their looms in the crypt of the Cathedral, and adjoining their workshops was their place of worship, which still exists, although lately it has been much altered, and is used by their descendants, good Englishmen all of them, but bearing their French names or the same oddly anglicised. The industry has now gone to Spitalfields in London, but so late as 1789 the silk for the decoration of the Prince of Wales's palatial Carlton House was from the Canterbury looms. These Huguenots also made lustreings, brocades, satins, paduasoys, black and coloured velvets, cutlery, instruments, hardware and toys.

During the reign of Elizabeth no less than forty-six statutes were passed for the regulation of the woollen trade. In 1576 a further impulse was given to it by the sacking of Antwerp, whereby the Antwerp trade came to England.

To a limited extent the Wealden iron trade flourished in Kent during this reign, but not nearly as much as that of Sussex. There were forges at Cranbrook, Hawkhurst, Goudhurst, Horsmonden, Cowden, Tunbridge, Biddenden, Ashurst and Lamberhurst. In 1573 there were 10 owners, 6 forges and 8 furnaces in the Weald of Kent, as against 42 owners, 40 forges and 32 furnaces in Sussex.

Considerable alarm, however, about the consumption of timber for fuel, which meant the diminution of the supply of timber for the other great Kentish industry, ship-building, brought about severe ordinances restricting the felling of timber for the iron manufacture, and limiting its exercise to certain places. Cannon were founded in large quantities, and even exported for the use of foreign Governments, and the discovery of this caused the passing of an ordinance by which no piece of cannon could be cast without a licence. Another evil resulting directly from the iron industry was the destruction of high roads wrought by the constant transport of timber, which was usually done in winter when the roads were naturally at their worst. To remedy this an Act was passed by which it was forbidden to use the roads for this purpose between October 12th and May 1st.

Queen Elizabeth, like her predecessors, always kept the old national festival on St. George's Day, which we modern Englishmen have unaccountably allowed to be utterly overlooked and forgotten. In the year 1561 it was celebrated with much circumstance at Greenwich, and a short description of it from Sir Henry Nicolas's History of the Order of the Garter may not be out of place.

"All her Majesty's chapel came through the hall in copes, to the number of thirty, singing 'O God, the Father of Heaven,' the outward court to the gate being strewed with green rushes. After came Mr. Garter, and Mr. Norroy, and Master Dean of the chapel, in robes of crimson satin, with a red cross of St. George, and after, eleven knights of the Garter in their robes; then came the Queen, the sovereign of the Order, in her robes, and all the guard following in their rich coats, to the chapel. After service they returned through the hall to her Grace's great chamber. The Queen and the lords then went to dinner, where she was most nobly served, and the lords sitting on one side were served on gold and silver." This was followed by the election of knights.

In 1564, towards the end of the war with France, great alarm was felt about the defenceless condition of the county. In January, Archbishop Parker reported to Cecil:

" Dover, Walmer and Deal are forsaken and un-
regarded for any provision. The people are feeble, un-
armed and commonly discorrupted towards the feared
mischief. If the enemy have an entry as by consideration
of our weakness and their strength, of their vigilance
and our dormitation and protraction is like, the Queen's
Majesty shall never be able to leave to her successors that
which she found delivered her by God's favourable hand."

Lord Abergavenny ordered a levy of the gentlemen of
the South-Eastern Counties, and as the result was not very
satisfactory, at any rate proved by the exhibition of his
own armoury at Bekesbourne that he was ready.

In 1573 the Queen made a Progress through Kent.
She started from Greenwich on July 14th and went to
Croydon, where she remained a week as the guest of
the Archbishop. From Croydon she went to Sir
Percival Hart's house at Orpington, where she was presented with a magnificent nautical masque which so
pleased her that she dubbed her host Bark Hart. Thence
she went to Knole, her own property, to Lord Abergavenny's at Birlingham, and to the same nobleman's
seat at Eridge, where she stayed six days.

It was probably about this part of the journey that
Burleigh wrote to the Earl of Shrewsbury, " The Queen
had a hard beginning of her Progress in the Wild of
Kent . . . . where surely were more dangerous
rocks and valleys and much worse ground than in the
Peak."

Thence she went to Bedgebury at Goudhurst, where she
was presented by Culpeper, her host, with a silver bowl.
From here she went on to Hemsted and Rye. Thence
to Sissinghurst, whose proprietor she knighted. From
Sissinghurst she went through Smarden (where the bell-
ringers were paid two shillings and ten pence—about
two pounds of our money, for welcoming her) to Boughton
Malherbe, Hothfield, and to her own house at Westenhanger. It is hard to realise from the remains now
extant, picturesque though they be, how magnificent a
house was Westenhanger three hundred years ago.

WESTENHANGER
HOUSE .

We are told that it had nine towers, one hundred and twenty-six rooms, three hundred and sixty-five windows, and a fine chapel. During the recent operations in connection with the formation of the new Folkestone racecourse many interesting relics have been unearthed, and it is pleasing to be able to record that not only are these carefully preserved, but that the whole of the buildings, after a narrow escape from being converted into a tripper's holiday resort, are to be maintained, and, where possible, judiciously restored by the gentleman at present in occupation.

From Westenhanger the Queen went to Folkestone—or, rather, skirted it, and was given a splendid welcome by the Gentlemen of Kent; from Folkestone to Dover and from Dover to Canterbury, where she lodged at the Episcopal Palace of St. Augustine. Her birthday happened to fall during her stay here, and was celebrated with the greatest pomp, no such assemblage of people having been in the City before—not even when Henry VIII. came here on his way to the Field of the Cloth of Gold. Elizabeth remained at Canterbury fourteen' days and went thence to Sandwich.

Here she met with a great reception, was presented with a cup worth a hundred pounds, and witnessed nautical sports, amongst which "certain Wallounds that could well swym had prepared two boates, and in the middle of each boate was placed a borde, upon which borde there stood a man, and so they met together, with either of them a staff and a shield of wood, and one of them did overthrowe another, at which the Queene had good sport." It must have been a pretty sight on the day of her departure when more than a hundred English and Dutch children were ranged on a turf bank and spun fine linen for the Queen's amusement.

From Sandwich the Queen returned to Canterbury, thence she went to Sittingbourne, thence to Rochester, where she stayed five days at the Crown Inn in order to inspect her ships; from Rochester she went to Chatham,

where she stayed at the house of Mr. Watts, the founder
of the charity made famous by Charles Dickens as that
of the Seven Poor Travellers, and was so well entertained
there that she desired the house to be known ever after as
Satis House.   From Chatham she passed on to Dartford,
where she lodged at Place House, erstwhile the residence
of Anne of Cleves, and so home to Greenwich.

In 1586 one of our most famous and beloved heroes,
Sir Philip Sidney, met his warrior's death on the field of
Zutphen in the Low Countries.   Sidney had been
appointed Governor of Flushing.   Spain and Holland
were then at war, and in 1585 Elizabeth promised to take
the Protestants of the Netherlands under her protection
and despatched a military force to their succour.   Sidney
was elected Colonel of the Dutch regiments and Captain
of 200 English foot and 100 cavalry.   He had gained
many small successes against the enemy, when on the
22nd September, 1586, a small detachment of English,
500 men, encountered a convoy of the enemy numbering
about 3,000, who were on their march to relieve Zutphen,
an obscure town in Guelderland.   An obstinate engagement took place under the walls of the fortress.   Sidney
performed prodigies of valour.   Early in the battle he had
a horse killed under him; he mounted another, rescued
Lord Willoughby from the most imminent peril, and
gallantly charged the enemy three times in one skirmish.
At length he received a musket shot from the trenches a
little above his left knee, which " so brake and rifted the
bone and so entered the thigh upward, so the bullet
could not be found before the body was opened."

We are told that an eccentric and chivalrous feeling of
emulation, caused by his having met the Marshal of the
camp only lightly armed, had induced Sir Philip to throw
off his cuisses before going into action, and thus to leave
exposed the parts of his frame which they protected. The
anguish of the wound and the loss of blood brought on so
much faintness that Sidney was obliged to leave the field.
Then comes the touching story of his relinquishing the

drink of water to the dying soldier, as told by his friend, Lord Brooke.

His uncle, the Earl of Leicester, in a letter to Sir Thomas Heneage, says :

"I was abroad that time in the field, and meeting Philip coming upon his horseback not a little to my grief. But I would you had stood by to hear his most loyal speeches to Her Majesty; his constant mind to the cause, his loving care over me, and his most resolute determination for death ; not a jot appaled for his blow, which is the most grievous that I ever saw with such a bullet ; riding so long, a mile-and-a-half to the camp, not ceasing to speak still of Her Majesty, being glad if his hurt and death might any way honour her; 'for her's he was while he lived, and God's he was sure to be if he died,' prayed all men to think that the cause was as well Her Majesty's as the country's, and not to be discouraged, 'for you have seen such success as may encourage us all, and this my hurt is the ordinance of God by the hap of the war.' "

Sidney lingered sixteen days in severe and unceasing pain, which he endured with the utmost sweetness and composure. We are told that in order to divert his mind he composed an ode (unhappily lost), which he caused to be set to solemn music. His wife was at his bedside and nursed him, and on October 17th he died.

Upon the news of his death the whole of England, from the Queen to the lowliest subject, went into mourning for him, an honour never before paid to any subject, and it is related that for many months no gentleman of quality ventured to appear in a light coloured dress, either in the resorts of business or fashion.

He is described as "a gentleman finished and complete, who trod from his cradle to his grave amid incense and flowers, and died in a dream of glory;" also as "a true model of worth, a man fit for conquest, plantation, reformation, or what action soever is greatest and hardest amongst men ; withal such a lover of mankind and goodness that whosoever had real parts in him found comfort, participation (sympathy) and protection to the uttermost of his power."

The following description of the hero's funeral is from the *Custumale Roffense :*

"In September at the releeving of Zutphen, he charged the enemye thrice in one skirmishe, and in the last charge he was wounded with a muskett shott whereof he died at Arnheme the 17th October, from whence he was brought by water to Vlishing, where he was kept eight days for his convenient passage. On November 1st, 1586, he was broughte from his house in Vlishing to the sea side by the English garrison, which were twelve hundred, marching three and three, the shott hanging downe their pieces, the halberts, pykes, and enseignes trayling along the grounde, drums and fyfes playing very softly.

"The bodye was covered with a paule of velvet, the burghers of the towne followed mourning, and so soone as he was imbarked the small shott gave him a triple vollye ; then all the great ordynaunce about the walles were discharged twise, and so tooke theire leave of theire well beloved governour. From thence he was transported in a pynnis of his owne, which is here portrayde.

"All her sayles, tackling, and other furniture were coloured blacke, and blacke cloth hanged rounde aboute her, with escouchions of his armes, and was accompanyed with dyvers other shipps. He was landed at Tower Hill, London, the fifth of the foresayde month, and carried to the Minorites."

On February 15th, 1587, the funeral was at St. Paul's.

"To sollempnize the same, there followed nexte unto the mourners the Lord Maior, Aldermen, and Sheriffs of the Cittye of London, ryding in purple ; after them the Company of Grocers, of which he was free ; and lastlye certaine young men of the Cittye, marching by three and three, in black cassokins, with their shott, pikes, halberds and enseigne trayling on the grounde, to the number of three hundred, who, so soon as he was interred, honored the obsequy with a double volley." The pall bearers were his 'dear loving friends,' Thomas Dudley, Fulke Greville, Wooton and Fryer. His brother, Sir Robert Sidney, acted as chief mourner. *(See Note E at the end of Tudor Kent).*

In 1580 there was an earthquake in Kent which was felt at Sandwich and Dover, where part of the cliff fell ; part of Saltwood Castle was destroyed, the Hythe bells were rung, and much damage was done at Great Chart and Ashford.

In 1583 the Earl of Anjou came wooing the Virgin Queen, and she coquetted with him, close upon fifty as she was, just as she had coquetted with Spaniards, and Hollanders, and Scotsmen in her political *rôle*, for, after all, it was a political game she was playing in keeping him in good humour as a representative of France. Even when he, disgusted, started on his homeward journey she accompanied him to Chatham and showed him her ships, and to Sittingbourne, and as far as Canterbury, where she bade him a tearful farewell, although she pursued the poor man with messages until he fairly embarked at Sandwich. *(See Note F at the end of Tudor Kent).*

We now come to the chief event of this reign, the arrival and the destruction of the Spanish Armada, and as the "Vanguard of Liberty" the County of Kent played a part in the national defence, certainly second to none, and perhaps more important than any.

The possibility of an invasion of England by Spain had long been present in the minds of Englishmen—so long that the only reason for the almost utter lack of preparation for it can only be the utter dislocation of national affairs under the papist reign of Mary.

"The shadow of Spain already stretched beyond the Andes," says Froude: "The shadow of this gigantic power fell like a deadly blight over Europe," echoes Green. It was in truth a blight, stifling, corrupting, blistering, befouling wherever it settled, and as it was settling over the greater part of the Christian world small wonder that the dread of it should be a hideous dream by day and night in our little island. The fanaticism which had turned the gentle, lute-playing, hysterical Mary Tudor into a bloody mad woman, was raging amongst all ranks of the Spanish people, and no more popular, because no more holy, enterprise was conceivable in their minds than the extirpation, if necessary, of the one European people which dared to be heterodox, and more, was proud of its heterodoxy, and actually flourished under its burden.

Briefly the causes of the sending of the Armada were:—

    1.—The hatred of Popery in England, intensified a hundred-fold by the atrocities of Alva and his lieutenants in the Netherlands, and by the stories of the doings of the Spaniards in the Indies brought home by the Adventurers.

    2.—English buccaneering.

On the first no comment need be made.

The second, buccaneering, had assumed such enormous proportions that it might almost without exaggeration be said to have become not only the staple industry of the people of our Southern and Western Coasts, but a form of speculation into which people of very high estate were not ashamed of dipping deeply. Our Kent people were not a whit behind those of the Western Counties in their zeal for this utterly indefensible yet much winked at business. Dover and Margate men in particular seem to have distinguished themselves, but Thomas Cobham of Cooling Castle was one of the most reckless of individual desperadoes. For attacking and sinking in the Bay of Biscay a Spanish treasure ship, with the cargo of which he made off, Elizabeth, who had hitherto paid but little attention to the Spanish remonstrances which poured in, sentenced him to be taken to the Tower of London, stripped naked, placed with a sharp stone under each of his shoulders, and on his stomach a gun too heavy for him to bear, but not heavy enough to crush him at once. There he was to be left till he died, with a few grains of corn to eat, and foul water to drink.

This sentence however was really never carried out.

The preparations for the Armada were long known in England. In January, 1584, the Governor of the Isle of Wight wrote to Walsingham, Secretary of State, that a ship master lately returned from Lisbon had informed him of preparations being made for a navy, carrying many thousands of men, to be commanded by the King in person, of which the destination was England. In December, 1585, this report was confirmed by a Devonshire captain from Lisbon. Thomas Rogers, *alias* Nicholas Berden, Walsingham's private agent abroad, kept his master fully informed by a series of letters which probably enabled Walsingham to checkmate Philip. During 1586 Sir John Gilbert reported that an army of 60,000 men was being trained for an expedition against England, and Sir Francis Drake reported similarly.

In 1585 active measures were taken in Kent. Watches were set at Hoo, Sheppey, Caule, Graystone, Elmes, Broadhull (Dymchurch), Seabrook, Sandgate and Shorn-cliffe, whilst a series of beacons was established which were to base their movements upon a signal from Fair-light, near Hastings. *(See Map, and Note G at the end of Tudor Kent)*.

In 1586 a demand was made upon the South Eastern Maritime Counties as follows :

Kent was to supply 1,500 men, 9,000 lbs. of powder, 9,000 lbs. of lead. Sussex and Hampshire, 1,600 men, 9,600 lbs. of powder, and 9,600 lbs. of lead.

The Cinque Ports, although much shorn of their ancient power and wealth, were rated thus :

Folkestone, 4 ships. Hastings, 15. Sandwich, 43. Hythe, 11. Faversham, 20. Ramsgate, 16. Deal, 6. Walmer, 5.

The following proportions borne by the Maritime Counties of Southern and Western England of the cost of these early preparations show how Kent came to the front.

Kent, £631 9s. 4d. Devon, £527 13s. 4d. Sussex and

Hampshire, £399 5s. 4d. each.   Dorset, £378 17s.   Cornwall £320 1s. 2d.

In April, 1588, Sir John Norris was appointed Royal Commissioner of the Forces in Kent and on the South East Coast; a great chain was fixed across the Medway to Upnor, and batteries erected at a cost of £1,470; and, at the same time, an extraordinary " aid " was levied, to which Kent gave £5,025, Sussex £4,535, and Hampshire £2,875.

The Kent command of land forces was as follows :

Sir Thomas Scott, of Scotts Hall, and Sir James Hales commanded respectively the infantry and cavalry of East Kent; Sir Henry Cobham and Sir Thomas Fane those of West Kent.   Altogether they had 13,000 foot and 1,000 horse, but this by no means represents the contribution of our county to the national armament.

Sir Thomas Scott's instructions were to remain on the watch at Shorncliffe until he was relieved by Lord Cobham with his trained archers, now armed with muskets or calivers, as per letter to the Lord High Treasurer dated July 12th, 1588.   At the same time Sir James Hales with the cavalry scouted along the Downs.

The East Kent force of 6,500 foot and 450 horse formed the Van, the West Kent men of about the same number were the " second battayl."   All cattle were driven inland and provisions in standing grain which could not be used were to be destroyed.

In this arming of the archers with muskets and steel bows we note the revolution wrought in warfare by the use of gunpowder.   A contemporary writer says :—" The bow is our national weapon, good at home, but naught abroad ; the cross-bow flieth far and striketh forcibly ; but above all the steel bow which flieth twenty score yards and can be discharged twice as fast as the cross-bow.   The most powerful weapon against all this enemy is the fear of God."

In order to get as exact as possible an idea of the part played by Kent in the defence of the country at this

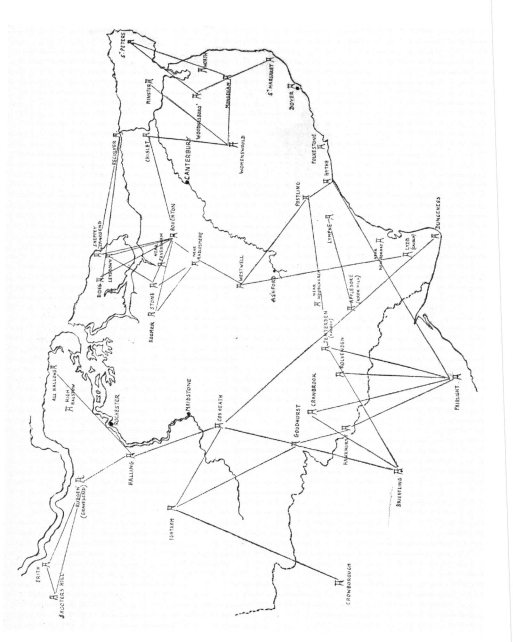

The Beacons of Kent, A.D. 1588
from the plan by Sir William Brooke, Lord Cobham,
Lord Chamberlain to Queen Elizabeth I

tremendous crisis, it is necessary to review the entire disposition of the national forces.

There were four armies.

    1.—The army for the defence of the Southern Coasts: —that upon which the brunt of invasion might be expected to fall.

        This consisted of 30,500 trained men, made up of about 25,000 foot, 6,000 horse and 18 guns.

        To this Kent sent 4,000 men, Hampshire 4,000, Sussex 4,000, Devon 3,000 trained and 2,000 untrained, Cornwall 2,000, Dorset 1,500 trained and 500 untrained.

        These were divided into "cornets" of horse and "ensigns" of foot. An "ensign" of foot consisted of 200 men thus divided :—60 pikemen, 30 musketeers, 100 harquebusiers and 10 halberdiers.

    2.—The army for the Queen's person.

        Consisting of 28,900 foot, 3,500 horse, and 36 guns.

        To this Kent contributed 2,000 men.

    3.—The army at Tilbury under the Earl of Leicester, designed for the defence of London, and made up of the London trained bands, stated variously at 11,000 and 16,000 men.

    4.—The army at Stratford-at-Bow, made up largely of Midlanders, consisting of 22,000 men from eleven counties, to act in conjunction with the Tilbury force.

        To this it is stated Kent was to send as many as 5,000 men, but we doubt if Kent could spare so many.

In addition, there was a cavalry force under the Lord Steward at Brentwood, consisting of 203 lances and 669 light horse, drawn from seven counties, to which Kent sent 50 lances and 100 light horse.

In order to secure the ports of the Kingdom, able, but not trained, men were drafted as follows :

Falmouth, 11,000. Plymouth, 17,000. Sussex Coast, 15,000. Sheppey, 20,000. Yarmouth, 13,800. Poole, 14,000. Portsmouth, 16,000. Harwich, 17,502. Suffolk Coast, 13,300.

So far as we have been able to gather after a long and minute examination of contemporary records the entire force, at any rate summoned, if not assembled, for the defence of the realm consisted of about 238,000 men, made up of armed men—trained and untrained—able men, pioneers, lances, and light horse.

Now if, in order to arrive at Kent's proportion of this force, we add up Kent's contributions to the various armies, we shall find the large total of 25,000 men, which, bearing in mind the population of the time, not even our patriotism will induce us to believe as correct. So we must infer that when, for instance, Kent is represented as contributing 5,000 men to the Stratford Army, if it was done at all, it was at the expense of the other armies to which Kent had contributed.

Possibly we are within, but not beyond, bounds when we say that Kent's proportion of the entire force was about 18,000 men, made up of 7,000 armed men—both trained and untrained—and 11,000 able men.

Even the clergy bore their share in the national move-ment, contributing 3,885 footmen and 559 horse. For in-stance, the Archbishop sent four light horse men fully equipped, besides having 100 of his servants trained and armed; the Chapter sent the same number, and the Dean two. The parson of Chartham was ready for two men or £105 ; the parson of Wrotham for two men or £134 ; the Prebendary of Canterbury for two men or £118, whilst the Bishopsbourne parson declared for two men or £202.

In a wealthy county like Kent this spirit of volun-teering aid was no doubt very general, and we may certainly add to the 18,000 men, who may be considered the regular force of the county, many hundreds of volunteers recruited from the gentry and their adherents, who, without actually taking up a position in the line of

battle, held themselves in readiness to move to the front
much in the same way as did the "Minute Men" of
Massachusetts at the outbreak of the American Revolutionary War.

Thus Somers speaks of a gentleman of Kent with a
band of one hundred and fifty others who were worth in
goods above £150,000, besides their lands, and he adds :

"Such men would fight stoutly before they lost their
goods."

We may be quite sure that when the "Warlike
errand"

"Roused in many an ancient hall the gallant squires of Kent,"

the same spirit actuated them which prompted the
aged Earl of Shrewsbury to write to the Queen, "Though
I am old, yet your Majesty's quarrel shall make me young
again ; though lame in body, yet lusty in heart to lend to
your greatest enemy one blow, to live and die in your
service," and Lord Morley to declare that, although his
estate had been very much reduced, he would have in
readiness 20 light horse, 30 muskets, and 70 calivers.

At Northbourne there was a camp under Captain Pike
of Walloons and Englishmen, all volunteers, consisting of
200 bow and billmen, and 20 caliver men.

The system of beacons was very elaborate, and we have
thought it interesting enough to re-produce a map of those
in Kent, drawn up for Elizabeth by Sir William Brooke,
Lord Cobham, the Lord Chamberlain. The name of
"beacon" still clings to many of these posts, and the
cresset of Tenterden long hung upon the church tower.

Nor was Kent behindhand in her contributions to the
naval force of the realm, although, owing to the decay of
the Cinque Ports, she could no longer bear the entire
brunt of invasion as in days gone by.

The English fleet was made up as follows :—

The Royal Fleet of 34 ships and 6,264 men.
Merchant   ,,   34   ,,   2,394 ,,
City of London ,,   29   ,,   2,140 ,,

London Merchant Fleet 33 ships and 1,561 men.
. Coasters   42 ,,   2,036 ,,
Volunteers   23 ,,   939 ,,
Total, 195 ships and 15,334 men.

Against this the Spaniards brought 166 larger ships with 27,128 soldiers and sailors, 180 priests, and 1,493 guns. The Spanish fleet consisted of 40 great hulks, 60 galleons, 30 great ships, 4 galliasses, 8 galleys, and 24 pinnaces, and the armed force was made up of 1,600 Castilians, 3,000 Portingalls, 6,128 mariners, and 2,000 pioneers.

In addition to the Cinque Ports Fleet of five ships, of which not one was under 60 tons, and a "handsome pinnace," thus distributed : Winchelsea, Hastings and members 1 ship of 60 tons, Rye and members the same, Romney the same, Dover 1 of 100 tons, Sandwich 1 of 80, Hythe the pinnace of 24 tons ; the Ports held in readiness smaller vessels as follows, manned by 1,195 men :

Sandwich, 33. Rye, 51. Dover, 26. Faversham, 27. Ramsgate, 13. Hastings, 12. Hythe, 12. Lydd, 11. Folkestone, 4. Deal, 5. Walmer, 3. St. Peter's, 6 ; and others.

These were probably but lightly armed fishing boats, as the average crew per boat was only six men.

Another large fleet of the same class of vessels was contributed by Whitstable, Milton, Rainham, Upchurch, Halstow, Sittingbourne, Tong, Queenborough and Minster, Gillingham, Rochester, Dartford, and Maidstone.

Some details as to the scale of victualling the soldiers prove that our Elizabethan ancestors must have been mighty trenchermen, and the exceedingly liberal scale for the army contrasts strongly with the miserable parsimony which made Elizabeth send the ships which were to fight. her battles to sea with no more than three days' provisions, and with ammunition only for one day. In fact we doubt if the troops ever got this allowance. At any rate Leicester wrote to Walsingham with reference to the troops under his command at Tilbury :

" There was neither a barrel of beer nor a loaf of bread for them, but they said they would abide more hunger than that to serve Her Majesty and the country."

These are the published scales of allowances :

Per day for a foot man—

Bread, 1½ lbs. Butter, ½ lb. Beer, 2 quarts. Wine, 1 quart. Cheese, 1 lb. Beef, 2½ lbs. "Biskett," 1 lb.

Per day for a horse man—

Bread, 2 lb. 4 oz. Beef, 3½ lbs. Butter, 12 oz. Cheese, 1½ lbs. Beer, 3 quarts. Wine, 3 pints. "Biskett," 1½ lbs.

A few details about the Spanish Armada may be interesting.

As the enterprise was essentially religious, the strictest regulations were laid down for the conduct of the men on board the ships. All personal quarrels were to be healed ; it was forbidden to blaspheme or renounce our Lord God, or Our Lady, or the Saints upon pain of being sharply punished. Every morning the ships' boys were to give the Good Morrow at the foot of the main mast, and every evening to say the Ave, and some days the Salve Regina, or at least every Saturday, together with the " Lathanie." Watch words were appointed for the days of the week ; for Sunday, Jesus ; Monday, the Holy Ghost; Tuesday, the Blessed Trinity ; Wednesday, St. James; Thursday, the Angels ; Friday, All Saints ; and Saturday, Our Lady.

That the rumours current in England about the intention of the Spaniards, if successful in their venture, to force their religion upon Englishmen by the same gentle methods practised in Spain, in the Netherlands, and in America, were not ill-founded, is proved by a list of instruments of torture found on the captured Spanish vessels, given by Fox in his Book of Martyrs, prominently chests full of thumb screws, "cravats," bilboes and poisoned swords.

It is unnecessary to re-tell the oft-told tale of the utter discomfiture of the Armada by a fleet, more than half of which, be it noted, was composed of merchant ships and volunteers. During the great fight between Calais and Dunkirk on Monday, August 9th, the coast of Kent, whence assuredly the battle could have been seen, was lined by the forces of Sir Thomas Scott and Sir John Norreys, drawn up so as to make an imposing show, but there was fated to be no opportunity granted for the men of Kent to show their mettle.

' How ready they were is evident from a letter, dated July 31st, from Barry, the Lieutenant of Dover Castle, to Walsingham, in which he commends the Cinque Ports for furnishing thirty boats at a day's notice.

The great danger passed away. The Spaniards fought as the Spaniards of that day always fought; not a ship surrendered during the actual fighting, and many went down with all hands on board and colours flying. But not even this great salvation seems to have loosened the Royal purse strings, for so late as September 14th Cobham writes to Burleigh on behalf of the Dover and Sandwich people, entreating the payment of two months' hire of their ships and mariners. This request had to be repeated, Hastings also claiming payment for her ship the "Anne Bonaventure."

In September, 1588, the Cinque Port contribution to the fleet for the "Narrow Seas" was:

Dover, 5 ships, 265 men; Sandwich, 4 ships, 150 men; Rye, 3 ships, 135 men; Faversham, 1 ship, 30 men.

There is nothing of importance connected with our county during the remaining years of this reign. In 1597 a Greenwich man named Squires, an old sea-dog, who had been captured by the Spaniards and actually tortured into fanaticism for the Romish faith—in other words, racked out of his mind, made a silly attempt to kill the Queen by rubbing poison into the pommel of her saddle, and, although he failed, he was executed with the usual barbarities.

The execution of Essex, the Queen's favourite, in 1602, produced a very marked effect upon her, and although on

May Day she went maying in the glades of Lewisham, and she affected to enter heartily into the revels and festivities of the Court at Greenwich, she was in a miserably depressed state.

Thus ended the reign of her whom poets and romancists still love to celebrate under the name of Gloriana. No other sovereign has left such indelible traces upon what may be called the side life of rural England: no other sovereign's name is linked with so many places or is associated with so many legends, tales and episodes: no other sovereign's relics—not even those of the so-called Royal Martyr—are treasured with such pride and care, and, be it added, of no other sovereign are so many relics —genuine and spurious—extant. The romance of her being a Virgin Queen has something to do with this immortality, but a more potent cause is the fact that she identified herself, socially as well as politically, with the lives of her subjects, high and low. Possibly in all the history of chivalry there is no more forcible example of absolute devotion to a mistress than was shown by the statesmen, the soldiers, the sailors, the writers, and the poorest and humblest of cottage dwellers, to Queen Elizabeth; and assuredly with no other county in England is she so continuously and intimately associated as with Kent.

GENERAL VIEW OF TUDOR KENT.

The claim of Kent to be considered one of the chief industrial districts of England was furthered during this period by the introduction of two industries which remain to this day especially characteristic of the county—paper making and fruit growing.

Even to the outsider it is obvious that some special reason must exist for the development of certain industries in certain places, and so it is with these two Kentish industries. In that part of Kent devoted to paper

making there happens to be an almost unlimited supply of
pure spring water which can be used without filtration ;
hence paper is made in Kent which can only be produced
in a few other districts of England.

The first paper mill in England is believed to have been
set up at Stevenage in Hertfordshire, but the next is
certainly that which Sir John Spielman started at Dartford early in the reign of Elizabeth.

From Teynham, where was the cradle of the Kentish
fruit industry, then limited to apples and cherries, it has
spread almost over the whole face of West Kent, and
Kentish fruit, strawberries in particular, is sent in huge
quantities to every part of the kingdom.

Lambarde thus sums up the fertility of Kent :

"The ile of Thanet and the Eastern parts are Grayner ;
the Weald. was the Wood ; Romney Marsh is the
Medow Plot ; the North Doune towards the Thamyse
be the Long Garthe or Warreine ; and this Tenham with
thirty other Parishes from Rainham to Blean Wood bee
the Cherrie Garden and Apple Orcharde of Kent."

The splendour of the Tudor Period generally, and of
Elizabeth's reign in particular, is abundantly reflected in
our County.

When, upon the accession of Henry VII., men began to
breathe freely after a period of strife and desolation, great
and rapid progress was made in the science of living.
Houses ceased to be fortresses and became stately and
beautiful homes, and with specimens of these Kent is
fairly rich, the most notable being Penshurst, Knole,
Cobham, part of Leeds, and manor houses such as Bedgebury, Hollingbourne, Godinton, Franks, Ightham Mote,
and Restoration House, Rochester. Chimneys came into
general use, carpets gradually replaced rushes in good
houses, although the German traveller Hentzner notes
that the floor of the presence chamber at Greenwich
Palace was strewed with "hay ;" pillows were used, silver
plate adorned the table, pewter vessels replaced wood and
horn, and glass windows ceased to be a luxury confined to
the exceeding wealthy.

Most of our Kentish Grammar Schools, like those elsewhere, were founded by the Tudors, although the most
ancient, that of Sevenoaks, dates back to 1418. These
are the principal :

Tenterden, 1520 ; Biddenden, 1522; Faversham, founded
in 1527, abolished at the Dissolution, and re-founded in
1576; Rochester, 1542 ; Canterbury, 1542 ; Wye, 1545 ;
Tunbridge, 1552 ; Maidstone, 1562; Sandwich, 1563 ;
Cranbrook, 1574 ; and Sutton Valence, 1578.

Some Tudor prices in Kent are interesting :

A bullock of 40½ stone, at 8lbs. to the stone, cost £2 5s.,
Tudor money ; a wether cost 6s. 6d. ; an ewe, 5s. 5d. ; a
lamb, 2s. 6d.

Bread, now at 7d. the 4lb. loaf, cost 2s. 6½d. ; beef, now
about 10½d. a lb., was 1s. 3½d. ; beer was much the same
price as now ; cheese was 1s. 3d. against about 9d.

A soldier received eight pence a day, a workman about
ten pence, a reaper three shillings per acre, a common la-
bourer from three half-pence to four pence a day. See also
a paper in Arch. Cant. XXII. by Revd. C. E. Woodruff
upon wages paid in Maidstone during Elizabeth's reign.

We described Elizabeth's progress through Kent in
1573, and we append some accounts from the Faversham
Registers of that year, which give some idea of how costly
a matter it was to entertain Her Majesty, and this without considering the expense incurred by the private
individual whose house she honoured, sometimes with a
sojourn of more than a week.

" Drum and flute coats, 4s. 8d. ; Bear wards, 6s. 8d. ;
1 dozen torches and 24 links, 16s. 0d.; couchemen, 10s. 0d.;
pursuivants, 10s. 0d. ; mummers, 10s. 0d. ; supper to Her
Majesty, £27 2s. 0d. ; Porters, £1 0s. 0d. ; Yeoman of
flagons, 10s. 0d. ; Green taffetee for Mr. Fynche's son that
made the oration before the Queen, £1 4s. 0d."

Towards the glorious literature of this period Kent
contributed her very fair share. Thomas Sackville, Earl
of Dorset, planned and wrote part of the Mirror for

Magistrates, a metrical biography of English historical personages from our earliest history, but his fame rests rather upon his tragedy of *Gorboduc or Ferrex and Porrex*, remarkable far more for being the first-known instance of the employment of blank verse in English dramatic composition than for its intrinsic merits.

Sir Henry Wotton, poet, statesman, and man of letters, best known perhaps by his lyric which opens

<blockquote>
" You meaner beauties of the night,"
</blockquote>

addressed to the Queen of Bohemia, daughter of James I.

Sir Thomas Wyatt, of Allington, the lover of Anne Boleyn, of whom his son, in Tennyson's Queen Mary, says :

<blockquote>
" Courtier of many Courts, he loved the more
His own gray towers, plain life and letter'd peace,
To read and rhyme in solitary fields ;
The lark above, the nightingale below,
And answer them in song."
</blockquote>

He was a friend of the unfortunate Earl of Surrey— another Sidney—and the acknowledged introducer of blank verse into our literature ; their poems were published together, and their names are usually linked as at the head of our new poetry.

There was Christopher Marlowe, of Canterbury, described as the greatest dramatic writer before Shakespeare, author of *Faustus, Tamburlaine the Great, The Jew of Malta, Edward the Second*, and many other plays.

There was Lyly, the inventor of that fantastic style known as Euphuism, ridiculed by Holofernes in Shakespeare's *Love's Labour Lost*, and later by Scott in the *Monastery*, as represented by Sir Piercie Shafton.

There was Sidney, the " warbler of poetic prose," as Cowper calls him,

<blockquote>
" Sydney, than whom a gentler, braver man,
His own delightful genius never feigned,
Illustrating the vales of Arcady
With courteous courage and with loyal loves,"
</blockquote>

as Southey writes, the author of *Arcadia*, addressed to

his sister, the Countess of Pembroke, the inspirer of the exquisite epitaph by Ben Jonson; of *Astrophel and Stella*, addressed to Penelope Devereux, daughter of the Earl of Essex, and of various songs and sonnets.

There was John Fletcher of Cranbrook, joint author with Beaumont of more than thirty plays, sole author of eleven, of which the best known is the *Faithful Shepherdess.* He is also an interesting personage from his intimate association with Shakespeare. When on June 29th, 1613, the Globe Theatre was burned down by the accidental discharge of the piece of ordnance which announced in Shakespeare's play of King Henry the Eighth, or, to be more correct, of the play called "All is true," in which was embodied Henry the Eighth, the masked visit of the King to Wolsey, Shakespeare's play was lost. Another play was written on the same subject by Shakespeare, Fletcher, and perhaps Massinger, and is that which is now included amongst Shakespeare's works.

It is easy to distinguish between the smooth and polished diction of Fletcher and the more irregular and impulsive work of Shakespeare, says a recent writer in the *Contemporary Review,* who apportions the play between the two writers so that Fletcher appears to have written the greater part of it.

As indirectly associated with our county it may be mentioned that Spenser wrote the *Shepherd's Calendar* when a guest at Penshurst, and that it was at Sayes Court, Deptford, that Raleigh was the hero of the cloak and puddle episode.

A brief notice of the progress of the National Navy under the Tudors may fitly close this period of our history. Royal Navy there was none until the reign of Henry VIII., when, in 1512, the Navy Office was instituted, and the work of building and equipping ships for the National service came under the immediate control of the Government. Until then the Cinque Ports really supplied the National wants in this department; the ships were built of Kentish timber in Kentish yards and manned by Kent and Sussex men.

However, the *Great Harry*, built at Chatham in 1488, may be considered as the first ship, properly speaking, of the Royal Navy. James, in his introduction to his Naval History, speaks of her as remaining the only three-masted ship in the Navy until 1545, and alludes to her having been well built, as she lasted until 1553, when she was accidentally burned at Woolwich. But we read elsewhere of a *Great Harry* built at Erith under Henry VIII., which had four masts, each with two round fighting tops, sails of cloth of gold damasked, the Royal Standard at each corner of the forecastle, St George's banner at each quarter of the deck, her quarters, sides and tops lined with "heater" shields, and the arms of England and France at bow and stern. Also, that her armament consisted of about 60 brass and iron guns of various kinds, that she had a 20 and a 22 inch cable and an 8 inch hawser, and that she carried 301 marines, 349 soldiers, and 50 gunners. Either there were two *Great Harrys*, or the old one was altered.

Also in Henry VII.'s reign was built the *Henry Grace de Dieu*, at a cost of £14,000, with 70 guns mounted on two decks. Under Henry VIII. was built at Woolwich the *Regent* of 1,000 tons burden, and at Erith a second *Henry Grace de Dieu*, also of 1,000 tons, at the exact cost of £6,478 8s. 0¾d.! Henry VIII. is rightly to be regarded as the father of the English Navy, for it was under him that the force assumed a national shape, and that the moral embodied in the following lines came to be recognised :

> "Cherish marchandize, keepe the Admiraltie,
> That we bee masters of the narrow sea ;
> The ende of battaile is peace sickerly,
> And power causeth peace finally.
> Keepe then the sea, about in special
> Which of England is the town wall ;
> Keep then the sea, that is the wall of England,
> And then is England kept by Godde's hand."

He spent £65,000 on Dover Harbour, enacted severe laws for the regulation of the growth and cutting of timber, founded the Royal Dockyards at Woolwich and Deptford, the Trinity House, and, as we have mentioned, the Navy Office.

After the first years of his reign, however, his zeal for the Navy cooled; we soon had practically no Navy at all, and foreign ships landed and sacked our coast towns at will. In 1536 we had scarcely a man-of-war in the Channel; the harbour construction works at Dover were constantly interrupted by French and Flemings, and ships were openly attacked and robbed under the very guns of Dover Castle.

In 1539 there was a re-awakening consequent upon Henry's open defiance of the Papacy, and therefore of all Roman Catholic nations. The lands belonging to the suppressed religious houses were sold, and the proceeds applied to the National Armament, so that when the King died in 1547 he left the Navy in a better state than it had ever been in before, consisting of 30 ships with a tonnage of 10,330, 15 "row barges," and the dockyards of Woolwich and Deptford in full swing.

Under Edward VI. there was a decline, chiefly owing to dissensions between the Protector and his brother the Lord High Admiral.

Under Mary the English supremacy of the sea was proudly asserted, even Philip of Spain being made to salute the flag by Lord Howard of Effingham when he came to marry the Queen. Still the Navy declined. At the beginning of Elizabeth's reign the Royal Navy consisted of but 21 ships, of which the largest was 800 tons, and of 45 merchantmen with enough arms for 3,000 men. In 1587 there were actually only nine ships in commission, and at the time of the Armada but 28, which was increased to 34 at the actual hour of crisis. There was an honourable competition between the three chief Elizabethan ship-wrights, Peter Pett, Matthew Baker, and Richard Chapman, with the result that ships were thoroughly well built. Thus, the *Elizabeth*, launched in 1588, was afloat in 1618; and the *Marye Rose*, launched in 1566, was only condemned in 1618. During the entire reign only two Queen's ships were taken by the Spaniards, and not one was lost by fire, or weather, or running aground.

Chatham seems to have been the chief Elizabethan ship-building yard—at any rate it cost the most.

Upon the accession of James I. the Royal Navy con-sisted of 42 vessels of 17,000 tons, manned by 8,400 men.

By this time the Cinque Ports had so decayed that the number of ships belonging to Hythe had dwindled from eighty to eight, and of Winchelsea it was reported "there are at present no ships, and the town is greatly decayed."

The rate of pay for the Fleet at the end of Elizabeth's reign was :

			£	s.	d.	
Lord Admiral	-	-	3	6	8	per day.
Vice-Admiral	-	-	2	0	0	,,
Rear-Admiral	-	-		15	0	,,
Captain	-	-		2	6	,,
Lieutenant	-	-	3	0	0	per month.
Boatswain	-	-	1	10	0	,,
Sailor	-	-		10	0	,,
Boy	-	-		7	6	,,

NOTES ON TUDOR KENT.

A.

The original seal of the City of Canterbury had on its obverse a complicated system of towers, and on its reverse the martyrdom of Thomas à Becket. In the Corporation entries, 1541-2, appears the following item :

"Paid to William Oldfield, belfounder, for puttyng out of Thomas Bekket in the common seale and gravyng agayn of the same."

A poor representation of the city arms was substituted.

B.

We are asked not to believe a good deal about the vengeance taken upon Thomas à Becket's remains under Henry VIII. The head so long presented to be kissed by pilgrims who could afford to pay the required fee is said to have been a sham of the early fourteenth century, indeed is as good as proved not to be the original by the 1888 discovery, which seems to point to the fact that the remains were buried entire under the round tower of St. Thomas's chapel—that is, in 1538.

This does away with the accepted story about the scattering of Becket's ashes by order of Henry VIII. At any rate the only evidence we have to go upon with respect, not merely to the desecration of the Archbishop's remains, but to his mock trial, is in the angry complaint of the Pope. Indeed the story of his trial is said to be no earlier than the seventeenth century. Henry concerned himself far more about the decorations and offerings at the shrine than about Thomas's personal relics, and there seems no reason to doubt that the latter were decently buried without let or hindrance.

C.

A love letter from Henry to Anne Boleyn :

" Myne owne sweetheart ;

"This shall be to advertise you of the great ellingness (solitariness) that I find here since your departing ; for I assure you me thinketh the tyme longer since your departing now last, than I was wont to do a whole fortnight. I think your kindness and my fervence of love causeth it, for otherwise I would not have thought it possible that for so little a while it should have grieved me ; but now that I am comeing towards you methinketh my pains have been half released, and also I am right well comforted. . . . Wishing myself (specially an evening) in my sweetheart's armes, whose pretty duckys I trust shortly to kysse. Written with the hand of him that was, and is, and shall be, yours by his will,

H.R."

Ordinance for the government of the Royal Palaces in the reign of Henry VIII., dated from Eltham :

"His Highness's attendants are not to steal any locks or keys, tables, forms, cupboards or other furniture, out of noblemen's or gentlemen's houses where he goes to visit."

"No herald, minstrel, falconer or other shall bring to the Court any boy or *rascal*."

"Master cooks shall employ such scullions as shall not go about naked nor lie all night on the ground before the kitchen fire."

"No dogs to be kept in the Court, but only a few spaniels for the ladies."

"Dinner to be at ten, supper at four."

"The proper officers are between six and seven o'clock every morning to make the fire in and straw His Highness's Privy Chamber."

" Officers of the Privy Chamber shall be loving together, keeping secret everything said or done, leaving hearkning or inquiring where the King is or goes, be it early or late, without grudging, mumbling, or talking of the King's pastime, late or early going to bed, or any other matter."

" Rhenish and Malmsey wines are directed and no other."

" Coal only allowed to the King's, the Queen's and Lady Mary's chambers."

" A gift to each officer of the kitchen who marries, and a gift to whosoever brings His Highness a present."

" The Queen's maids of honour to have a chet loaf, a manchet, a gallon of ale and a chine of beef for their breakfasts."

" Injunction to the brewer not to put any hops or brimstone into the ale."

" Among fowls for table are crocards, winders, runners, grows and peions, but neither turkey nor guinea fowl."

Peions are no doubt peacocks, and *runners* may mean ordinary fowls, but for the others ——— !

" Twenty-four loaves of bread a day are allowed for His Highness's greyhounds."

D.

According to an Ashford pamphlet the exact distribution of the Kentish martyrs between the years 1554-1558 is as follows :

Canterbury	- -	35 men and 15 women burned.
		2 men and 1 woman starved.
Wye	- - - -	2 men burned.
Ashford	- - -	2 men burned.
Dartford	- - -	1 man burned.
Rochester	- -	2 men and 1 woman burned.
Maidstone	- -	4 men and 5 women burned.
Tunbridge	- -	1 woman burned.

Total 48 men and 23 women = 71 persons.

E.

At the risk of being considered tedious I transcribe a letter from Sir Henry Sidney to his son Philip, then a little boy at school in Shrewsbury, and a postscript added by Lady Sidney :

" SON PHILIP,

" I have received too letters from yow, one written in Latine, the other in Frenche, which I take in good parte, and will yow to exercise that practise of learninge often ; for that it will stand yow in moste steade in that profession of lyf that yow are born to live in.   And, since this ys my first letter that ever I did write to yow, I will not that yt be all emptie of some advyses which my natural care of yow provoketh me to wishe you to followe as documents to yow in this your tendre age.

PENSHURST.

" Let your first action be the lyfting up of yowr mynd to Almightie
God by harty prayer, and felingly dygest the woords yow speake in
prayer with continual meditation and thinkynge of Hym to whom
yow praye and of the matter for which yow praye : and use this at
an ordinarye hower, whereby the time ytself will put yow in
remembrance to doe that which yow are accustomed to doe in that
tyme. Apply yowr studye suche houres as youre discrete master
doth assign you, earnestlye, and the time, I knowe, he will so
lymitt as shall be both sufficient for yowr learninge and safe for
yowr health. And mark the sense and the matter of that yow read,
as well as the woordes, so shall yow both enriech yowr tonge with
woordes and your wytte with matter, and judgement will growe as
yeares growyth to yow. Be humble and obedient to yowr master,
for unless you frame yourselfe to obey, yea, and feale in yowrselfe
what obedience is, yow shall never be able to teach others how to
obey yow. Be curtees of gesture, and affable to all men, with
diversitie of reverence, accordinge to the dignitie of the person.
There is nothing what wynneth so much with so lytle cost. Use
moderate dyet, so as after yowr meate yow may finde yowr wytte
fresher and not duller, and yowr body more lyvely and not more
heavye. Seldom drinke wine, and yet sometimes doe, least, being
enforced to drinke upon the sodayne, yow shall find yowrself
inflamed. Use exercise of bodye, but suche as ys without peryll to
yowre jointes or bones, it will encrease yowr force and enlardge
your breathe. Delight to be cleanly as well in all parts of yowr
bodye as in yowr garments. Yt shall make yow grateful in yche
company, and otherwise lothsome. Give yowrself to be merye, for
yow degenerate from yowr father if yow find not yowr self most
able in wytte and bodye to doe anything when yow be most merye,
but let yowr myrthe be ever void of all scurilitee and biting woords
to any man, for a wound given by a woorde is oftentimes harder to
be cured than that which is given by the swerd. Be yow rather a
hearer and bearer away of other men's talke than a begyner or
procurer of speeche, otherwise yow shall be counted to delight to
hear yowr self speake. Be modest in yche assemblee, and rather
be rebuked of light felowes for a medenlyke shamefastnes than of
yowr sad friends for pearte boldness. Thinke upon every woorde
that yow will speake before yow utter hyt, and remember how
nature hath rampared up, as yt were, the tonge with teeth, lippes,
yea, and here (hair) without the lippes, and all betokening for loose
raynes or bridles, the use of that membre. Above all things tell no
untruthe, no not in trifels, the custome of hyt is naughte. . . . . .
Remember my sonne, the noble blood yow are descended of by yowr
mother's side, and thinke that only by vertuous lyf and good action
yow may be an ornement to yowr illustre famylie.

" Well, my litell Philippe, this is yuough for me, and to much I fear for yow; but yf I shall find that this lighte meale of digestione nourishes anything the weake stomache of yowr younge capacitee, I will, as I find the same growe stronger, fead yt with toofer foode.

" Farewell. Yowr mother and I send yow our blessing, and Almightie God grant yow his, nourish yow with his feer, guide yow with his grace, and make yow a good servant to yowr prince and country.

" Yowr loving father, so longe as yow lyve in the feare of God.

HENRY SIDNEY."

P.S. to above letter by Lady Sydney.

" Your noble and carefull father hath taken paynes (with his owne hand) to give you in his letter so wise, so learned, and most requisite precepts, for you to follow with a diligent and humble, thankefull minde, as I will not withdrawe your eies from beholding and reverent honouring the same, no, not so long time as to read any letter from one, and therefore at this time I will write unto you no other letter than this whereby I first blesse you with my desire to God to plant in you His grace; and secondarily warn you to have alwaies before the eyes of your mind these excellent counsails of my lord, your deere father, and that you fail not continually once in foure or five dais to read them over. And for a finall leave taking for this time see that you shewe yourselfe as a loving, obedient scholar to your good maister, to governe you yet many yeers, and that my lord and I may heere that you profite so in your learning as thereby you may encrease our loving care of you, and deserve at his handes the continuance of his great joy, to have him often witnesse with his owne hand the hope he hath in your well doing.

" Farewell, my little Phillip; and once againe, the Lord blesse you.

Your loving mother,

MARIE SIDNEY."

F.

The Earl of Anjou was only one out of 28 suitors whom Elizabeth had either more or less encouraged herself, or who had been suggested to her, or had been pressed to marry. No clearer idea of the all-important part played in the politics of the Elizabethan age by those so-called " coquetries " of the Queen can be gained than from a study of Mr. Martin Hume's book, " The Courtships of Queen Elizabeth."

Here is a list in chronological order of Elizabeth's suitors:

1.—Duke of Angouleme.
2.—Earl of Arran.
3.—Philip of Spain.

4.—Lord Seymour of Sudely.
5.—Duke of Guise.
6.—The Son of the Duke of Florence.
7.—The Son of Frederick of Saxony.
8.—Lord Courtney.
9.—Earl of Arundel.
10.—Duke of Savoy.
11.—Crown Prince of Sweden.
12.—Earl of Westmoreland.
13.—Lord Howard's Son.
14.—Sir William Pickering.
15.—Adolphus of Denmark.
16.—Earl of Oxford.
17.—Robert Dudley, Earl of Liecester.
18.—Archduke Charles of Savoy.
19.—Duke of Finland.
20.—Son of Duke of Nevers.
21.—Duke of Nemours.
22.—Hans Casimir.
23.—Don Carlos.
24.—Charles IX. of France.
25.—Duke of Anjou.
26.—Henry of Navarre.
27.—Duke of Alençon.
28.—Don John of Austria.

G.

Instructions concerning the management of Beacons :

"Inprimis, that all beacons, especially of the East and West Forelands, be dubled, garded with such watchmen as shall be of judgment and discretion, upon the fyrst occasion of appoache offered by the ennymie to rayse the laram by bells or hoblers (light horsemen), and if they shall procead forthe to landing to fire the beacons.

"That yow shall appoynt the serchers (inspectors) of every beacon dilligentlye to attend ther charge from tyme to tyme, to advertise yow the centioners (sentinels) what shal be descryed and that uppon anny matter discovered yow advertise me with diligens what shal be seen.

"That yow appoint the beacons sufficientlie, to be supplied with fuell, and that yow appoint for every day watche a *gare* (signal of warning) reddy uppon the fyrst occasion to be hanged up.

"That yow take order in all the perrishes within yowr centen that no bells be ronge in the churche for service, christeninge, or burriall, but only on bel during this tyme, and uppon the alaram al the bells to be ronge out.

"That yow charge all yowr centens as they wil answer to the contraire at their perrills to provide themselves with powder, shott, and matche sufficient, and that they be in reddiness uppon the fyrste strocke of an alaram to marche to the place of their fyrst assembly, but that all that can com on horsebacke repayre in al hast to meet me at the place from whence the alaram shal be first raysed.

"That every man carry into the feelde with him when he goethe abroad, his furniture (armour and arms) that he may soner be in reddiness to answer the alaram.

"That every householder make provision in a reddiness of meale or breade for on monthe, accordinge to the proportion of his householde, that he may kepe the feeld yf we shall see occasion.

GEORGE CAREY."

Drill orders issued by Walsingham :

"That the strongest and squarest men exercise muskets, the leest and most nimble, harquebuses.

"An order for the readie and easie trayning of shott, and the avoyding of great expence and waste of powder :—The leaders and captaines who are appointed to instructe and traine them shall cause an holbert to be sett up in the plaine, whereby every shott maie passe in that order which the french men call "a la file," or as we terme yt, in ranke like wild geese, and so passing by the halbert, to present his piece, and make offer as thoughe he would shoote, and those which doe not behave themselves with their pieces as they oughte, maye receyve particular instructyon and teaching. This exercise would be used two or three metings at the least for ignorant people, in which time may be discerned those that cannot frame themselves in any likelihood to prove shott, in whose roomes the captaines maie require others to be placed who are more apt thereunto. Afterwards to teach them how to hold their pieces, for endaungering themselves and their fellowes, to put in their matches, and to acquainte them with false fyres, by priming only the panne, and not charging the piece which will enure their eye with the flashe of fyre, embolden the partyes, and make everything famillyer and ready unto them. Then to give the piece half his charge, and acquaint them in skyrmishing wise to come forward and retire orderly again. After to proceed to the full charge, and lastly to the bullet, to shoote at a marke for some tryfle to be bestowed on him that best deserveth the same. With this order and pollecye, men shall in shorter time be exercised, and with the tenth part of the charge, to the great ease of the cuntrye and saving of powder, for that in this manner yt is found that two lb. of powder will serve one man for the foure daies exercise of trayning. And a number which by reeson of the churlyshenes of their pieces, and not being acquainted therewith by degrees, are ever after so discouraged and fearefull, as either they wincke or pull their heads from the peece, whereby they take no perfect levell, but shute at random, and so never prove good shotte."

LOSELY M.S.S.

STEWART KENT.

PART I.—JAMES I. AND CHARLES I. TO 1642.

JAMES I. 1603-1625.

JAMES, strange contrast mentally and physically to the majestic, imperial Tudors who preceded him, was very fond of Greenwich Palace, and passed much time hunting in the Park after his own peculiar fashion, propped and bolstered up on his horse so that he could not have fallen off if he had tried to, as described in Scott's *Fortunes of Nigel.*

It may be noted that the first Protestant baptism of a Royal infant in England, that of the Princess Mary, took place at Greenwich.

This was an age of plotting and intrigue, and we find the tenth Lord Cobham deeply involved with Raleigh and others in a couple of plots known respectively as the Main or Spanish Treason, and the Bye or Priests' Treason.

The real character and object of the first have always been veiled in obscurity, but although it was supposed to have hinged upon the placing of Arabella Stewart, cousin of the King, upon the throne, it was probably but a plot of Raleigh and Cobham against their political enemy Essex, who was now in favour and was making them feel his influence, in which France was to play a part.

For this Cobham and Raleigh were condemned, and their trials are not edifying and not very creditable to either, for Cobham turned on Raleigh, who, under examination, had hinted at Cobham's implication, and Lingard says that Raleigh betrayed Cobham as having had secret communications with Arenberg, the ambassador of the Archduke. Raleigh denied it, but when he was confronted with his own letter to Cecil, in which Cobham was alluded to, he was guiltily amazed and confounded.

Cobham got off with going through all the horrors of death on the scaffold without being actually executed, and was sent to the Tower, whence he was released on sick leave in 1617, to which he returned in 1618, and where he died in 1619, not, as has been often stated, starved and deserted in a Minories hovel.

Raleigh's sentence was also commuted and he was sent to the Tower, whence he was released to go upon his luckless voyage to Guiana, and returned to be executed in order to gain the favour of Spain.

The Bye Plot or Priests' Treason had for its object the seizure of the King's person. Cobham, and his brother George Brooke, were concerned in this, as, is believed, was Raleigh, but nothing came of it, and the priests concerned were executed.

A Muster of the County of Kent for 1603 shows :— 7,500 able men, 3,000 armed men, 250 pioneers, 20 demi-lancers and 200 " high horses."

In this year the King's father-in-law, King Christian IV. of Denmark, paid a state visit. He landed at Gravesend, proceeded thence to Greenwich, and whilst there spent much of his time hunting at Eltham—this being the last record of a royal visit to this ancient palace. On his return journey he was presented at Greenwich with various sports—bear and bull-baiting, and tilting, and inspected the Royal fleet at Chatham during his stay at Rochester.

We get a fair notion of the character of the Court at Greenwich at this time from Harington's description of a masque held in honour of Christian. He says :

" After dinner the representation of Solomon's Temple, and the coming of the Queen of Sheba was made, or meant to have been made. But alas! as all earthly things fail to poor mortals in enjoyment, so proved this. The lady who played the Queen's part carried precious gifts to both their majesties; but, forgetting the steps arising to the canopy, overset her caskets into his Danish Majesty's lap, and fell at his feet, or rather into his face. Much hurry and confusion ensued, and cloths and napkins made all clean. His Majesty then got up and would dance with the Queen of Sheba; but he fell down and humbled himself before her, and was carried to an inner chamber, and laid in a bed of state, which was not a little defiled with the presents which had been bestowed upon his garments; such as wine, cream, jelly, spices, and other good matters.

"The entertainment and show went forward, and most of the presenters went backwards, or fell down, wine so occupied their upper chambers. Then appeared in rich dresses, Faith, Hope, and Charity. Hope tried to speak, but wine so enfeebled her endeavours that she withdrew, and hoped the King would excuse her brevity. Faith followed her from the royal presence in a staggering condition. Charity came to the King's feet, and, seeming desirous to cover the sins of her sisters, made a sort of obeisance; she brought gifts, but said she would return home again; she then returned to Hope and Faith, who were both sick in the lower hall. Next came Victory in bright armour, and presented a rich sword to the King, who waved it away, but Victory persisted in a strange medley of versification, till, after much lamentable utterance, she was led away like a captive, and laid to sleep on the outer steps of the ante-chamber. Peace took offence in endeavouring to get up to the King, and wielded her olive branch in warlike assault upon the heads of the attendants."

Prince Henry at this time resided with his tutor, Adam Newton, at Charlton House. He was a young prince of great promise and was dearly beloved by the people; of him the elder Disraeli says :—" He would have proved an heroic and military character. Had he ascended the throne the days of Cressy and Agincourt would have been revived, and Henry the Ninth had rivalled Henry the Fifth."

He was an all-round athlete as well as a scholar, and it was no doubt under his auspices that the Royal Blackheath Golf Club was founded. He also took a patriotic interest in naval matters, and, knowing that his father's favourite, Carr, and his faction had a spite against Phineas Pett, the Chief Constructor, determined that on the occasion of the launch of the *Charles*, one of the largest ships ever built for the Royal Navy, at Woolwich in 1611, the Court should be present at the ceremony in order to prevent any malicious action. Unfortunately there was a hitch, and the ship stuck on the stays, so that the Court, after waiting a long time, had to go off; this, in an age of witchcraft belief, was attributed to Carr's evil influence, and had not the ship got afloat that evening he would probably have heard of it. Prince Henry died this same year to the universal grief.

In 1617 James paid a visit to his native land, and during his absence the Queen resided at Greenwich. Whilst here the young ladies of a Deptford boarding school presented a Masque before Her Majesty entitled *Cupid's Banishment*. There is nothing notable about this fact except that this is believed to be the first mention of a ladies' boarding school in English history, it having been the custom heretofore for girls to be educated in convents.

Saturated with that notion of the Divine Right of Kings, which he had enlarged upon in his *Discourse on the True Law of Free Monarchies*, and the application of which led to the disastrous events of the next reign, James was engaged in a constant conflict with his Parliaments, although it was his own conceit rather than a hankering after power which inspired him. Amongst the many grievances which vexed the people was the arbitrary imposition of taxes upon merchandise by the King, of course without any reference to Parliament, in which he was backed up by venal and favour-currying judges. The manufacturing districts of Kent felt this very severely. In 1616 the exportation of white or undyed cloths was prohibited, although there is little doubt that those who were willing to pay for the privilege could export so much as they liked. As this particular trade had always been an important branch of the Kentish industry, it meant something like stagnation, and, in consequence, some 3,000 Kentish cloth-weavers emigrated to the Palatinate and there started factories.

Similar statutes injured the woollen industry, and, although in response to the high duties levied by the Dutch on imported wool an effort was made to foster the inland trade by such measures as the renewal of the order that all people of a certain position should be buried in shrouds of sheep's wool only, the trade gradually decayed.

In 1625 the Plague seems to have raged virulently in Kent. Ashford and Kennington suffered severely, and we find record of an order that the Half Hundred of Cale-hill contribute £1 19s. 6d. to assist the inhabitants of these places. The Plague increasing, the justices report that the inhabitants of Ashford "are not able to relieve and orderly to attend the sick, and to beare about the charges of theyr other poore Artificers who, for want of trade, must of necessity be provided for, or els they will be forced for the succor of theyr lives to breake forthe of that towne to the danger of the country."

So the said Half Hundred had to collect £3 for a month's provision of Ashford.

We may note that Sir Thomas Knevett, Steward of Westminster, who arrested Guy Fawkes, was a Kent man.

During this reign the picturesque so-called Jacobean style of domestic architecture came into vogue. In Kent, perhaps, the most notable examples are Chilham Castle, and parts of Cobham, Knole, and Lullingstone.

CHARLES I. 1625-1642.

We are now arrived at the most momentous and interesting period in the History of England, and by no means the least interesting in that of our county, and this must be our excuse for its treatment at some length, and for what may occasionally seem digressions beyond our defined limits.

So few are the pleasant scenes that we shall be able to record during this eventful reign that we must be pardoned for opening with one of them at the risk of its being deemed unworthy of what is called the " dignity of history."

It is the meeting at Dover of Charles with his bride, Henrietta Maria, the beautiful, iron-willed woman who was so fatally to influence the Royal destiny. Charles was at Canterbury when the Queen arrived at Dover after a stormy passage, and the messenger who brought him the news is said to have performed the journey of fifteen miles in thirty-six minutes, which we don't believe for a quarter of a minute. Charles hastened to Dover Castle to greet her, and, noticing her to be taller than he had expected, he glanced at her feet to see if she wore high heels, which she perceiving, said : " Sir, I stand upon my own feet : I have no help from art : thus high am I, neither higher nor lower."

Leaving Dover for Canterbury they halted on Barham Downs, where a banquet awaited them ; the gentry of Kent were mustered on horse, and .the English ladies of the Royal Household assembled to be presented.

At Canterbury they went to the Palace (of which the only relic to-day is an arch in Palace Street), where was held a magnificent entertainment at which the King himself carved for the Queen. Here they were married on June 24th, 1625. From Canterbury they went to Gravesend, and thence by water to London, where, although the Plague was raging, they had a great reception.

From the very outset it became evident that Charles was even more fully imbued with the notion of the Divine Right of Kings than had been his father, and was more determined to assert it—an unfortunate resolve, as Parliament happened to contain a number of very able and strong-willed men, and was in no mood to be bullied. So we find the King in the first year of his reign in conflict with the Commons.

Sir Dudley Digges, of Chilham, was one of the eight managers of the impeachment of the Duke of Buckingham, the King's favourite and master, and for this he and the famous Sir John Eliot, "the most illustrious confessor in the cause of liberty whom that time produced," as Hallam calls him, were arrested by the King's order and thrown into the Tower.

This unwarrantable attack upon its privileges aroused the House, and it refused to proceed to business until its members were released. As business in the King's mind meant simply the granting him supplies, he yielded, admitted his error and the prisoners were released.

It was on this occasion that Sir Dudley Digges, incensed at the jaunty way in which Buckingham received the news of his impeachment, made the famous remark :

" Do you jeer my Lord ? I can show you when a greater man than your Lordship, as high as you in place and honour, and as deep in the King's favour, has been hanged for as small a crime as these articles contain ! "

It was this same Sir Dudley by whose will originated the quaint old custom, observed until comparatively recently, of the race on Old Wives Lees at Chilham between a young man and a young woman for £10 a side.

In 1626 the King, in the absence of regular supplies from Parliament, made a demand for a general loan, with promise of repayment within eighteen months, to be levied according to the rate at which the people were assessed for the last subsidy ; and the Commissioners appointed for the collection thereof were instructed to certify the names of refractory persons to the Privy Council and not to accept any abatement of the amount demanded.

This produced an uproar. In Kent the loan was peremptorily refused—" Kent stood out to a man," on the principle that no subsidy had received the assent of

Parliament and that it had nothing to do with loans levied without such assent.

The result of this was that five knights—Darnel, Corbet, Hampden, Heveningham and Earl—were arrested and imprisoned, and upon their appeal to be brought up on a writ of *Habeas Corpus*, with the articles of their indictment fully shown, it was refused upon the grounds that they had been committed by special command of the King without particular cause being shown.

To this case, known as Darnel's, we owe the continued assertion by Parliament of the fundamental immunity of English subjects from arbitrary detention, and its subsequent establishment by 31, Car. II.

But judgment was given for the Crown, and the five knights were remanded to prison. By this decision every statute from the Great Charter downwards became a dead letter, and the wound was the more deadly because the notorious cause of imprisonment was a refusal to pay an illegal exaction.

The prisoners, however, were released in June, 1628, in which year the King called his third Parliament.

In the vehement discussions which took place upon the various tyrannies and misdeeds of the Crown, and in the conference held by the two Houses which led to the Petition of Right, Digges took a prominent part, and was one of the managers for the Commons.

Briefly, the Petition of Right dealt with :

    1.—Illegality of forced loans. 2.—Commitment of those who refused. 3.—Billeting of soldiers. 4.—Martial law.

Whilst it absolutely deprived the King of the power of committing those who refused to contribute.

In 1630 the King endeavoured to add to his revenue by prohibiting the export of wool, although he sold the privilege. This put a premium upon smuggling, which was carried on to an enormous extent on the Kentish coast, especially from Romney Marsh and the lone creeks and inlets about the mouths of the Stour, in the neighbourhood

of Sandwich, liquor being received from the Frenchmen and
Dutchmen in exchange, nor could the Statute of 1674,
which made it felony to export wool, stop the practice.

The abuse of the levy of ship-money was the next stroke
widening the gap between King and people. This was
calculated to produce about a million per annum, modern
money. The first writ was issued in 1634 for £10,400, and
was pretty generally paid. Noy is credited with the dis-
interment of this ancient right of our sovereigns to levy
ship-money upon coast towns, but Finch is responsible for
its extension to inland places.

The ordinary form of writ was for a ship of a certain
tonnage, armed with so many guns, equipped with so many
crew, and supplied with provisions for six months, to be
ready for the service of the King at a certain seaport on a
certain day. The cost was levied by a "distress," and
refractory people were imprisoned.

James Mann, of Bromley, declined to pay for Kent on
the plea that he was already contributing as a citizen of
London. He was ordered to appear before the Privy
Council, but history does not record the result.

In April, 1636, we find a petition from Canterbury
praying for an abatement of assessment, having already
paid £550 and £400; and in 1640 Maidstone objects to
pay more than the proportion of £100 per 100 tons, and is
reprimanded by the Privy Council.

In 1639, Sir John Colepeper, of Leeds, as distinguished,
although moderate, a Royalist as was Digges a champion
of Parliament, was amongst the foremost in forcing the
resignation by the King of the iniquitous monopoly
system. His speech, so loyal, yet so emphatic in its
declamation of wrongs, which Rushworth gives in full,
makes the perversity and pride of Charles all the more
detestable.

In 1640 there was an attempt to raise soldiers in Kent
to serve against the Scots, but such as were enlisted,
composed of farmers and yeomen, were reported to be
restive, unruly and insubordinate.

In the same year Sir Edward Dering, described as "an honest but not very enlightened man," brought up a petition from the County of Kent, complaining of the abuse of power by archbishops, bishops, deans and archdeacons, "who suspend and punish good ministers without reason, that few of them preach the Word themselves, but countenance Papists, hinder the printing of good books, deform churches with Popish pictures and altars, revive antiquated ceremonies, such as standing at hymns and at the Gloria, turning to the East, bowing to the altar; that they abuse the power of excommunicating, claim their office *jure divino*, occupy temporal places, awe the judges, hinder Habeas Corpus, &c., profane the Lord's Day by tolerating sports thereon, and suspend ministers for not reading the Book of Sports." The petition prays for the abolition of episcopacy, and the second reading of the bill which was consequently brought in was carried on a division by 139 to 108. But there was a strong feeling in the County that this was too much of a concession to Puritanism, and a second petition was presented in 1641 on behalf of "The gentrie, ministers, freeholders and subsidy men within the County of Kent" for reform, which should stop short of the abolition of episcopacy.

It is absolutely necessary in order to enter upon an intelligently comprehensive survey of events affecting our county first briefly to consider the Long Parliament.

It met in November, 1640. Its first session lasted rather longer than ten months, and almost entire unanimity prevailed owing to its resolve that the abuses which had existed during so many years of misrule should be abolished and redressed, and the instruments of the King's tyranny punished.

It received petitions and complaints, and enacted that all canons unsanctioned by Parliament were illegal: that a Parliament should be summoned every three years, and sit for thirty days. The Courts of Star Chamber, High Commission, and of York were abolished. The judgment in favour of Ship Money reversed: Finch, Laud and

Strafford were impeached, and on the day on which the Act passed the King assented to a law binding him not to adjourn, prorogue or dissolve Parliament without its own consent. After a recess of six weeks the Houses met again, and it was evident that it was now divided into two Parties, Royalist and Popular, afterwards Cavaliers and Roundheads, and, later still, Tories and Whigs. The former were of opinion that enough had been done for the present, abuses redressed, rights vindicated and surrounded with new securities, and that it was necessary to take care that the victory over despotism should not end in anarchy.

The latter knew that no real securities had been given, nothing but the King's word, on which they could not rely, and that he was no more likely to respect the new laws than he had the old.

Whilst thus separating, news came which excited the passions and confirmed the opinions of both—the Irish Rebellion.

The Cavaliers maintained it a duty rendered by this that every good Englishman and Protestant should strengthen the hands of the King : the Roundheads that no precaution was necessary, that they had no security that if an army was raised for the reduction of Ireland it would not be turned against the liberties of the country.

Now came the first great Parliamentary struggle. The Roundheads moved that a Remonstrance should be presented to the King, enumerating the faults of his Government, and expressing the distrust with which it was still regarded. It was carried by eleven votes, and this result shows that if the King had been prudent there would soon have been a majority for his side. His first steps promised well. He announced his intention of governing constitutionally, and called Falkland, Hyde and Colepeper to his councils.

Then he committed the great error of his life. Irritated, it is said, by some hints which were dropped of impeaching the Queen, he attempted to seize the five members—

Hollis, Hazlerig, Hampden, Pym, and Strode—whilst Parliament was in session.

This breach of the privileges of Parliament, that is, this outrage upon the liberty of the subject, for it must be remembered, as Mr. Harrison says, that "Parliament as a legislature had ceased to exist; it was a committee of safety of the nation charged with the duty of forcing the King to submit," produced an explosion of anger to which all previous outbursts had been mere fire-works, united again the two parties in one phalanx of opposition, put all London in arms, roused the city to such a fury that in a few days the King left it, and brought addresses of fidelity to Parliament from a score of counties.

That from Kent to the peers was carried bodily by a number of freeholders; this was its tenor:

"Wherein His Gracious Majesty, seduced by the Malevolent Counsell of an ill affected party of Malignants and Cavaliers; the Protestant Religion, his Royall Person, and Honour, the Priviledge of Parliament, and the subjects' liberty are threat'ned with too apparent hazard and ruine:

"Wee, the knights, gentry, and commonalty of the County of Kent, according to the duty of Loyall Subjects and good citizens, are not only willing to contribute our best wishes and votes, but even to the utmost of their endeavours, both with their lives and their fortunes, for the redressing of His Majesty from such hands, and our Liberty and Religion from such perill and danger.

" May it please this Honourable House to consider that wee do apprehend themselves in a condition and posture nothing suitable to this their Resolution, being deprived and left naked by the taking of our arms from us, and therefore beseech your provident care to impower us with such a proportion of arms and ammunition to be magazined in these parts, whereby wee may be inabled to manifest our affection and obedience to the Counsel of King and Parliament."

It was added that the petitioners endorsed the action

of Parliament in taking away the votes of the prelates, and disabling them from temporal employments, and asserting that they will defend Parliament to the utmost so long as it should be in accord with the Commons.

The Parliament expressed itself much pleased with this address, and in acknowledging it wished that all other counties would follow the example of Kent.

Immediately after the King's departure from London the Houses assumed all the powers of government: they raised money and forces for their support, seized the arsenals and ports, fortified London, dispatched Sir John Hotham to be governor of Hull, where there was a large magazine of arms, instructed the governor of Portsmouth to take no orders but from them, placed the Tower under the command of one of their own adherents, and passed a Bill by which the command of the militia was entrusted to men of their own choosing.

But there was a strong Royalist party in Kent which was willing yet to give the King every chance and which viewed with apprehension the decided measures of Parliament. Many of the County nobility and gentry not only declined to recognise the above address to the Peers as representing County feeling, but in April, 1642, instructed their member, Augustus Skinner, to say in reply to the rumour that there would be disturbances at the Assizes, that the County was in perfect peace, and that the assertor to the contrary should be punished.

They offered the following advice in an address " on behalf of the gentry, ministers and commonalty of the County of Kent agreed upon at the General Assize of that County."

1.—-That Hull should be restored to the King.

2.—That the Militia question should be laid aside until good law could be passed wherein care may be taken as well for the liberty of the subjects as for the defence of the Kingdom.

3.—Adjournment of Parliament to an "indifferent place" where all might meet and discuss."

Parliament resented this ; Sir William Boteler and Captain Lovelace, who had presented the address, were detained and the chief signers of it ordered to be arrested.

This, as may be imagined, did the Parliamentary cause in Kent very little good.

Part II.—Charles I.   1642-1649.

Before we treat particularly of the part played by Kent in the Civil War it is as well to state as nearly as possible how the two parties of King and Parliament were distributed.

For King :—Were most of the greater nobles, many of the lesser gentry, some rich citizens, the townsmen of the West, and the country people generally of the North and West of England.

For Parliament :—The peers and the greater gentry, the great bulk of the lesser gentry, the townsmen of the richer part of England, the Eastern and Home Counties, and the City of London.

Roughly : — For King — Aristocracy and peasantry, church and universities, the world of culture and pleasure.   For Parliament — Gentry, yeomanry, law, commerce and trade.

At the outbreak of the War, Parliament acted promptly in Kent.   Dover Castle was secured and garrisoned; suspected royalists were arrested and their estates confiscated, and the houses of Sir William Boteler and Sir Edward Dering plundered.   The Parliament soldiers broke into Canterbury Cathedral, battered down the organ, pulled up the communion rails, hacked the image of our Lord out of the altar cloth and made a target of our Lord's figure over the south door.

On October 23rd, 1642, the indecisive battle of Edgehill was fought.   The prayer of the Kentish knight, Sir Jacob Astley, who commanded a battalion of the Royal Foot Guards under Lord Lindsey, is well known :

"O Lord, Thou knowest how busy I must be this day. If I forget Thee, do not Thou forget me.   March on, boys!"

In 1643 there was a meeting of Royalists at Sevenoaks

—written in contemporary documents, "Synocke." Parliament troops under Colonel Brown were marched thither, but finding that the Royalists had gone, learned that they had retreated to Tunbridge. Brown went on to Tunbridge and sent in a summons to surrender, the reply to which was that "they stood for their ancient laws and customs, without which they refused to lay down their arms, but were willing to treat."

Brown pithily replied that he would come himself and treat with them; marched on Tunbridge, and after some stiff fighting, during which the Parliament forces were once nearly annihilated by an ambuscade, the Royalists were beaten and the town taken. Meanwhile some five hundred of the "malignants" had assembled at Yalding, and the Tunbridge people, who had welcomed the Parliamentarians, went out and dispersed them.

At Tunbridge the Parliament General took 150 prisoners. Evidently the Royalists in the town had expected assistance from outside, for during the fighting the town bells were "rung backwards." Sir George Sandys, who had undertaken to raise Faversham, Sittingbourne, Milton, Boughton and Rainham, was taken prisoner.

It was at this time that the churches of England suffered such irremediable mischief at the hands of the Puritan soldiers. The edict of August, 1643, for the demolition of "monuments and objects of idolatry and superstition" was followed by a still more sweeping one in May, 1644. This ordered that all representations of any Person of the Trinity, or angel, or saint, shall be taken away, defaced and utterly demolished; that all raised chancels be levelled, chancel rails removed, together with all tapers, candlesticks and basons. No copes, surplices, hoods, rood-lofts or holy water fonts to be used, and all organs taken away. These orders did not apply to images, pictures and coats of arms put up as memorials and not as objects of veneration. The search for objects of superstition was made an excuse for all sorts of out-

rages and violations of domestic life.   In Sir Richard
Fogge's family chronicle there is the following entry :
"11th July, 1644. My daur Ann died of convulsive fits
occasioned by Sir Ed^d Boys, his troops comming to my house
often to search for mee and plunder mee." In this year
the commanders of the Parliament forces in Kent, being
apprised of Rupert's march towards Worcester, were
warned to be in readiness to join Sir William Waller at
Kingston with the Militia of the five Lathes.

Whereupon the Committee of Kent, sitting at Knole,
drew the attention of the "Committee of both Kingdoms"
to the excessive charge which the county had borne for the
levy of forces. "What we do," it says, "And what we
have done, is all out of our own purses, without any
additional help." It remonstrates that after a cost of
£2,000, Kentish troops should not be sent into other
counties and so leave the county defenceless. It resents
the imprisonment of Captain Scott because some of his
Kent men had left Waller without his knowledge, and
states, "We have observed for a long time a plot of the
malignants to blow up their county into a high discontent."

However, Waller writes of the Kent men who had
joined him, "Those who are here are as gallant men and
as well provided as any I ever saw in the field, but they
have brought their mouths with them," meaning that he
was puzzled how to provide for them.

In short, there is abundant evidence that after the first
year of the war the Parliament Party in Kent was growing
weaker, and that it was with the greatest trouble that
order could be kept, much less recruits obtained. For
instance, at Horsmonden there was a gun foundry—still
commemorated in the name of the Gun Inn—kept by one
John Browne, who was ostensibly turning out munitions of
war for the Parliament. He was suspected of transactions
with the Royalist faction, called up for examination, and it
came out that Lord Walsingham had advised Lord Dorset
that the county was loyal, that the King should at once

march 4,000 men into Kent, and that Browne would at ten days' notice have cannon and bullet ready, the King's people to bring bullet moulds and Browne to find the lead. Browne, under pressure, admitted that in his dealings with the Parliament authorities he had always given them short weight. The last Royal stronghold to defy the Parliament during the first Civil War was Donnington Castle in Berkshire, under the command of the Kentish Knight, Sir John Boys. From September 29th, 1644, to April, 1646, this staunch hero, with a garrison of two hundred men, kept at bay a continuously besieging force which sometimes numbered three thousand.

His replies to invitations to surrender are worth quoting.

When Horton, the Parliament General, summons Boys for the second time and refuses to give quarter if the Castle has to be stormed, Boys answers :—

" SIR,

Neither your new addition of Forces, nor your high threatening language shall deterre mee nor the rest of these honest men with mee from our Loyalty to our Soveraigne, but do resolve to maintaine this place to the uttermost of our powers, and for the matter of quarter yours may expect the like on Wednesday, or sooner if you please. This is the answer of

Sir,
Your Servant,
JO. BOYS."

Oct. 7th, 1644.

On November 1st Horton sent an ultimatum, to which the gallant Boys replied :

" His Sacred Majesty had entrusted that place to his custody, and though they would give him liberty to take whatever was in the Castle, and (if possible) to carry the Castle it selfe away, yet would he not forsake his ground, but till his Majesty, who sent him thither, should command him thence he was resolved to live or dye in the place."

Although as yet there had been no very open, much less united, manifestations of a change of feeling in Kent, it is impossible to read the contemporary literature, and, above all, the Domestic State Papers, without perceiving that the county was a continually rankling thorn in the side of the authorities. The pages which refer to Kent are full of little but punishings, arrests, takings of precautions, monitory addresses and episodes and incidents, clearly showing that from "Foreland Point to Westerham" the people were fuming and setting their teeth and clenching their fists in an unmistakable manner which boded ill for a not very distant future.

To call this a popular feeling is to misrepresent it. The people certainly felt deeply and bitterly, but with them were the aristocracy and gentry almost to a man, and it is unnecessary to say that the aristocracy and the gentry of Kent formed a very large, wealthy and influential political body.

At the Christmas of 1644 it was ordained by Parliament " that all men should keep it humbly, bemoaning the great national sin (of feasting) which they and their fathers had so often committed on that day." Apparently no open opposition was made to this, but assuredly it did not tend to bind a jovial, sport and feast-loving people to their masters.

In 1645 Parliamentary recruiting in Kent was forcibly resisted. Five hundred recruits halted at Sevenoaks on their way to London, rose upon their guards, marched to Sir Percival Hart's house at Orpington (or Lullingstone ?), shut themselves up in it, and for some days stood a regular siege by two troops of horse and two cannon. In April there was a meeting held at Croydon by the Kent men who had been pressed to serve in Waller's army on the sore subject of being compelled to serve away from their county, with the result that Sir Michael Livesey's entire regiment quietly marched themselves over the border and nobody could stop them. Then there appeared upon the scene the new model army, under Sir Thomas Fairfax as general,

and stout old Skippon as sergeant-major-general, consisting of 6,600 horse, 1,000 dragoons, and 14,480 foot—that
marvellous force of Englishmen which was never to know
defeat, and which, in the words of Macaulay, was to "drive
before it in headlong rout the finest infantry of Spain, and
force a passage into a counterscarp which had just been
pronounced impregnable by the ablest of the Marshals of
France."

Some of us may be Royalists at heart and like to have
a sneer at the Puritans as canting rascals who acted in
everything in the spirit which moved them to stop a sport
like bull-baiting, not because it gave pain to the bull,
as Macaulay said, but because it gave pleasure to the
spectators. But as Englishmen we can but feel a genuine
glow of national pride when we read of the heroism and
determination of these farmers, yeomen, and tradesmen
generally against odds and against the best fighting blood
of Scotland and Europe.

The result was Naseby.

Even after Naseby there remained a chance for Charles.
His affairs were in irretrievable ruin ; he might have
considered the deep and wide-spread suffering which his
prolonged resistance was causing, and could either have
abdicated or have fled to France.

But a bigotry closely allied to insanity hedged him
round with an immovable conviction that he could yet
emerge from the toils with dignity, that success *must*
eventually reward him and the faithful gentlemen who
were hazarding their all in his cause, and to the very last
he prevaricated and plotted.

It was Kentish Colepeper, one of his trustiest counsellors,
who at length lost all patience with him, and in reply to
his assertion that religion and episcopacy were coincident,
said : " Come ! the question in short is, whether you will
choose to be a king of presbytery or no king ? "

Then came the publication of his letters to the queen,
which were damning enough, and the discovery of the
Glamorgan Treaty by which Charles authorised Ormonde

Q

to abrogate all penal laws against Roman Catholics in
Ireland, and commissioned him to coin money and to
raise men, which completed the chain of proof of his
utter insincerity.

"Many good men," says a commentator, "were sorry
that the King's actions agreed no better with his words ;
that he openly protested before God with horrid impre-
cations that he endeavoured nothing so much as the
preservation of the Protestant religion and rooting out of
popery, that he abhorred to think of bringing foreign
soldiers into the kingdom, yet he promised the Irish rebels
an abrogation of the laws against them, and solicited the
Duke of Lorraine, the French, the Danes, the very Irish
for assistance." ·

Yet this is the man whom some people still revere as a
martyr !

We now come to the Kentish rising of 1648, but ere we
enter upon an account of it it will be as well to describe
briefly the state of affairs.

The King, who had been delivered up by the Scots,
amongst whom he had sought refuge after Naseby, upon
the payment by Parliament to them of £400,000 due
for their services, and not, in all fairness to the Scots
be it said, in return for this money, had been lightly confined at Hampton Court, whence he had escaped, and had
gone to Colonel Hammond in the Isle of Wight, who
respectfully made him a prisoner in Carisbrooke Castle.

On March 20th Charles made an attempt to escape from
Carisbrooke, but found that he could not pass through the
window. On May 28th he was to have made a second
attempt, but it was frustrated by two soldiers who had
been counted upon as accomplices, and who gave timely
information to Hammond.

Many districts in England were ripe for revolt against
the dominion of the Army. The Scots, anxious to redeem
what they deemed was considered a slur upon their
national character, corresponded with Charles through the

Earls of Lanark and Lauderdale, and proposed that they should invade England, whilst simultaneous risings should take place, not merely in the country districts of England, but in London, hitherto the centre of the Parliament power, where some Royalist riots had already taken place.

Warwick Castle was to be seized; Nottingham and Oxford were to be surprised; Lancashire, Cheshire, and North Wales were to declare directly the Scots crossed the border; and Essex was ready for a rising.

Kent, as has been shown, had completely veered from the attitude she had adopted at the commencement of the struggle, and a very little stirring was needed to set the combustible matter in her in a flame.

The stirring took place in the City of Canterbury at the Christmas of 1647.

A week before Christmas the Mayor of Canterbury published the following ordinance :

"This is to give notice that the ordinance of the most Honourable Parliament is to be strictly enforced; and, whereas Saturday next is the 25th December, all persons whatsoever in this city of Canterbury are to take heed and remember that Christmas Days and all other superstitious festivals are utterly abolished.

"Wherefore all ministers and churchwardens and others are warned that there be no prayers nor sermons in the churches on the said 25th December, and whosoever shall hang at his door any rosemary, holly or bayes, or other superstitious herb, shall be liable to the penalties decreed by the ordinance of last year, and whosoever shall make or cause to be made either plum pottage or nativity pies, is hereby warned that it is contrary to the said ordinance. This is also to give notice that the usual weekly mercate will be held in this City on Saturday, 25th December, and all persons are required to open their shops on the said day."

Canterbury rose at this. Crowds swarmed through the streets shouting, "For God, King Charles and Kent!" The mayor knocked a man down, and in consequence was half killed by the mob. On Christmas Day not a shop was opened, not a stall was occupied in the market, and not a house but had its decorations without, and its good cheer within.

The Mayor sent for help, the citizens shut the gates, the troops came, broke in the gates and breached part of the walls, and, seizing the ringleaders of the riot, sent them off in custody to Leeds Castle.

In January, 1648, a Commission sat in Canterbury Castle to try the rioters. The Grand Jury ignored the bill against the prisoners and persisted in so doing. Still the prisoners were not released.

Whereupon a Petition was drawn up; it started with the signatures of two hundred gentlemen of Kent, and in a very few days twenty thousand names were appended to it, and it was arranged that on May 29th the petitioners should assemble on Blackheath and carry the document to London.

The Preamble ran thus:

"We, the Knights, Gentlemen and Freeholders of the County of Kent, the most free people of this late flourishing nation, by the wisdom and valour of our Ancestors delivered from the laws of a Conqueror, and, to these late days of unhappy confusion and distraction, enjoying the same through all the reigns of the most glorious, victorious Kings and Princes of this nation, do hereby declare and manifest to all the world:

"1.—That the King be admitted to treat with Parliament.

"2.—That the present army be paid and disbanded.

"3.—That we be governed by the laws of the kingdom and none other.

"4.—That all illegal burdens and taxes be taken off."

The ending of the Petition was:

"In the mean time we shall look upon all opposition as the provocation of a conscious and enraged Committee, and in respect of the invasion lately made upon the persons of our neighbours we think fit not to lie at the mercy of soldiers, but to have refuge in our arms, from which no threats or face of soldiery shall drive us, knowing well the justice of our cause and the temper of our own hearts."

The Committee of Kent condemned this petition and orders were issued against all signing it.

The authorities now became really anxious : orders were issued to prevent the Blackheath meeting and to secure the strong places of the county, whilst the trained bands were called out, but not twenty per cent. reported themselves.

Further, irritated by the rumour that Parliament intended to make an example of Kent by hanging two petitioners in each parish, the Kent men sent up the following bold declaration :

"We do solemnly and religiously oblige ourselves with our lives and fortunes to oppose effectually what persons soever shall presume to interrupt us in the just and legal presentment of our humble desires to the two Houses of Parliament . . . . . In case any single person shall be for this engagement persecuted, all of us shall rise as one man to the rescue."

The author and printer of this were ordered to be whipped and imprisoned. Three Members of Parliament came into Kent with a letter to the Mayor of Rochester, explaining that there was no intention to repress festivity by force, but only to disperse tumultuous assemblages. But the Kent men distrusted the excuses and stood their ground. All efforts at reconciliation failed, the Parliamentary fiat went forth that "everything should be left to the General " (Fairfax), and the news spread from end to end of the land that Kent was up for the King.

All now depended upon the movements of the Scots who, it had been arranged, should act so as to draw Fairfax's formidable army away from London. But they only came southward in time to be completely rolled up by Cromwell at Preston, so that Fairfax was at liberty to deal with the Kent rising.

The fleet in the Downs declared for the King, for dissatisfaction had long been stirred up by the issuing of Commissions without the name of the King, by the appointment of landsmen to sea commands, and by "the insufferable pride, ignorance, and insolency of Colonel Rainsborough." Colonel Rainsborough, the Parliamentary Vice-Admiral, was refused aboard his flagship, to which he had hurried upon seeing from the shore a commotion. About twelve ships revolted, and Cavalier Kent exulted and sang a wild song with the refrain,

> " For the castles on the sea
> Are faithful to their King : "

which supplanted the older one :

> " We shall not think our Coyne and blood ill spent,
> For the glory of God, King Charles, and Kent ! "

This revolt of the fleet, which is an especially notable event when we remember that the fleet had been generally for the Parliament—sea-faring people being chiefly from the Puritan parts of England—might have led to a turning point in the Royal fortunes, but all was marred by incapacity and want of unity amongst the chiefs. If they had sailed for the Isle of Wight and rescued the King, as they might easily have done, it is impossible to say what might not have been the effect upon the stunned and bewildered Royalists of England.

So they sailed over to Holland—seventeen sail now, and took on board the Prince of Wales and the Duke of York, and intrigues became rife for command, and such a medley of silly stories ran from quarter-deck to foc'sle that the Jacks got muddled and half wished they had never stirred in the matter. The plan of rescuing the King was actually suggested, but, instead of carrying it out, the chiefs decided to sail up the Thames, which they did, captured a few ships, which they sold to the City, and returned to find the Parliamentary Admiral, the Earl of Warwick, waiting for them, and spoiling for a fight. But the Prince and the Duke got away to Holland somehow

DEAL
CASTLE

without fighting : writers generally let Royal Commanders down easily, if they can, and Campbell says that a sudden shift of wind took the Royalists out of Warwick's way, but more candid historians hint at something else.

Of course Warwick went after them, but the Hollanders sent deputies to pray the fleet commanders not to engage upon their coasts, and so the matter ended, and Warwick returned to England.

On land the Royalists of Kent seized arms ; men were enrolled fast and encamped on Barham Downs ; Deal, Sandown and Walmer Castles were occupied, but the Parliament Commander at Dover refused to surrender and prepared for a siege.

We can only form an idea of the intensity of passion between the two parties at this period by examination of contemporary diurnals and Mercuries. Not even in a later age against the " Corsican Ogre " was poured forth such a torrent of invective and slander as during this part of the Civil War was poured out against Cromwell and his party by the Royalists, and against the King by the Roundheads. (See Note A at the end of Stewart Kent).

This warfare of the scribblers of course only reflected the warfare of the fighters. The names of Cromwell and his followers have been handed down as those of the authors of indescribable brutalities and miseries, but there is not a shadow of doubt that the balance of shame on this score remained with the Royalists. Even in Royalist counties, commanders like Rupert, Goring, Maurice, and Wilmot behaved like fiends, and the excesses of their ill disciplined followers led to associations for mutual protection irrespective of party, like the " Clubmen " of Wiltshire.

Fairfax now started on his errand.

The Royalist officers in Kent were :

General, Mr. Edward Hales, utterly unfitted for the post, but under the influence of his wife and his friend l'Estrange, and so full of zeal that he is said to have spent £80,000 in raising and equipping men.

Major General, Sir John Many; Lieutenant General, Sir Thomas Peyton; and with them were Sir Robert Tracy, Sir John Darell, Sir Richard Hardres, Sir Thomas Palmer, Sir James Hales, Sir William Many, Sir Thomas Godfrey, Colonel Washington, Colonel Hammond, Colonel l'Estrange, Colonel Culpeper, Colonel Hacker, and James Darell.

The Earl of Thanet raised men from his estates at Hothfield, Charing, Westwell, and Ashford, but seceded, not from want of heart, but because he preferred a compromise to the risk of a conflict between the yokels of Kent and the trained battalions of Fairfax.

On May 30th the Royalists marched on London by way of Gravesend and Dartford, but halted when they heard that Fairfax with 7,000 horse and foot was at Blackheath. At Dartford they received a warning from the Parliament not to proceed with the Petition to London, and ordering them to treat with Fairfax. This they determined to do after consultation; Fairfax declined to treat, but advised them that if they dispersed peaceably he did not doubt that they would be leniently dealt with.

But from Head Quarters at Rochester came the following defiant note to Fairfax :

"We invade not your right, but stand firm to secure our own, which is neither tumult nor rebellion. We are determined to stand and fall together, being rendered incapable of any fear save only of relapsing into our former slavery."

The main body of Royalists then fell back on Rochester, which was defended by four cannon at the bridge foot, and forty in works along the river bank.

Fairfax, in the meanwhile, advanced from Blackheath, sent Gibbons on to relieve Dover, which was being besieged by Sir Richard Hardres, and made towards Rochester.

A contemporary Royalist news letter here speaks of a great success for the King's arms : says that at Rochester there was a stiff fight in which as many as five hundred men were killed on the Parliament side owing to the fire kept on them by the *Rainbow* and *Swallow* men-of-war in the river, that the Parliament troops retreated, whereupon the Royalists sallied forth, pursued them, took twelve cannon, arms, prisoners and carriages.

The fact is that Fairfax marched from Blackheath to Eltham, where he passed the night, sent one wing under Colonel Husband towards Rochester, and marched himself *viâ* Meopham to Malling, where he halted.

Husband's division had some stiff fighting at Northfleet, and especially at Gravesend, where a bridge was held by eighty London 'prentices, sailors and countrymen, of whom twenty were killed, many wounded, and thirty taken prisoners. But, seeing how strongly defended Rochester was, Husband turned southward to join Fairfax at Malling.

Meanwhile a Royalist force of 6,000 foot and 1,000 horse were assembled on Penenden Heath, and here a change of command took place, the Earl of Norwich, better known as Lord Goring—a typical Cavalier of the period—replacing Edward Hales.

This was at noon, June 1st, 1648.

At five o'clock in the afternoon Fairfax's battalion was seen "through perspective glasses" on the west side of the Medway. The Royalist commander at once sent 1,000 men to guard the ford at Aylesford, and threw 3,000 into Maidstone, towards which, it was as clear as anything could be to an army which had not the crudest shadow of an Intelligence Department, Fairfax was moving.

The Parliament troops moved in excellent order: Fairfax's proclamation against plundering or taking goods without payment ensuring the safety of the country people, the men being in high spirits and "every man three in courage." With the design of turning the Royalist Left, Fairfax had turned South from Malling, crossed Barming Heath, down the lane by Barming Rectory, and the Medway at Farleigh Bridge, Norwich in the meantime remaining unaccountably inactive on the Downs by Kits Coty House. At Farleigh Bridge and all along the river there was skirmishing, and possibly a lane near the bridge, called Gallants Lane, may preserve the memory of this, but the Royalists were reserving themselves for the defence of Maidstone, and retreated towards that town.

A stronger resistance was made in the fields at the top of Upper Stone Street, but the Royalists always had the worst of it, and, although the taking even of hastily thrown up barricades cost time and life, the onward progress of the Roundheads was steady.

There was more hard fighting at the point where the Tovil brook runs into the Medway, and at the Len Bridge, which then marked the limit of the town.

Two hours had been occupied in winning these two miles from Farleigh Bridge, and it was 9 p.m. when Fairfax prepared to storm the town.

From all accounts, of the victors and of the vanquished, the resistance in the Maidstone streets was most stubborn and the fighting most desperate, and it should be borne in mind that the Royalists had but 2,000 men to oppose to four times that number. Every house was a fortress or a nest of sharp-shooters, barricades crossed Stone Street at frequent intervals, and at the top of Gabriel's Hill, where the four main streets of the town converge, was a battery.

A Parliament man who took part in the affair writes :

"The result became very questionable till almost twelve at night. Though I have been a member of the army ever since its first going out, and have seen desperate services in several stormings, the like service I have not seen before ; every street in the town was got by inches, but the Lord completed the victory for us."

At midnight the defenders, outnumbered, were driven foot by foot into the churchyard and into the church, where, finding that no succour could be had, they surrendered.

The losses of the Royalists amounted to 300 men slain and wounded, 1,300 prisoners, 500 horse, 3,000 arms, eight cannon and nine colours. The Parliamentary loss in killed and wounded was probably still greater.

The Parliament thought so much of the victory that it ordered a thanksgiving for it in all the churches of London and Westminster.

News of the fall of Maidstone did not reach the Earl of Norwich until the next day, when, of course, it was too late to help; indeed he had marched as far as Barming Heath with the intention of reinforcing the troops in Maidstone when he heard of the disaster. A Council of War was held, and he determined to march on London with his men, now about 10,000 in number. But the passage over the Thames to the capital being refused him, he crossed over into Essex from near Greenwich.

Fairfax's success had somewhat subdued the spirit of the Essex men, and they were not zealous in playing the part which had been assigned to them of acting simultaneously with their neighbours of Kent, but Norwich induced the country gentlemen under Sir Charles Lucas to assemble and to muster the trained bands, and, being joined by the Hertfordshire men under Lord Capell, the united forces marched by Chelmsford to Colchester.

Of the famous siege of Colchester by Fairfax, who, having disposed of Maidstone, had at once marched after Norwich, and of its gallant defence, and the heavy punishment inflicted upon the leaders and the town by Fairfax, we have nothing to do.

Practically the Kentish rising ended with the capture of Maidstone. Sir Richard Hardres, however, was still besieging Dover Castle, but Rich and Hewson coming to its relief the siege was raised. Canterbury, with a large store of arms and many prisoners, surrendered to Ireton; Deal, Walmer and Sandown Castles were closely blockaded.

Prince Charles made an attempt to relieve Deal Castle, and landed with a thousand sailors and soldiers, but the absolute want of generalship which had distinguished the Royalist military movements throughout the war was here again manifest; the Royalists walked into the simplest of ambuscades, two hundred of them were killed, a hundred made prisoners, and the Prince embarked in all haste, narrowly escaping capture, and sailed with the fleet to Yarmouth.

The personal influence of Fairfax being withdrawn, the Parliament troops quartered in Kent were guilty of much outrage and mischief in the county, but, as has been already remarked, they were probably not a whit worse than the Cavaliers were elsewhere.

Somner describes Canterbury Cathedral at this time as looking more like a ruined monastery than a church, for there was little left but bare walls and roof, and these shaken and defaced, the windows were all broken, the choir stripped and robbed of its hangings, the organ and organ loft, communion table, screen, and monuments defaced, rifled and robbed of brasses and iron gates. The present font is the original which was destroyed by the Puritans, but the fragments of which Somner gathered and saved and had pieced together after the Restoration.

The deer in Greenwich and Eltham Parks were killed, and the timber cut down; private residences, such as Surrenden, Knowlton and East Sutton, were plundered, and scarcely a parish church exists but does not show some traces of the sacrilegious proceedings of the vehement fanatics of this period.

It was during this year that a stranger landed at Sandwich, giving himself out to be the Prince of Wales. The Sandwich people were completely deceived by him; he took up his quarters at the *Bell*, and old servants of the Prince seemed to recognise him, although the Prince was a dark swarthy man and this visitor was fair.

Tailors and sempstresses were set to work to make him decent garments, "for the clothes in which he came were hardly worth three pence, and he did weare a shirt as black or blacker than his cloathes."

He then appeared in church in a suit lined with crimson satin and laced with gold and silver; was carried round the town in state, had many presents made to him, and in return promised all sorts of berths and rewards when he should enjoy his own again. And all this in spite of the facts of his complete want of resemblance to the Prince, and that he spoke English imperfectly and in a strange dialect.

Sir Thomas Dishington, an old servant of the Prince, came over from Dover to see him, found him hunting duck in the Town Haven, confronted him, called him a counterfeit rogue, and asked permission of the Mayor to kick him. The Prince appealed to the infatuated Mayor for protection, and Sir Thomas was arrested, but being released went to Dover and returned with letters from the real Prince. The Mayor, however, refused to see the imposition and the "Prince" was entertained at the town's expense. Eventually he turned out to be one Cornelius Evans, a low-bred Welshman, born in Marseilles, and "well known to the police," so he was ordered into custody.

The sentence of death upon Charles the First was read by Broughton, clerk of the court, a Maidstone man, and the King's body was embalmed by a Maidstone doctor.

Whether the following Petition existing in manuscript in the Library of Crundale Rectory, and now, I believe, published for the first time, may be accepted as evidence that there really was a considerable Parliamentary party in our county, or whether it must be regarded as merely a politic stroke on the part of time-servers it is difficult to say. It is not dated, but evidently it was just after the suppression of the Kentish Rising of 1648.

" To the Supreme Authority of the Nation, · the Commons of England in Parliament assembled.

" The humble petition of the well affected in the County of Kent.

" Humbly sheweth :

"That your Petitioners cannot but in all gratitude declare how much their spirits are refreshed and heightened upon the observation especially of the late unparalleled actings of this honourable house far above all others formerly, insomuch as your Petitioners are encourag'd to believe that the second year of this nation's freedom (thro' God's blessing upon your endeavours) is begun, and in order hereunto we cannot but express our hearty and highest acknowledgement of thanks to thy honourable house for their vindicating and preserving of the just power of the people in the late votes that declared that your legislative power was originally in the people, and derivatively in the House of Commons as their representative, and also for the forwardness of thy honourable house to satisfie the just and earnest desires of this and other counties for the bringing of the person of the King with the rest of the grand delinquents to a speedy Tryal.

" And forasmuch as we are not ignorant of the plottings and practises of those that are ill-affected to retard (and if possible) make void the proceedings of this honourable house, and the High Court of Justice in the said business, and also to foment and raise (as much as in them lies) another war, we are forc'd omitting other great and necessary particulars for the present in all earnestness and submission to propose these two ensuing particulars to your serious and speedy considerations.

" 1.—That notwithstanding all suggestions to the contrary the Tryal of Charles Stewart, King, may be vigorously prosecuted, and that no pretence or overtures what soever may cause thy honourable house and the High Court of Justice to be satisfied for the blood of three States with less than the blood of those persons who have been the principall authors of its effusion, forasmuch as God himself hath said that who sheddeth man's blood by man shall his blood be shed.

" 2.—That for the prevention of future insurrections and rebellions thy honourable house will be pleas'd to commit the militia of this and other counties to his Excellency the Lord Fairfax, general & cet, so to be new modelised as that the commissionating and arming of all forces what soever may by mediate pow'r and authority from him be deputed, and put into the hands of such and none but such as adhere unto your Parliament and army in their present proceedings.

Wm. Kenwicke, ⎫ etc. to the number
Richd. Bowen. ⎭ of 1,135."

PART III.—INTERREGNUM ; CHARLES II. ; JAMES II. ;
WILLIAM AND MARY.

THE INTERREGNUM.   1649-1660.

The "news out of Kent," as the old papers phrased it,
during the Commonwealth is depressing reading.   The
county, although sorely bent by Fairfax and his captains,
was by no means broken, and the record of this period is
just a continuance of the state of affairs in the county
after the Christmas of 1647.   The country was full of
soldiers, who were as little disposed to be gentle and
forbearing towards a people who were giving them so
much trouble, as were the people little disposed to sit
down meekly under the coarse rule of men with whom
they had nothing in common but birthright.

Typical Cavaliers in every particular, the gentlemen of
Kent found it impossible to accept their defeat as the
natural issue of the struggle.   " We were too soon "
was their cry, " Had we but waited until Wales and the
West and the Midlands were ready, Charles would have
been on the throne now "—the same cry which was raised
after the failure of Wyatt.   For our part we do think that
the Kentish Rising was premature, but that the postpone-
ment until other districts were equally ready would have
led to anything more substantial than a prolongation of the
struggle, a careful comparison between the two parties
forbids us to believe.   In one respect the English civil
wars of the seventeenth century always remind us of the
Franco-German war of the nineteenth—never was such a
chance offered for genius to arise and tear victory from the
very jaws of defeat as during the Franco-German war ;
yet the name of not one single French commander will be
handed down to the admiration, much less the worship,

of posterity. So with the Cavaliers of our Civil War. From 1642 to 1648 not one captain of anything more than the most ordinary merit emerged from the mass of dashing swordsmen in whose hands was placed the Royal Cause.

Nor was there any comparison between the rank and file of the two armies except in the matter of animal courage. Without in the smallest degree wishing to minimise the glory of the defence of Maidstone in 1648, we do not hesitate to say that had the positions been reversed, not only would the Royalists never have taken Maidstone, but they would never have been allowed to come within ten miles of the town.

But the Cavaliers of Kent refused to accept the situation, and so under the Commonwealth the county was continually seething with impotent impatience and dissatisfaction, and for this reason possibly no other county was so hardly treated.

In 1653 a groan was raised about tythe paying, in these terms :

"That we, a number of poor labouring people in the county of Kent, having been for many years before, and during the whole time of these wars persecuted and prosecuted to the ruine of many of our families, through imprisonments unjust, tedious and vexatious suits at law, and often sub-pœna'd up to London, not sparing us seed time nor harvest, to our inexpressible prejudice by the priests and clergy of this nation, for our refusing to pay them tythes, though it were an equal tenth part of all the increase of the ground, whereas indeed it is above the fifth part, all charges, labour, losses and servants' wages being deducted."

After the execution of Charles the Princess Elizabeth and the Duke of Gloucester were placed in the charge of the Countess of Leicester at Penshurst. Possibly from some fear that their presence in the heart of a strongly-disaffected county might be the cause of Royalist disturbances it was ordered that they should be transferred to Carisbrooke. This was done under the charge of Major-

General Harrison, in two coaches each with six horses, with plate, bedding and all necessaries, and Harrison was strictly enjoined to use no ceremony towards them beyond "what was fit for and due to a gentleman."

The Princess died soon after her arrival at Carisbrooke, and as freedom of movement of the Prince was deemed as unwholesome here as it had been at Penshurst, he was confined to the Castle precincts, and an allowance of £1,500 a year was made him.

The domestic state papers of this period are full of ordinances against all sports and pastimes which brought people together in any numbers, such as horse races, cock fighting and football, and on one occasion when the authorities heard of a horse race to be held at Dover they sent the Militia to stop it.

One of the greatest difficulties to be overcome by the Government at a most critical time was the manning of the Fleet. Although the press was at work at all times and at all places—neither churches nor hours of divine service being held sacred—the men pressed received their conduct money and then refused to serve. On one occasion fifty men were pressed at Dover, of whom twenty came up to receive their conduct money and then refused to go, and as the whole country was on their side their flight was easy and their capture difficult, and this in spite of heavy penalties imposed on householders for harbouring runaways.

Despite this difficulty of procuring seamen it is remarkable that at this period—as at the later and more humiliating period under Charles the Second, presently to be described, the Honour of the Flag at sea was strictly insisted upon and maintained by English commanders, and it may be noted that during this and the succeeding period the deficiency of our seamen was somewhat atoned for by the splendid quality of our commanders—not a few of them military men—and our maritime supremacy established.

This high-handed principle of the maintenance of the Honour of the English Flag in home waters—and sometimes in very far away from home waters—is of ancient origin. In John's reign it was ordered that if English captains met foreigners at sea who refused to strike to the Royal Flag they might attack them, even if the foreign ships belonged to a friendly Power.

Edward the First insisted upon it. The Flemish towns recognised Edward the Second's claim; Edward the Third, as he held Calais, could assert it in the Channel. When Philip of Spain came to marry Mary of England, Lord William Howard, who had to escort him, refused to call on the Spanish Admiral until the latter had hauled down his colours. It is said that Howard also fired a shot across his bows, but Mr. Hume (*not* David) can find no contemporary evidence for this. Sir John Hawkins made the Spanish ships which escorted Anne of Austria from Flanders do the same. In 1605 Sir William Monson, one of the finest of our seventeenth century sea-dogs, made the Dutchmen off Dover strike to the English Flag in the presence of the Spanish fleet. Charles the First insisted rigorously on the right. In 1652 Tromp came into Dover Roads with forty-four sail. Blake was there with fifteen. Tromp kept his flag mast-headed. Blake hinted that he should strike it. The tough old Dutchman replied with a broadside, the two parties went hard at it, the bad gunnery of the Dutchmen alone saved Blake, and by some writers this has been deemed the origin of the first Dutch War. On this occasion the Council of State thanked the Mayor, jurats, and seamen of Dover for having volunteered to reinforce Blake, and promised an advance of part of the £4,000 required to build their new pier.

In the same year Commodore Young fell in with a Dutch squadron off the North Foreland. The Dutchman declined to lower his flag, saying that if he did the authorities at home would cut off his head. So Young attacked him and gained his point.

By the peace of 1654 it was agreed that the Dutch should always strike flag where the English dominion was recognised.

In 1652 the first Articles of War were published in the fleet. They numbered thirty-nine, and seem to us excessively severe, inasmuch as the penalties in thirteen cases was death unconditionally, and in twelve others death or a lesser punishment.

It is curious to note that during these troublous times people had leisure to attend to witches. Thus in 1645 Joane Williford, Joan Carriden and Jane Hott were executed at Faversham for witchcraft. In 1652 five women from Cranbrook and one from Lenham were hung " for the devilish crime of having bewitched nine children, one man and one woman, caused the loss of £500 worth of cattle and much corn at sea."

CHARLES II.   1660-1685.

On May 25th, 1660, Charles the Second landed at Dover. Let us quote the special reporter of the *Mercurius Publicus* on the occasion :

" On Friday, about 3 o'c in the morning, they were in sight of Dover, whereupon an express was sent to the General (Monk) then at Canterbury, to hast to Dover, which he did accordingly, and about 1 o'c came thither. His Majesty landed about 3 in the afternoon at the Beech, near the Peer of Dover with the Duke of York, Duke of Gloucester and many of his nobles. Now did all put themselves in a posture for to observe the meeting of the best of kings and the most deserving of subjects ; the admirers of Majesty were jealous on the king's behalf of too low a condescension, and the Lovers of Duty, fearfull on the other side of an ostentation of merit, but such a humble prostration was made by his Excellency kneeling, and so fitting a reception by His Majesty kissing and embracing him that all parties were satisfied. . . . . . His Majesty walk'd up with the General, a canopy being carried over his head and a chair of state by him towards his coach.

"In his passage the Mayor and Aldermen of Dover, with Mr. Redding, the minister, met His Majesty, and after a short speech presented His Majesty with a large Bible with gold clasps. . . . . . About two miles beyond Dover His Majesty took horse to Canterbury." On Barham Downs richly attired troops of horse were drawn up, and the Kentish regiments of foot. Charles rode to the head of each troop, which, bowing to him, kissed the hilts of their swords and then flourished them above their heads.

At Canterbury the Mayor, Aldermen and Recorder met him, inflicted a speech on him, but made up for it by presenting him with a gold tankard, value £250, and conducted him to the Palace, where he stayed until Monday.

"On Monday, 28th of May," says another 'special,' "His Majesty came into Rochester about 5 o'c of the afternoon, and went immediately to Colonel Gibbon his house (built 1587: still existing and known as Restoration House), where the Dukes of York and Gloucester also lodged. After His Majesty had in his chamber eat something to refresh himself, he went to Chatham to see the *Royal Soveraigne* and the rest of his ships, where he gave Commissioner Pett so much honour as to receive a banquet from him. Thence he returned to Rochester, and about 8 o'c supped. The next morning the Mayor and Corporation presented him with a bason and ewer of silver gilt of a good value, which was well received.

"His Majesty took his journey from Rochester about betwixt 4 and 5 in the morning; the militia forces of Kent lining the waies, and maidens strewing herbs and flowers, and the several towns hanging out white sheets."

Rochester was decorated with beautiful garlands curiously made of scarves and ribbon, decorated with spoons and bodkins of silver and small plate, and some with gold chains.

At Dartford Monk's horse regiments presented the King with an address. On Blackheath were drawn up troops of horse, and a performance of a morris dance to pipe and tabor was given with "all agility and cheerfulness imaginable." Several bonfires were made as the King came along, and one more remarkable than the rest for its bigness, where the States Arms were burned. Here the Earl of Winchilsea presented a congratulatory address from the nobility and gentry of Kent, and His Majesty replied that during his journey through the county the evidences of loyalty had been all sufficient.

"At Deptford on the King's right hand were ranged one hundred 'proper maids' clad all alike in white garments, with scarves about them, who, having prepared many baskets covered with fine linen and adorned with rich scarves and ribbons, which baskets were full of flowers and herbs, which they strewed before him." Done into doggrell to the air "When the King enjoys his own again:"

> " At Deptford the maidens they
> Stood all in White by the high-way,
> Their loyalty to Charls to show,
> They with sweet flowers his way to strow ;
> Each wore a Ribbin blew,
> They were of comely hue ;
> With joy they did him entertain
> With acclamations to the skye,
> As the King passed by
> For joy that he receives his owne again."

Small wonder after it all, at the end of the London reception, the Court Jeames has to record that "His Majesty, wearied with the heat and long continued solemnity of the day, was diverted from his pious intention of going to Westminster to offer up his Devotion of Prayer and Praise in publick."

For down-right flunkeyism, hardly excusable even at such an effervescent period as this, commend us to the two following addresses from the Cinque Ports to the King and the Duke of York respectively :

To the King.

"That with all possible gratitude we do adore the Wise and Gracious Providence of Almighty God in the peaceable restoration of Your Gracious Majesty to the exercise of your kingly government within all Your Majesty's dominions and territories and as we do upon the bended knees of our hearts offer up our sincere thanks to God for the same, so we earnestly implore Your Sacred Majesty to receive this our address (though but an evening obligation in respect of others, the accustomed time of our convention not sooner happening) is the effect of that Duty, Loyalty, and Subjection, which we acknowledge by the Laws of God, Man, and Nature to owe and yield to Your Majesty : and we do take the humble boldness to assure Your Majesty that in the midst of the greatest defection from Your Majesty's Government, our hearts were never tainted with so great disloyalty, as by any address or application whatsoever to testify our assent to any Government imposed on us, but faithfully retained (though forced to lie hidden in their own ashes) those lively sparks of Loyalty, Love, and Affection towards Your Majesty as our only Supreme Sovereign, which by Your Majesty's happy return and presence do enliven all our hearts, and break forth into flames, never to be extinguished, but to be daily revived and renewed in our Supplication at the Throne of Grace for Your Majesty's preservation and long and happy reign over us."

ʼ To the Duke of York.

" That next unto that never to be forgotten mercy of restoring your Petitioners the breath of their nostrils and the joy of their lives, His Sacred Majesty, their Gracious Sovereign, your petitioners are filled with joy in the sense of their extraordinary favor which His Majesty hath been graciously pleased to confer on your petitioners in granting Your Highness the office of Warden of the Cinque Ports.

" Whereby so great a door of hope is opened to your Petitioners, that in their own thoughts they seem to be in actual possession of their antient, but of late infringed liberties and priviledges, and dare not let a distrustful thought surprise their spirits, but hope that by the

interposition of Your Highness with His Majesty, His
Majesty will be pleased to confirm and renew unto your
Petitioners the Charters of the Cinque Ports, two ancient
towns, and their members, granted, confirmed and renewed
by His Majesty's noble progenitors, and also that His
Majesty will be graciously pleased to give speedy and
effectual relief to your petitioners in the several grievances
in the schedule thereunto annexed."

Most of the English counties sent up addresses of
welcome to the King, but we believe that the one
presented by the Earl of Winchilsea on the part of the
County of Kent, was, and fittingly should have been, the
first.

The outburst of thanksgiving and rejoicing which
followed the Restoration has had no parallel in our own,
or, we should imagine, in any other country's history, until
the two celebrations of our present Gracious Queen's
Jubilees in 1887 and 1897. In its extravagance it was
absolutely un-English, but it was thoroughly English in
its genuineness. And the reason is not far to seek. Sober-
minded, steady, phlegmatic as the Englishman has always
been, the yoke of Puritanism weighed heavily on the neck
of a people famous as pleasure loving, even if in foreign
eyes its manner of taking pleasure was sad.

As we have tried to show with regard to the County of
Kent, the dominion of the Roundhead was one of continual repression. The people put up with silly kings,
with avaricious kings, with unjust kings, even with
bullying kings, but a ruler who stopped the course of the
flowing bowl, who tabooed manly sports, who saw
crime in rustic festivals, and idolatry in church and house
decoration, it could not stand.

Directly Charles the Second set foot on Dover beach
the reins were cast loose, and the nation from Tyneside
to Lands End capered and frolicked in its revived ecstasy ;
all bounds of reason and decorum were outstripped, with
the melancholy results to be told hereafter.

We are not perhaps far wrong in attributing the

disgraces which a year or two later befell our arms to the intoxicated condition of the nation, which rendered all order and organisation in public departments impossible.

That the operations against the Dutch in the years 1664 and 1665 were creditable to us is entirely owing to the capacity of captains, such as Lawson, Bourne, Spragge, Kempthorne, Ayscue, Montague Earl of Sandwich, Jeremiah Smith, Monk, Thomas Allen, and especially Blake, for the ships themselves were ill-manned and ill-found to a degree only credible when contemporary records are examined.

Despite the press, there was a great dearth of seamen. Pett, Commissioner of Chatham Dockyard, described the recruits as "pitiful pressed creatures who are fit for nothing but to fill the ships full of vermin."

Prisoners multiplied so that Leeds Castle was hired of Culpeper as a receiving place, and Evelyn, who was in charge of the work, records how he "flowed the drie moate, made a new drawbridge, and brought spring water into the court of the Castle." Maidstone at the same time petitioned to have no more wounded men sent for fear that the Plague, now raging in London, should break out.

In the spring of 1666, Rupert and Monk, Earl of Albemarle, with 77 ships, fought a four days' battle against Michael de Ruyter with from 80 to 100 ships, the scene of battle being along the Flemish coast from Ostend to Dunkirk, and the Downs. On the first day the English suffered severely, but showed themselves the better fighters and manœuvrers. The second day was signalised by the bad behaviour of some of the Dutch captains, by the independent action of Van Tromp from De Ruyter, and by the loss of the English *Prince Royal* of 100 guns on the Galloper, being burned by the Dutch On the third day there was stubborn fighting, Sir Christopher Myngs and Berkeley being killed. On the fourth day the English retreated to the river, and the Dutch had the sea clear. Altogether we were defeated: we lost or had disabled 20 ships, and nearly 5,000 men were killed, wounded, and missing.

The year 1667 marks the most disgraceful page in English History. The Dutch knew that we were completely unprepared for war. Many of our captains were young court rakes, who took to commanding frigates as a fashionable diversion. It was with the greatest difficulty that men could be pressed for a deservedly unpopular service, as much as two years-and-a-half of pay being sometimes due to seamen, as is testified by the touching petition of the officers and seamen of the *Harp* frigate and *Mary* yacht for pay "that their families may not be starved in the streets, and themselves go like heathen with nothing to cover their nakedness."

One captain complains that for want of pay, instead of a "young commander," he is rendered an "old beggar." The Chatham shipwrights and caulkers marched up to London to appeal to the Navy Board "as their families are denied trust and cannot subsist." At Woolwich the Commissioner said, " I am almost torn to pieces by the workmen at the yard for their weekly pay." The caulkers and shipwrights at Deptford "fell on the foreman of the yard, and only by God's mercy they had not spoiled him." The credit of the Government was *nil;* it was impossible to buy stores; Commissioner Pett tried to buy tallow and candles at Maidstone for the navy, but "found the country so shy that, though assured of good payment, they refused to have any dealings."

At the close of the war ships had to be kept in Commission longer than was necessary because men could not be discharged without being paid off. One anchorsmith delivered goods to the value of £6,000, and only got £800 on account.

On June 9th, 1667, De Ruyter, with a carefully selected fleet of fifty-one men-of-war, three frigates and fourteen fire ships, appeared at the Nore, "all this," says Evelyn, "thro' our unaccountable negligence in not setting out our fleete in due time."

On June 10th the news came that a detached squadron
of seventeen powerful ships was in the Swale, and that a
party had landed in Thanet, but had been repulsed by the
Scots soldiers there. The trained bands of Canterbury
and Sittingbourne were hurriedly called to arms and sent
towards Chatham; the beacons were fired and the country
generally put into a ferment of aimless, unordered
running to and fro, whilst reinforcements brought the
Dutch fleet up to 60 sail at the Nore, and 60 at the
Gunfleet.

The detached squadron sailed up the Thames, showing a
knowledge of the river's navigation which the English
themselves did not possess ; by the first tide it reached
the Middle, landed a force on Canvey Island, burned
some houses and barns, but were driven off by the
locals ; got by the second tide to within two miles of
the Lower Hope, seeing the masts of the English ships
at Gravesend, and anchored. Next morning the English
ships had disappeared higher up the river, and the Dutch
Admiral, fearful of being decoyed too far, retired to the
mouth of the Medway, and joined De Ruyter, who was
here with ten men-of-war.

Sheerness was next attacked. A miserable new fort
there was soon knocked to pieces, and the garrison fled at
the approach of the Dutch storming party of eight hundred
men, who carried off guns, stores and the flag, blew up the
rest of the fort, and returned in triumph to their ships.

At this news all was confusion and consternation in
official quarters, and a more humiliating and disgraceful
picture of sloth, corruption, inability, utter unprepared-
ness, and, worst of all, cowardice, cannot be imagined
than that which is faintly drawn by the more or less
official pen of Samuel Pepys.

Monk, Earl of Albemarle, came hurrying from London with the Guards and any troops he could pick up.
A chain was thrown across the river opposite Gillingham, batteries were raised at Chatham, and Upnor
Castle was reinforced. Seven hulks were sunk by the

chain and fireships prepared, but the forts were badly constructed, the block-houses were of no good, for some wanted guns, some carriages, whilst there were either no bullets at all, or they were too big for the guns.

As for the ships which were sunk, this was done in such a hurry that afterwards there were discovered to have been among them the *Franklin*, laden with stores for other ships, and another " hulk " with a cargo on board her worth £80,000 !

To complicate matters further, the dockyard men refused to work ; the streets were filled with men and women clamouring for back pay, and the officials, conscious of having failed miserably in their duty, shifted the responsibility and blame on to one another's shoulders.

On June 11th the Dutch advanced up the Medway. The *Unity* was attacked and captured, and a channel being shown the Dutch, no doubt by Englishmen on their ships, they sent fireships at the chain and broke it, in doing which one of them went against the *Matthias*, set her on fire, and she blew up. The *Charles the Fifth* was taken, and the *Monmouth*, not liking the ugly look of things, sailed away.

At Gillingham the Dutch landed, and behaved very well —far better indeed than had the English soldiers quartered in the village.

All the Dutch squadron now sailed through the gap off Upnor Castle, the *Royal Charles* — a pet ship of the navy, formerly known as the *Naseby*, which had brought the King to Dover from Holland—and the *Mary*, which had been left, were taken. The former might have been saved in time, but she had no boats for towing her, it being reported that the boats had been used by the officers and crew for escaping ! At any rate, she was captured by a boat with nine men ; they found nobody on board, so they struck her flag, played " Joan's placket is torn," on a trumpet, and towed her off, but she grounded later on and had to be abandoned.

Upnor Castle kept up a brisk fire upon the invaders for some time, but its powder failed. Here the Dutch burned the *Royal James*, the *Loyal London*, the *Royal Oak*, and the *Santa Maria*, the first three being 80-gun ships which had been sunken by Monk, but showed their upper works.

Captain Douglas of the *Royal Oak* stuck to his ship and perished in her, so remarkable an instance of heroism at this degenerate period that it inspired Andrew Marvell to write a poem entitled " The Loyal Scot."

The Dutch now retired, carrying the *Royal Charles* and the *Unity* with them, but, as has been mentioned, the former had to be abandoned, and, although the difficult passage of the river was skilfully made, three of the Dutch ships ran aground and were burned to prevent their falling into the hands of the English. The Dutch anchored in a line which extended from the North Foreland to the Buoy at the Nore. "A dreadful spectacle as England ever saw, and never to be wiped off," says Evelyn.

Altogether our losses consisted of five men-of-war burned or taken with loss of life, three burned without loss of life, and thirteen ships sunk or ashore, but not taken.

The Dutch lost all their fireships, and three men-of-war destroyed by themselves.

The terror spread to the Capital. " The alarme was so great," says Evelyn, "that it put both country and citty into a paniq, feare, and consternation such as I hope I shall never see more; everybody was flying, none knew where or whither."

The Dutch were expected at Woolwich: the inhabitants of Greenwich and Blackwall packed up and fled by hundreds into the country crying " we are betrayed ! " although the real reason for the catastrophe was the parsimony of the ministers who had counselled the laying up of first and second rate ships, and the carrying on of a defensive war. More ` than this : incapacity and even cowardice were rife. One English soldier-captain actually went into action with the tompions in his gun muzzles;

ships were deserted and even set on fire without striking a blow, and from top to bottom the Government departments were incapable and rotten.

On June 29th the Dutch were still at the Nore. Complaints of all kinds from all sides were poured into the ears of the stupified, bewildered Admiralty and ordnance officials. It was asserted that treason was rife; that there were three thousand English and Scots seamen in the Dutch fleet; Englishmen had been heard talking on the Dutch ships and saying: "We did heretofore fight for tickets, now we fight for dollars." Swarms of seamen patrolled the streets declaring that they were willing to do their utmost against the Dutch if only their tickets were paid, but otherwise they would not venture to be killed and lose all they had already fought for. It was asserted that those in charge of the land defences had been acquainted with the enemy's designs, and that in spite of all the drumming and trumpeting there were not three hundred trained men to defend the Kentish coast and to man the Castles of Deal, Walmer, and Sandown.

Let us close the humiliating scene. By the Treaty of Breda, in 1667, peace was made, De Ruyter withdrew his fleet, after having swept the English seas for six weeks almost without let or hindrance, and the Dutch must have had a good laugh in their sleeves when they agreed to the clause by which the honour of the English flag should be respected!

The plague which ravaged London in 1665 was also virulent in Kent, having been conveyed thither, no doubt, by refugees from the Capital. Greenwich and Deptford particularly suffered, and it is recorded that Eastwell House was shut up, one house in Westwell, and seven in Canterbury.

In 1670 was concluded the shameful Treaty of Dover, a secret affair conducted chiefly by the Duchess of Orleans, sister to the King, by which Charles agreed to announce his conversion to Roman Catholicism, and if any trouble therefrom should arise in England, Louis would help him

COSHAM HALL

with an army; he and Louis were to declare war upon Holland, Louis paying Charles £200,000, and if the King of Spain should die without an heir Charles was to back up the French King's claim on Flanders. So in 1672 war was declared upon Holland by England and France, and, to show how sincere they were, the French allowed us to fight the battle of Southwold Bay unaided, in which, although the Dutch fleet had the worst of it and retired, we lost two of our best captains, the Earl of Sandwich and Sir Edward Spragge.

The naval service was still most unpopular, and to avoid the press-gangs seamen fled from the coast and concealed themselves in the inland towns and villages. Major Darell, at Sheerness, writes to Secretary Williamson :—" A great many seamen, lusty, able men, are run away from Feversham and Milton and other maritime places into the Wild of Kent." Consequently the most unsuitable men were forced to serve. Of eighty men sent to the fleet from Cambridge and Huntingdon, not three men were sailors, and they often arrived on board in so filthy and ragged a condition that the officers refused to receive them.

In this year Evelyn the Diarist paid a visit to Scotts Hall. He went by barge from Gravesend to Deptford, posted to Rochester, and then by coach and six to Scotts Hall. He describes the ancestral home of this noble Kentish family, of which eighteen generations lie buried in Brabourne Church :

"A right noble seate, uniformly built, with a handsome gallery. It stands in a Park well stor'd, the land flat and good. We were exceedingly feasted by the young Knight, and in his pretty chapell heard an excellent sermon by his chaplaine"

Assuredly, according to the old distich, Scotts Hall has had a fall, for all that remains of it is part of the stable wall, close to the Ashford and Hythe road between Smeeth and Sellinge.

Evelyn also notes the farming in Thanet as "far exceeding any part of England for the accurate culture of their ground, in which they exceed even to curiositie and emulation."

Mary of Modena, the bride chosen by the Earl of Peterboro for the Duke of York, arrived at Dover in 1673, and, unlike another royal spouse who had been chosen by proxy, charmed her husband-elect with her "surpassing grace and loveliness." The Duke himself says that he married her at Dover; Peterboro, who would have known almost as well, says that the ceremony took place in London. York, who knew as a sailor how much the English people loved a show, purposely did not hurry over the journey by Canterbury, Rochester and Gravesend to London, so that the Kentish folk had plenty of time to give the bridal party a good reception, and, from all accounts, a right royal one it was.

Not so agreeable a Kentish experience was that of another Mary, the Princess of Orange, who in 1678 was on her return journey with her husband from a visit to the King of England, and got stranded at Canterbury without any money! Worse than this, the Corporation of the City on being applied to for temporary assistance declined. Dean Tillotson, however, came to the rescue, and the future sovereigns of England stayed four days at a Canterbury inn, having declined Tillotson's offer of the Deanery. This must have been rather galling to the Corporation people, especially as the gentry of Kent came flocking in to pay their respects. This same lady had another Canterbury experience later on.

In 1683 Algernon Sidney, son of the Earl of Leicester, was brought to trial on account of complicity in the Rye House Plot. He had the brutal Jeffreys as his judge, his trial was a disgraceful proceeding throughout, and only his high connexion saved him from having executed upon him the whole of his horrible sentence, which was that he should be " hanged by the neck, and, being alive, cut down, his members mutilated and burned before his face, his head severed from his body, which should be quartered," and he was simply beheaded.

Kingsgate, formerly Bartholomew's Gate, gained its present name in this year from the circumstance of the landing here of the King and the Duke of York.

Charles the Second built the observatory at Greenwich, and, with the idea of having a new Placentia, that western wing of the palace which afterwards became the royal hospital.

Wool smuggling was carried on to an enormous extent on the coasts of Kent at this time in consequence of the Act of 1674, by which it was proclaimed felony to export wool. Everybody, from highest to lowest, was concerned in it; no place was sacred to the smugglers; the belfries of churches were favourite store-houses or places of temporary concealment of cargoes, St. John's Church, Margate, Snargate, Lydd and Erith, amongst others, being noted. In 1671 it was calculated that no less than 40,000 packs of wool had been smuggled into Calais alone during two years.

It is interesting to note that the new iron railings round Wren's Cathedral in London were cast at the Gloucester furnace in Lamberhurst. We believe that the Gloucester furnace itself is actually just in Sussex, but it is near enough to Kent for our purpose. The price was sixpence a pound and the total cost was £11,200.

JAMES II. 1685-1688.

The case of Sir Edward Hales, son of the Kentish "general" during the opening scene of the "Forty Eight," was important as deciding that the King had the power of dispensing with penal laws. Sir Edward Hales was appointed Governor of Dover Castle, but, being a Roman Catholic, he could not take the oaths of supremacy and allegiance under the Test Act. The King, in the usual Stewart style, dispensed with this qualification, but public opinion was aroused and a test action was brought against Sir Edward, in the name of his coachman, to show cause why he should not pay the full penalty of £500. He was tried and convicted, but upon appeal the judges of the

s

King's Bench reversed the judgment, it being laid down as law that the King had the right of dispensing with penal laws under certain circumstances.

In 1685 the Revocation by Louis of the Edict of Nantes, by which Henry IV. had restored his Protestant subjects to equality with Roman Catholics, sent large numbers of refugees into England, Hume says 50,000, and a great many settled in Kent.

So far as our county is concerned there is nothing during this miserable reign to detain us until the last Act. James from the very beginning showed his resolution to enforce his Romanist opinions, and the people were equally determined to have none of them. The struggle ended in the Prince of Orange being invited to come over and assume the sovereignty, whereupon James resolved upon flight.

On December 11th, 1688, accordingly he disguised himself, and, attended only by his faithful Sir Edward Hales, sneaked out of a back door from Whitehall, taking the Great Seal with him, which he dropped into the river, and crossed over to Vauxhall. All through the night he travelled, and at ten the next morning arrived at Elmley Ferry, opposite to Faversham. Here he embarked in a custom house hoy for the French coast, but it being dirty weather the master, requiring more ballast, put in to shore near Sheerness.

Here Sir Edward Hales, who besides being a well-known Papist was a most unpopular man, was recognised by a lot of the blackguards who were constantly on the look out at Kentish ports for refugee Papists. They boarded the craft, robbed the King, ransacked the boat and brought it up to Faversham.

At length a seaman recognised James, and instantly awe of royalty overcame all other considerations, and those who had been foremost in the work of robbery now came forward offering to restore their plunder and to guard the person of the worthless individual whom they regarded still as their King, and a Kentish peasant willingly took the following note from the King to the Privy Council, or rather, to the Earl of Winchilsea :

"Faversham, December 12th, 1688.

" I am just now come in here, having been last night seized by some of this town, who telling me you were to be here this day, I would not make myself known to them, thinking to have found you here ; but, that not being, I desire you would come hither to me, and that as privately as you could do, that I might advise with you concerning my safety, hoping you have that true loyalty in you as you will do what you can to secure me from my enemies, of which you shall find me as sensible as you can desire.

"JAMES R."

The result is an extraordinary instance of the deep-rootedness of loyalty to the reigning sovereign in the English heart. Instead of being hounded for a runaway poltroon, as he deserved to be, James's progress to London and through the city was almost triumphal, bells were rung, cheers were raised, and the very people who a few days back had cursed him were now beside themselves with enthusiastic joy at his return.

But it was too late. The Prince of Orange was fast advancing on London, and Dutch troops were already in London, so that the poor man's reception was but a respite, and on December 18th he was off again, attended by five gentlemen and escorted by Dutch guards.

"The Englishmen were very sorrowful at seeing him depart," says Barillon, " most of them had tears in their eyes." Even Evelyn says :—" I saw the King take barge to Gravesend, a sad sight ! "

To us, such devoted loyalty to three such Kings as these Stewarts seems incomprehensible, but the confirmed fact of its existence simply shows what chances they blindly and wickedly threw away. Even at this crisis if James had behaved as a Tudor assuredly would have behaved, instead of giving way to childish despair, the people would have flocked to his standard and the Dutchmen have been sent about their business.

But it was not to be. James went to Gravesend; the next morning he was at Rochester, and remained three days in the house of Sir Richard Head. Dundee here counselled him to play the man and strike a blow for himself and his kingship, but he refused. On the evening of the 22nd he drew up a paper of moan and snivel to be printed and published as soon as he was gone, and early the next day he dropped down to Sheerness and sailed for France, landing at Ambleteuse on Christmas Day.

WILLIAM III. 1688-1702.

There is as little history connected with our county during the greater part of this reign as in the last, and we begin to find the history of Kent becoming more and more merged into that of England.

In 1693 William started for Holland, and Queen Mary accompanied him as far as Margate, his port of departure. The weather, however, being foul, he determined to wait at Canterbury, and so, not being expected, says Hooper, they drove to the largest house in the city. This happened to belong to a lady who was an ardent Jacobite, and she, having received notice of the coming of the King and Queen, not only took herself out of the way, but removed as many articles of necessity and convenience as she could.

Consequently the Royal pair had to seek another lodging. They were advised to go to the deanery, and thither they went, and remained there for some days. The Dean was absent, and, when the Queen returned to town, he called to express his regret.

"It was impossible," said the Queen, "for you to know that I was there. Yours is the cleanest house I ever was in. . . . . The people were very solicitous to see me, but there was a great walnut tree before the windows, that I could not gratify them." She then described how on Sunday she had gone to one of the parish churches, and that the people stood on the Communion table to look at her. Hooper gallantly cut down the walnut tree in case the Queen should come again, but she did not.

In return for the hospitality shown her, the Queen, observing how shabby the hangings of the Cathedral altar were, replaced them by a magnificent cloth of rich velvet figured with gold and silver, valued at £500.

It was on the occasion of this Canterbury visit that William so disgusted a local boy with his cold, unresponsive manner. This boy gathered the flowers out of his own garden and several more to adorn the High Street as the King came along, and with a number of companions ran about two miles alongside the coach cheering enthusiastically and crying, " God bless King William ! " at which the King put his hand on the glass of the carriage window with a deprecating gesture and said, " It is enough ! "

In 1694 the Queen founded Greenwich Hospital for sailors. Hasted quotes the legal instrument : " That the King and Queen granted to Sir John Somers, lord keeper, and other great officers of state, eight acres of their manor at Greenwich and that capital messuage lately built by their Royal uncle, King Charles the Second, and still remaining unfinished, commonly called the Palace of Greenwich, and several other edifices and buildings standing upon part of the aforesaid ground bounded by the Thames, and by admeasurement along that river 673 feet, to the east end of an edifice called ' The Vestry,' southward on the old Tilt Yard and the Queen's Garden, and westward on the Friar's Road."

The Queen, however, did not endow the building, and it actually remained unfinished until 1752 for want of funds, whilst the endowment of £8,000 made by William in 1695 was taken out of the civil list. Not to rob Mary, however, of the credit due to her it is fair to state that she had intended to dwell at Greenwich whilst the works were in progress so that she could personally inspect them, that she died shortly after her bequest, or there is no reason to doubt that she would have made a suitable endowment.

At Hurst, on the hills near Lympne, was arranged the Jacobite Plot of 1696, known variously as Barclay's or Fenwick's, the object of which was to attack the King and kill him as he was hunting in Richmond Park. The plot was betrayed, and Fenwick tried to escape to France. In the words of Macaulay, "The bells of all the parish churches of Romney Marsh rang the alarm; the country was up; every path was guarded; every thicket was beaten; every hut was searched; and at length the fugitive was found in bed."

He was beheaded on Tower Hill.

In 1698 the Czar Peter came to Sayes Court, Deptford, then occupied by the famous Admiral Benbow, who had leased it of Evelyn. He and his retinue wrought such havoc in the house, and, above all, in the beautiful garden, which had been the loving study and pastime of the author of *Sylva*, that the two gentlemen memorialised the lords of the Treasury for compensation for the injuries done. The result was that Evelyn received £162 7s. 0d., and Admiral Benbow £133 2s. 6d. Evelyn had been prepared for some damage to his house. A servant wrote to him, " There is a house full of people, and right nasty." Loudon, His Majesty's chief gardener, the earliest English gardener of any reputation, who had been called to assess the damage done, thus reports :

    1.—All the grass work is out of order and broke into holes by their leaping and showing tricks upon it.

    2.—The bowling green is in the same condition.

    3.—All that ground which used to be cultivated for eatable plants is all overgrown with weeds, and is not manured nor cultivated, by reason the Czar would not suffer any men to work when the season offered.

    4.—The gravel walks are all broken into holes and out of order.

    5.—Great damages are done to the trees and plants, which cannot be repaired, as the breaking of the branches of the wall fruit trees, spoiling two or three of the finest true philleras, breaking several hollys and other fine plants.

111111111111111

(This last item no doubt includes the five-feet thick holly hedge through which the barbarian genius loved to drive the wheelbarrow with Prince Menzikoff in it.)

In the last year of William's reign, 1701, was presented the famous Kentish Petition to Parliament. Kent, like other counties, was exceedingly dissatisfied with the want of energy shown by Parliament in the granting of supplies on the eve of a momentous war, and in general attention to public business; but Kent, unlike other counties, resolved to express openly what she thought.

On April 29th, 1701, the freeholders of Kent, at the Quarter Sessions held at Maidstone, got the consent of the Grand Jury to the presentation of the following Petition:

"We, the gentry, Justices of the Peace, Grand Jury, and other Freeholders, at the General Quarter Sessions at Maidstone in Kent, deeply concern'd at the dangerous estate of this Kingdom, and of all Europe, and considering that the fate of us and of our posterity depends upon the wisdom of our representatives in Parliament, think ourselves bound in duty humbly to lay before this Honourable House the Consequence of this Conjuncture, of your speedy resolutions and most sincere endeavours to answer the Great Trust reposed in you by your county.

"And in regard from the experience of all ages it is manifest no nation can be happy without union, we hope that no Pretence whatsoever shall be able to create a misunderstanding between ourselves, or the least Distrust of His Majesty, whose great actions for the nation are writ in the Hearts of his subjects, and can never, without the blackest ingratitude, be forgot.

"We most humbly implore this Honourable House to have regard to the voice of the people, that our Religion and Safety may be effectually provided for, that your Loyal Addresses may be turned into bills of supply, and that His Most Sacred Majesty may be inabled powerfully to assist his allies before it be too late."

The Chairman and twenty-three justices signed this, and the freeholders of the county came in so fast to follow their example that the parchment was filled up in five hours.

William Colepeper (the chairman), Thomas Colepeper, Justinian Champneys, David Polhill, and William Hamilton were selected to present it.

They arrived in London and showed the Petition to Sir Thomas Hales, a Kent M.P. Hales took it, promising to return it, but showed it to other members and detained it some time, whereupon Colepeper told him he had broken his word and served his country very ill.

They applied to the other Kent member, Meredith, who said that he dared not consider it as there was already a ferment about it in the House.

In truth the House was exceedingly angry about it. Still the Kent men determined to persevere in presenting the Petition, and Colepeper declared "if every tile on the chapel of St. Stephen's was a devil, he would present the Petition ; " the others stood by him, and swore they would carry it in themselves if their representatives declined to. So Meredith consented.

After half-an-hour the Presenters were called to the bar of the House, and admitted the Petition to be theirs. They were told to withdraw. Members came out and warned them of the serious consequences of what they were doing, and entreated them before it was too late to throw themselves upon the clemency of the House. Still they held out, knowing that they were within the law, and sent answer, "We are humbly of opinion that it is our right to petition this Honourable House, according to the Statute 13, Car. II. As to the matter of our Petition, we declare that we intend nothing offensive to this Honourable House ; " but they refused to add that they were sorry,—"because we will have no ' sorry.' "

After five hours' debate the Petition was declared scandalous, insolent, and seditious, and the presenters were ordered into custody.

At first they were well treated, and William Colepeper was allowed to go to Hollingbourne to comfort his wife, but afterwards the four gentlemen were separated and rigorously confined. Colepeper and Champneys were shut up in a wretched garret in Fox Court, Holborn; Polhill and Hamilton in a cellar so vile they could hardly breathe; all were bullied by the Serjeant who had the custody of them.

Thinking to make their conditions worse the Serjeant complained that his prisoners behaved so disorderly that he feared a rescue; but this complaint turned out to their benefit, for they were removed to the Gate House, where they were well treated.

Then came the presentation to the House of a petition still more violent than the original, and known as the Legion Paper *(See Note B at the end of Stewart Kent)*, by, it is said, Daniel Defoe, disguised as a woman, and escorted by sixteen lords. This so alarmed the anti-Petitioners that the whole matter was dropped, and after prorogation the prisoners were released.

They instantly became popular idols, and were regarded as martyrs in the public cause. The Mercers' Company feasted them before their departure for their homes, and their progress through Kent was one triumphal procession. At Blackheath, where Polhill left them to go to Otford, 500 horse met him and escorted him home. The other three went on to Rochester, where they were met by horsemen from all parts of the county, "so that all the inns could not entertain them."

Four miles from Maidstone, on Boxley Hill, the people met them. At Sandlin, two miles further, the gentry of the entire neighbourhood came in their coaches, attended by an enormous crowd. They entered Maidstone in triumph, " with such exclamations as had never been seen in the place since the Restoration ; " and all night bonfires blazed and healths were drunk; the Grand Jury, of which twelve were justices of the Peace, publicly in a body thanked them.

At Bearsted all the countryside was assembled; bells rang, and all night the crowd waited for Colepeper, intending to escort him to Hollingbourne, but the extraordinary reception at Maidstone had delayed him so that he passed the night there.

That this Kentish remonstrance against the waste of time by Parliament, and its lethargy in the business of putting the nation ready for the crisis at hand—a crisis which produced the War of the Spanish Succession—was not without just cause appears likely from the following letter, bearing upon the national unreadiness for war, written at this time by a Gentleman of Kent, either to the Earl of Godolphin, Lord Treasurer, or to Henry Boyle, Chancellor of the Exchequer:

"Upon peril of my head I would undertake, old as I am, to land with about 20,000 foot and 2,000 dragoons on next Monday morning in any part of Kent or Sussex, from Dover to Chichester, and quarter my troops in London, Westminster, and Southwark, by Saturday next, so as to hear High Mass on Sunday morning at Saint Paul's, and dissolve your Parliament on the Monday following."

The Bishops' Palace at Bromley was the scene of the discovery of the so-called Flower Pot Plot against the Prince of Orange. The name of Bishop Sprat, of Rochester, was affixed to a paper containing the details of a plot for the restoration of James II., which paper was placed in a flower pot, so that it might be found by Government spies. Sprat was arrested and kept in confinement for a short time, but no proofs of his guilt being produced, he was released.

SUNDRIES OF THE STEWART PERIOD.

Mrs. Hutchinson, the noble wife of the noble Puritan Colonel Hutchinson, thus speaks of James the First and the influence of his vile court at Greenwich:

"The honor, wealth and glory of the nation, wherein Queene Elizabeth left it, were soone prodigally wasted by

this thriftlesse heire, the nobillity of the land utterly
debased by setting honors to publick sale, and conferring
them on persons that had neither blood nor merritt fitt
to weare, nor estates to beare up their titles, but were
faine to invent projects to pill (pillage) the people, and
pick their purses for the maintenance of vice and lewd-
nesse. The generallity of the gentry of the land soone
learnt the court fashion, and every greate house in the
country became a sty of uncleannesse. To keep the
people in their deplorable security, till vengeance overtook
them, they were entertain'd with masks, stage playes
and sorts of ruder sports. Then began murther, incest,
adultery, drunkennesse, swearing, fornication and all sorts
of ribaldry, to be no conceal'd but countenanc'd vices ;
because they held such conformity with the court
example.

"And now the ready way to preferment there was to
declare an opposition to the power of godlinesse, under
that name ; so that their pulpits might justly be called
the scorner's chair, there sermons only pleasing that
flatter'd them in their vices, and told the poore King
that he was Solomon ! that his sloth and cowardize, by
which he betray'd the cause of God and honour of the
nation, was gospell meeknesse and peaceablenesse, for
which they rays'd him up above the heavens, while he lay
wallowing like a swine in the mire of his lusts. He had
a little learning—and this they call'd the spirit of wise-
dome, and so magnified him, so falsely flatter'd him,
that he could not endure the words of truth and sound-
nesse, but rewarded these base, wicked, unfaithfull
fawners with rich preferments, attended with pomps and
titles."

Charles the First as a King was despicable, but at any
rate he was a gentleman, and his court was pure. Of him
Mrs. Hutchinson says :

" The face of the court was much chang'd in the change
of the King, for King Charles was temperate, chast and
serious, so that the fools and bawds, mimicks and

catamites of the former court grew out of fashion; and
the nobility and courtiers, who did not quite abandon
their debosheries, had yet that reverence to the King
to retire into corners to practise them. Men of learning
and ingenuity in all arts were in esteeme, and receiv'd
encouragement from the King, who was a most excellent
judge and a greate lover of painting, carvings, gravings
and many other ingenuities, less offensive than the
prophane abusive witt, which was the only exercise of the
other court."

Jeffrey, in the *Edinburgh Review*, thus speaks of the
grossly exaggerated portrait of the Puritan which has
been handed down to us:

"Instead of a set of gloomy bigots waging war with
all the gaieties and elegancies of life, we find ladies of
the first birth and fashion at once converting their hus-
bands to anabaptism, and instructing their children in
music and dancing,—valiant Presbyterian colonels refuting
the errors of Arminius, collecting pictures, and practising,
with great applause, on the violin,—stout esquires, at the
same time praying and quaffing October with their godly
tenants,—and noble lords disputing with their chaplains
on points of theology in the evening, and taking them out
a-hunting in the morning.

"There is nothing, in short, more curious and instructive
than the glimpses which we here catch of the old hospitable
and orderly life of the country gentlemen of England
in those days when the national character was so high
and so peculiar, when civilization had produced all its
effects but that of corruption, and when serious studies
and dignified pursuits had not yet been abandoned to a
paltry and effeminate derision. Undoubtedly, in review-
ing the annals of these times, we are struck with a loftier
air of manhood than presents itself in any after era."

The list of famous Kent men during this period is not
long. Harvey, discoverer of the circulation of the blood,
may fairly occupy the first place. He was born in Folkestone, was chief physician to James I. and Charles I.

and published his famous treatise in 1628. Many other important works by him were destroyed in the wars.

Sir Richard Baker, whose chronicle of the Kings of England is so valuable to historical students, was a Sissinghurst man. Lovelace, the cavalier poet, was born at Woolwich, but the family seat was near Bethersden, where a farmhouse called Lovelace still marks the site. It was whilst imprisoned in the Westminster gatehouse for having been one of the presenters of the Kentish Royalist Petition of 1642 that he wrote the lyric to Althea, in which are the oft-quoted lines :

> "Stone walls do not a prison make,
> Nor iron bars a cage ;
> Minds innocent and quiet take
> That for an hermitage."

Edmund Waller, the turncoat poet, who wooed Lady Dorothy Sidney under the name of Sacharissa, was of a Kentish family, as was Sir Hardres Waller, the somewhat distinguished Parliamentary commander.

Grinling Gibbons, if not Kent born, was at any rate unearthed in Kent, near Sayes Court, Deptford. Of the ill-fated Algernon Sidney and of Sir Dudley Digges we have already spoken. Sir Heneage Finch, who occupied various high positions under Charles II., is famous chiefly as having been the Amri of Dryden's *Absalom and Achitophel*, and for his oratory was known as the "English Cicero" and "Roscius."

Will Adams, the first Englishman who landed in Japan, was a Gillingham man. In 1600 he was chief pilot to the Dutch fleet which annually went to Nagasaki in the service of the Dutch East India Company, and when out there won the favour of the great Shôgun Iyeyasu, who employed him as a ship-builder and even as a diplomatic agent, and raised him to high honour. Prevented from returning home, Adams married a Japanese girl and settled down as a naturalised subject of the Emperor.

The writer was living in Japan when his friend Walters discovered on a charming hill near what is now the busy dockyard of Yokosuka the tombs of this Kentish exile and his wife. The tomb of Adams is uninscribed, but that of his wife bears the usual Buddhist posthumous name. The view from the tombs is one of the most lovely on this coast of lovely views.

It was during this period that Wrotham in Kent became famous for its pottery. The earliest dated specimen is 1612, the latest 1710. It was known as the " Slip decorated ware," and consisted of coarse, reddish clay, upon which a " slip " of thin creamy mixture of clay and water was allowed to trickle through a small tube, producing all sorts of fanciful and quaint designs. On this a glaze of sulphuret of lead, often mixed with manganese, was applied before firing, which gave a rich yellow tone and transparency. The principal articles of Wrotham ware are " tygs "—cups used by all the guests in common before the introduction of separate drinking vessels, with double and triple handles ; posset cups, jugs, plates, dishes, candlesticks and cradles intended for gifts. Jull was the great Wrotham potter, and the site of his manufactory is still pointed out. The drinking vessels generally had mottoes on them, such as " Be merry and wise," "The best is not too good for you," " Obeay the King ; " " Brisk be to the med you desier, as her love you may require ; " " Com, good weman, drink of the best, John, my lady, and all the rest."

NOTES ON STEWART KENT.

A.

Here are samples of contemporary Kentish verse—that is to say, verse of which Kent is the subject. From the *Mercurius Publicus*, May 22nd-29th, 1648.

" Courage, Courage, brave soules, and now revive
Your country's ancient glory, may you thrive,
In enterprise of equall honor may your name
Stand fair with theirs in the monuments of fame.
May you unconquer'd still remaine ! Tread downe
The Common Foe, and help the King to the crowne :
May after ages say thus : Noble Kent
Gave the great'st blow to that curs'd Parliament !"

A Kentish Cavalier song :

" Kentish men, keep your King,
Long swords and brave hearts bring ;
Down with the rebels and slit their crop ears !
Hell now is wanting rogues,
Send there the canting dogs,
Ride to the scurry, my Kent cavaliers !

God and our King for grace,
Leave now your wives' embrace,
Up and avenge all their insults for years !
Ironsides ! Who's afear ?
Pack 'em to Lucifer,
Ride to the scurry, my Kent cavaliers !"

Then there is Browning's swinging chaunt :

" Kentish Sir Byng stood for his King,
Bidding the crop-headed Parliament swing,
And pressing a troop unable to stoop
And see the rogues flourish and honest folks droop,
Marched them along,
Fifty score strong,
Great-hearted gentlemen, singing this song !"

This is a typical morsel :

" Look to your eyes, War Kite, I say,
You carren Parliament,
For yet before Midsummer Day
Your houses shall be rent.
All loyall hearts now join with Kent,
And revenge Surrey's wrongs ;
Come, all you counties with intent
And thrash them with your prongs !"

B.

The " Legion Paper " was addressed to the Speaker, and was accompanied by the following—well, threatening letter :
" Mr. Speaker,
"This memorial you are charged with in behalf of many thousands of the good people of England. There is neither Popish, Jacobite, seditious, court, or party interest concern'd in it ; but honesty and

truth.   You are commanded by two hundred thousand Englishmen
to deliver it to the House of Commons, and to inform them that it
is no banter, but serious truth, and a serious regard to it is
expected ; nothing but justice, and their duty, is required, and it is
required by them who have both a right to require and a power to
compel, viz : the people of England.   We could have come to
the House strong enough to oblige them to hear us, but we
have avoided any tumults, not desiring to embroil, but to save
our native country.   If you refuse to communicate it to them you
will find cause in a short time to repent it."

The claims of the Petition, if so dictatorial a composition can be
called a Petition, were that the people had a perfect right to
censure and direct their representatives in Parliament: that the
House of Commons has no separate right to suspend the laws of
the land : that the House has no power to imprison any person
except its own members.

The " Petition" concluded thus:

" Thus, gentlemen, you have your duty laid before you, which,
it is hoped, you will think of ; but if you continue to neglect it you
may expect to be treated according to the resentment of an injured
nation ; Englishmen are no more to be slaves to Parliaments than
to Kings.   Our name is Legion, and we are many."

VIII.—EIGHTEENTH CENTURY KENT.

$\mathcal{A}$S we approach modern times we find that naturally the history of a county becomes more and more merged in that of the country generally, and this is the reason for the course we shall now pursue to the end of this work, of dealing *seriatim* with the principal events touching the county of Kent without any arbitrary divisions into reigns.

The great storm of 1703—that alluded to by Addison—"such as of late o'er pale Britannia passed"—was most disastrous on our Kentish coasts. Schomburg says that thirteen men-of-war were destroyed, and 1,519 seamen drowned. Sandwich suffered to the extent of £3,000, and we know that Deal, Ramsgate and Margate were stricken in proportion. The Downs, at the time when the gale burst, were crowded with shipping, and upon the Goodwins drove the full force of the south-westerly wind. So fierce indeed was the blow that ships actually sank at their anchorages. Sir Cloudesly Shovel, however, with eight sail of the line, managed to weather it, although, of course, at a vast loss of masts and rigging. Amongst the men-of-war lost were the *Mary* (60), *Northumberland, Restauration* and *Sterling Castle,* each of 70; and of all their crews only 80 men were saved.

In 1722, Atterbury, Bishop of Rochester, was engaged at Bromley Palace, together with the Earls of Arran and Orrery, and Lords Lansdowne, North and Gower, in a Jacobite Plot. Their design was to get a force under the Duke of Ormonde to land on the South Coast, whilst

T

Atterbury and his friends got possession of the Tower, the Bank and the Exchequer Office, and James the Second should be proclaimed simultaneously all over the country. But the French Government gave information of the preparations to the British authorities; Atterbury was arrested and sent to the Tower, sentenced to deprivation of all his ecclesiastical offices, and to perpetual banishment.

The middle of the Eighteenth Century marks a low point in our National History. The spirit of the people seemed to be absolutely dead, the upper classes abandoned themselves to frivolity and vice, the lower classes were hardened and brutal to a degree only to be appreciated by a study of the contemporary newspapers. A startling instance of this temporary degeneracy is afforded by the apathy and indifference with which the movements of the Pretender in 1745 were regarded by all classes of English society, until the advance to Derby caused a contemptible and disgraceful panic in the City of London, only once before or after paralleled in our history.

"England," wrote Henry Fox, "is for the first comer. . . . . If 5,000 French had landed in any part of this island a week ago, I verily believe the entire conquest of it would not have cost them a battle!" Another writer speaks of the "Forty Five" thus: "Those of any rank above a constable, instead of arming themselves and encouraging the people, generally fled before the rebels, while a mob of ragged Highlanders marched unmolested to the heart of a populous Kingdom." And this was not from sympathy with the Pretender's cause, for the feeling against it was very strong.

Yet we may note that it was in 1740 that were composed "God save the King," "The Roast Beef of Old England," and "Rule Britannia," and in 1759—the year of Granby's, Hawkes' and Wolfe's glories at Minden, Quiberon Bay and Quebec—was written "Hearts of Oak."

Kent, however, was held in readiness in case the Pretender's adherents should attempt a landing from

'A FAMOUS OLD.
KENTISH INN.
(NOW DEMOLISHED)

France; and a general levy of all capable of bearing arms was arranged for, the rendezvous being Barham Downs. Admiral Vernon sent a warning to the Governor of Deal Castle to be ready for an invasion of Irishmen, whereupon the Deputy-Lieutenant of the County issued a proclamation calling upon all able men to assemble the next day upon Swingfield Minnis, near Dover; all parishes within twenty miles of the coast were to send well armed men, and the men of the immediate neighbourhood were to bring intrenching tools. So well did the people respond that at the appointed time there were two thousand well-armed men assembled.

Smuggling was the chief industry of Kent at this period. In spite of severe penal laws the clandestine export of wool was enormous and continued until 1793. In 1743 " Riding Officers " were appointed for Romney Marsh, whose especial duty it was to look after the " owlers " as the wool smugglers were called.

So long as the smugglers stuck to their own trade the sympathy of all classes in the countryside was with them, but when, encouraged by their success and the futility of the Preventive service, they became mere robbers, Society awakened to the existence of a terrible tyranny in its midst, and took measures accordingly. Such paragraphs as the following, taken from the " Gentleman's Magazine " for 1745, were common in all contemporary journals :

" At Folkestone a body of smugglers enter'd the house of Mr. Jordan, a custom house officer, arm'd with carbines and pistols, destroy'd his goods, and carry'd off his plate, but one of them, who had ruffles, was shot dead."

" At an ale house at Grinsted Green, Kent, a gang of twelve or fourteen smugglers assaulted three Custom House officers, wounded them in a barbarous manner, and robb'd them of their watches, money, and other things of value."

"Some smugglers enter'd the house of a farmer near Sheerness and plunder'd it of 1,500 pounds of wool."

Ransley's gang, the exploits of which are commemorated in G. P. R. James's novel, " The Smuggler," were men and

women principally from the villages of Bonnington,
Bilsington, and Aldington, and their operations lay in
the country between Sandgate and Dungeness.   Legends
of their brutality still linger in the neighbourhood,
especially of their cruel attack upon a poor old woman at
Ruckinge.   The gang was broken up by the 'treachery'
of one Spratford, and the grave of Quested, the biggest
blackguard, who was hung, may be seen at Aldington, in
which village there is still a Ransley living.   But the chief
pest in the Weald was the Hawkhurst gang, which
flourished until 1747, when the people of Goudhurst
leagued themselves together for mutual protection, calling
themselves " The Goudhurst Band of Militia."   Between
them and the smugglers a regularly arranged encounter
took place, which terminated actually in the storming of
Goudhurst church, whither the smugglers had been driven,
during which three of the latter were killed, many
wounded, and the rest dispersed.   So famous was this
Hawkhurst gang that it was hired by the Dorsetshire
smugglers in order to recover a valuable cargo of two tons
of tea and 39 casks of spirits which had been captured
from them by the Preventive men and lodged in Poole
Custom House.   The attack was made, the goods recovered,
and two men, suspected of being informers, killed.   I give
the sequel in Mr. Furley's words :—

   " Being betrayed by one of their gang a special Commission for the trial of seven of the murderers was held at
Chichester in January, 1748.   They were convicted and
executed the day after their trial, except one, who died
within a few hours of his conviction.   Apprehensions,
trials and convictions of other members of the gang
followed.   Some of the Hawkhurst gang, including
Captain Kingsmill and his second in command, William
Fairall, aged twenty-eight, born at Horsendown Green in
Kent, who described himself ' of no business, but inured to
smuggling from his infancy,' were not tried until 1749,
when they were indicted at the Old Bailey for breaking
into the Custom House at Poole.   One of the accomplices

at the trial stated that the Hawkhurst gang were called the ' East Country People.' 'There were 31 horses and 30 men of us ; the odd horse belonged to the East country-men and carried their arms.' "

Another witness said, " Some had pistols, some had blunderbusses : all the Hawkhurst men had long arms slung round their shoulders."

Three of them were hung at Tyburn ; Kingsmill's body was hung in chains on Goudhurst Gore, Fairall's on Horsendown Green. Four more of the gang were after-wards hung for highway robbery, after having been rescued from Newgate by brother smugglers. Later still, four more were executed on Penenden Heath for house-breaking and horse-stealing, and so this particular gang was broken up, although the business continued to flourish until well into the next century.

In 1759 our Kentish hero, General Wolfe, was killed at the storming of the heights of Abraham before Quebec. I subjoin literally a letter from a Louisburg Volunteer who was present at the last :

" When the General receved the Shot I Caut hold of him And Carried him of the Feild : he Walked About one Hundred yards And then beged I would Let Sit Down, which I Did. Then I Opened his Breast, And found his Shirt full of Blood At Which he Smiled, And When he Seen the Distress I Was in, My Dear, Said he, Dont Grive for me. I Shall be Happy In a Few Minutes : take Care of your Self As I see you are Wounded. But Tell me O Tell me How Goes the Battle Their. Just then Came some Officers Who told him that the Freinch had given Ground and Our troups Was pursuing Them to the Walls of the town, he Was then Lying in my Arms, Just Expirin. . . . . . Raised himself up on this News And Smil'd in my Face. Now, Said he, I Die Contented, from that Instant the smile never Left his Face till he deided."

From 1766 the American War occupied the attention of

people exclusively, and it is remarkable how general the feeling was against it, especially in Kent.

In 1778 there was a large Camp of Regulars and Militia on Coxheath, about which we get some interesting details from contemporary newspapers.   For instance, we find the prices of provisions as supplied to the soldiers :—Beef and mutton 4 pence a pound, bacon 6 pence, Cheshire cheese 4 pence, butter 8 pence, peas and beans 2 pence a peck. Complaints from the smugglers are heard that the vicinity of this wild Heath (whence is obtained one of the finest views in the county), once a happy hiding place for their goods, is now, owing to the existence of the Camp, no longer so, as the goods hidden in woods and hedges are stolen by the soldiers.

Duelling seems to have been so prevalent amongst the officers that most stringent regulations against it were issued from head-quarters, but without effect.

On November 5th, 1778, a Royal Review was held here.

"Their Majesties arrived at Montreal, escorted by a large body of the inhabitants of Sevenoaks and neighbouring places, wearing in their hats cockades of oaken boughs, the emblem of the moving woods before William the Conqueror and their unconquered state.   The whole county concurred in giving them a hearty welcome . . . . . They stopped at Queen Elizabeth's Free School at Sevenoaks, where an elegant Latin oration was delivered to the honour of the Men of Kent.   It was allowed by their train that their Majesties were never received with greater, if they have with equal, respect and attention as they have been here in any tour they have made." Coxheath was enclosed early in the present century, and all that remains to tell of the Aldershot of our grandfathers is the old Clock House, which used to be officers' quarters.

In this year the great Earl of Chatham died at Hayes Place, where in 1759 had been born his equally illustrious son, William Pitt.

OLD CLOTH MANUFACTORY
BIDDENDEN

The Canterbury silk industry was in a sad condition at this time. Only one-third the number of hands were employed, which meant that £4,000 a year was now only circulated in the city instead of £12,000 as formerly. The weavers petitioned the ladies of England to patronise them instead of buying printed, painted, stained and dyed "callicoes," and even hinted pretty broadly that it was illegal to do so, quoting in support of their assertion the Act 7 George I., by which the wearing of such calicoes was forbidden under penalty. But the trade was doomed. Whereas in 1719 there were in the City of Canterbury 334 looms, 58 master weavers and 51 apprentices, in eighty years the number had dwindled to some ten master weavers, and we may suppose that one of the last big orders which the Kentish silkmen got was in 1789 for the silk used in the decoration of the Prince of Wales's magnificent Carlton House.

The transfer of silk weaving to Spitalfields really ruined the Kentish trade.

So with the Kentish broadcloth manufacture and that of baize. Scotland and the Yorkshire and Lancashire towns were coming to the fore in this industry by leaps and bounds, so that by the end of the 18th century, says Hasted, there was not a manufactory left in the Weald, although a worsted establishment at Hawkhurst was carried on for a few years later.

The Kentish iron trade had never been important when compared with that of Sussex; still, one little corner of our county had been a busy hive of grimy industry for many centuries. In 1740 there were 60 furnaces at work in England, of which Sussex owned 10 and Kent 4; the output respectively was 1,400 and 400 tons. In 1796 there were 104 furnaces in England, not one in Kent and only two in Sussex—the Ashburnham, which was only "blown out" in 1809, and one near Rye, which was kept on until 1825.

In the place of these good old industries the active, restless men of Kent followed two callings in particular of questionable morality, although the fact cannot be disguised that contemporary, aye and modern, sentiment was all in their favour. As smugglers and as privateersmen the men of the coast throve exceedingly, and, as a natural consequence, the effects of their prosperity were manifest amongst not only the country folk generally, but the yeomen and gentry. People embarked their money in a "run," or in a privateer, just as they do now in stocks and shares, and there was an element of risk and adventure about both which gave the speculation a peculiar zest.

The following are samples of advertisements which appeared in all the newspapers during the French wars. These are taken from the *Kentish Gazette* of 1778 :

"For a Six Months' Cruize

" Now fitting out at Dover and will sail with the utmost expedition, the *Active* privateer, 224 tons burthen, mounting 18 six pounders, swivels, etc., in proportion.

William Watson, Commander,

So well known for his extraordinary success during the late war, and the short period of time in which the prize money was shared. All able and ordinary seamen, landsmen, etc,, desirous of trying their fortunes in the said cutter, let them instantly repair, etc. It is unnecessary to inform a seaman what must be the advantages of such a cutter at the commencement of a French war. The commander is determined to distribute the prize money within one month after the condemnation sale, and the receit of it. A weekly allowance will be made for the support of the families of the seamen belonging to the above vessel."

From subsequent announcements it would seem that those who embarked in the *Active* had plenty of fun, and that those who invested in her had no reason to be disappointed.

This is another :

" All gentlemen sailors and able-bodied landsmen who are willing to enter on board the *Joseph* Privateer, a prime sailer, carrying 12 carriage guns, and ready to proceed on a cruize against our enemies, will meet with due encouragement by applying," &c.

As for the smugglers, the more stringent duties on imports gave a tremendous spur to their energy. By the law of 1779 a shipmaster from any country except the East Indies was liable to a fine of £300 if more than one hundred pounds of tea, or more than one hundred gallons of foreign spirits in casks, were found on board his vessel. Dealers in tea, coffee, chocolate, and spirits were obliged under heavy penalties to have the fact announced on their shop fronts. French wines, rum, and brandy paid £1 per gallon duty. All lace goods had to bear the Government stamp as a proof that duty had been paid upon them, and imitation of this stamp was punishable by a fine of £200. At the end of the century tea was twelve shillings a pound, even after much of the duty had been taken off and put on windows, so that it was quite customary for guests at tea parties to bring their own tea with them.

So smuggling went on apace all round our Kentish coasts, and hardly a newspaper was published without some paragraph concerning a fight between smugglers and Preventives, like the following:

"Rowley, a riding officer of the Customs, met a gang of smugglers near Sevenoaks, Kent, but the night being exceedingly dark the Dragoons separated from Rowley and three of his servants, the latter of whom engaged with the smugglers, who were armed with cutlasses. The affray was desperate. Seven of the smugglers, after being horribly mangled, deserted their horses and goods without any material hurt to their antagonists, save the loss of a cheek by one of the officers' servants."

Nor was the fun of the contraband trade confined to the coast and the by-roads. Here are two stories from "Baily's Magazine" in connection with the old Dover Road:

An announcement appeared in the papers that an English lady, wife of a celebrated foreigner, had died abroad, and that her body was to be brought home for burial. The coffin duly arrived by packet from Calais and was met at Dover by a hearse with six horses, and two mourning coaches with four, all decked with the orthodox trappings and plumage. Slowly and with befitting solemnity the funeral procession passed out of Dover on its way to London, just at the time that the Preventive authorities had learned that a great shipment of lace might be looked for. Of course the lace was in the coffin.

On another occasion the authorities knew that a large lot of lace had been landed at Dover, but all scent of its whereabouts was lost, until it was whispered at head-quarters that a special order had been received by a Dover inn for a post chaise to be in waiting at a point outside the town to take a single gentleman with a portmanteau, and ready to make a fast journey.

The officers made their plans, and accordingly at the named time a post-chaise dashed through Dover on the road to Canterbury as fast as four horses could lay hoofs to ground, and after it sped the officers.

At Canterbury they arrived a few minutes after the suspected chaise had left; they followed it through Faversham, Sittingbourne, Rochester and Gravesend. Here they met the return night heavy coach which travelled slowly.

"Seen a post-chaise and four pass you?" asked the officers of the old driver.

"Yes," replied he, "And one of their last change horses was lame, so you may catch them."

Off they went, and found the chaise at Deptford. The passenger was having supper. In walked the officers, and found a quiet, gentlemanly man who asked them their business.

"We must search your carriage in the King's name," they replied. "Search, and be d——d," said the passenger, Which they did, and found nothing.

All the time the lace was in the slow night coach, the fossil driver of which was, of course, a confederate of the smugglers.

However, the smugglers were pretty hardly hit now and then. In September, 1773, for instance, French silks and lace to the value of £15,000 were seized by the revenue people and the Dragoons in a house at Hawkinge, near Folkestone, probably the famous Hockley Hole Farm, known as "Smugglers' Hall." In the same year the officers met a party of smugglers with thirty horses laden with tea and lace near Dartford. There was a fight, but the stuff was captured. But the severest blow was dealt by Mr. Pitt himself in 1784.

It was December, and the weather had been too coarse even for Deal smugglers, and most of their boats were drawn up high and dry on the beach. Pitt was told that this would be a splendid opportunity for destroying them. Pitt at once applied to the War Office for a regiment of soldiers, for he knew with what desperate characters he had to deal. Mr. Clark Russell shall tell the rest of the story :

"On the arrival of the regiment at Deal the officer in command discovered that, although the people had no exact knowledge of the object of the presence of the soldiers, there was everywhere current an ugly suspicion that something injurious to the interests of the place was menaced. Every publican had pulled down his sign that the soldiers might have no quarters. The hunt after accommodation proved of no avail. There was a large barn hard by the town, large enough to accommodate the troops, and the quarter-master rode off to talk to the landlord about it, but the man refused to let it on any other terms than for two years certain. The commanding officer accepted the proposal and marched his men in, but he was put to his wit's ends to obtain provisions for the soldiers.

"Next morning a naval officer named Bray was ordered to station a few cutters off the beach, and when this was done the troops marched down to the water's edge. The notion amongst the people of Deal was that the cutters were there to receive the soldiers, and that the place would be cleared of the troops very shortly. A considerable crowd gathered to view the proceedings. Meanwhile the soldiers, with loaded muskets in their grasp, were so ranged as to cover the row of luggers. An order was then given, and in a very short while every smuggling craft along the beach was in a blaze. The people could only look on, pale with wrath, but helpless."

In 1794 Wilberforce brought before the House of Commons his proposal for the Abolition of the Slave Trade. He was encouraged to do this "after a conversation with Mr. Pitt in the open air at the foot of an old tree at Holwood, just above the steep descent into the Vale of Keston:" so may be read in the back of the stone seat close to the old tree, which is still standing—a wonder, considering that, not being protected in any way until within the past few years, it was rapidly being destroyed by visitors.

The chief event of the year 1797 so far as our county is concerned was the Mutiny of the Fleet at the Nore. It was an unfortunate and humiliating proceeding from beginning to end, inasmuch as it was irrational, ill planned, ill carried out, and might have caused a national catastrophe.

It was preceded by a mutiny at Spithead on April 15th —a mutiny to which Jack had been goaded after long years of patient suffering, and which, however reprehensible as a means to right, must claim the sympathy of every fair-thinking man. The causes of complaint were the smallness of pay and of the Greenwich pensions, which had not been augmented since the time of Charles II.; the unequal distribution of prize money, and last, but by no means least, the tyrannical power exercised by too many captains.

The ships' companies appointed two delegates each, petitions were drawn up in moderate language and presented, with the result that the men's demands were complied with and the King's pardon granted. Further concessions were made later on, and apparently the cloud had passed away. But on May 20th a mutiny broke out on the ships at the Nore. Two delegates were chosen from each of the twenty ships and Richard Parker, a "sea lawyer," one of those men of superior education and glib speech who are at the bottom of most popular discontents ashore and afloat, was chosen president, besides a committee of twelve on each ship. A statement of supposed grievances in eight articles was drawn up, couched in peremptory language, and presented to the Admiralty. The very first article sufficiently showed upon what imperfect ground the mutineers had taken their stand, for it demanded that every indulgence which had been granted to the fleet at Portsmouth should be granted elsewhere.

The authorities refused to comply, upon the very just grounds that sufficient concessions had already been made, and that what applied to the fleet at Portsmouth necessarily applied to the entire Royal Navy.

This exasperated the mutineers; the red flag was run up, and the ships at Sheerness ordered to drop down to the Nore. A committee from the Admiralty came to Sheerness, but all conciliatory efforts failed, and it withdrew, convinced that there was no course open now but force The mutineers drew their ships across the river and stopped all merchant vessels passing up and down, in reply to which the authorities took up the buoys at the mouth of the river, constructed batteries on the shore which were garrisoned by the Gravesend Volunteer Artillery, the Northfleet Volunteers, the Cobham and the West Kent Yeomanry Cavalry, besides regulars, and cut off all intercourse between the ships and the shore. Then the mutineers began to waver, especially when they found that their comrades at Plymouth and Portsmouth disapproved of their proceedings. Strange to relate, on June 4th, the King's birthday, the whole fleet showed its loyalty by firing a royal salute and by dressing ship, and by keeping the red flag flying only on the *Sandwich*. Then some of the ships slipped away, and by June 13th the Red flag had disappeared. The *Sandwich* ran under the guns at Sheerness, and a party of soldiers sent off to arrest Parker was allowed to do so.

Parker was tried, condemned and executed, as were two or three other ringleaders, a few men were flogged through the fleet or imprisoned and the rest pardoned.

About these mutinies Nelson said : " I am entirely with the seamen in their first complaint. We are a neglected set, and when peace comes are sharply treated, but as for the Nore scoundrels, I should be happy to command a ship against them."

On the eve of the great Irish rebellion of 1798, Kent came in for a prominent share in the public excitement. Arthur O'Connor, who had been long "wanted" in connection with the Brotherhood of United Irishmen, and who was suspected of being in correspondence with the French General Hoche concerning the invasion of Ireland, was arrested at Margate, together with a priest O'Coigly and three others, on the point of embarking for France. On O'Coigly was found a seditious address from the Secret Committee of England to the French Executive Directory, so all were arrested, taken to Maidstone and committed for trial.

Enormous interest was taken in the case. Fox, Sheridan, Erskine, Whitbread, and the Duke of Norfolk attended as witnesses on behalf of O'Connor, whose defence was that he was flying the country simply for his own good. The result of the trial was that O'Coigly was found guilty and sentenced to death, O'Connor and the others were acquitted.

Then ensued a remarkable scene in Court. O'Connor, upon hearing the verdict in his favour, sprang out of the dock, and tried to make his way through the Court. A scrimmage ensued, during which a couple of swords which lay on the witnesses' table were seized and used. O'Connor was held by a constable and dragged back to the bar, and a warrant for his arrest on the charge of high treason produced. So he was re-arrested, taken to London, and ultimately banished.

O'Coigly was executed on Penenden Heath. The usual barbarous accompaniments of executions for high treason were omitted, and he died professing his innocence,

This same year, 1798, renewed alarms of invasion from France kept our county in constant agitation from end to end. The most elaborate schemes were drawn up for the means of offence and defence to be adopted in case of an emergency, for driving off the live stock from the exposed parts of the county, for the saving of property, and for making every available man and woman useful in some way. Detailed accounts of the stores of grain and forage, of horses and carts, were collected. Enthusiastic meetings were held all over the county, at which the parishioners offered themselves for service *en masse*.

Every newspaper published subscription lists in aid of the raising and equipping of forces. The Corporations of Gravesend and Milton resolved to give up all civic feasting and entertainment and to apply the funds to the public cause. Armed associations were formed in every direction. The Canterbury Volunteers, in reply to a circular from the Lord Lieutenant asking what dispositions they could make at an emergency, replied that they were ready to march anywhere at any time. At a great meeting held at Sittingbourne on April 18th Lord Romney announced his intention of forming a corps of rifles and sharpshooters at his own cost.

Of course, there were ludicrous incidents. A Bromley volunteer almost blew his front rank man to shreds by firing off his musket with six charges in it. It was reported that one Sunday morning, whilst Divine service was being performed in the Dover churches, sounds of firing were heard, which produced a panic and emptied the churches, when it was found that the cause of the alarm was the firing of a salute. In fairness to Dover, however, be it said that the report was indignantly denied in the newspapers.

In 1799 a grand review of Kentish Volunteers was held at the Mote Park, Maidstone. The King left Kew at 5 a.m., breakfasted with Lord Camden at Wildernesse, and, as the breakfast was prolonged and the roads were bad, it was 11.45 before the Royal Party arrived in heavy

rain at the Mote. There were present the King, the
Prince of Wales, the Queen, the Dukes of Cumberland and
Gloucester, and the Princesses Augusta and Elizabeth, all
wearing sprigs of oak.

There was a march past, and a sham fight lasting an
hour-and-a-half, and at 3.30 p.m. a banquet, to which 6,000
people sat down. The Court Newsman tells us that the
length of the tables was $7\frac{1}{2}$ miles, the value of the wood
used in their construction £1,500, that Gunter, of Jermyn
Street, was caterer, and that Johnny Townsend, the
famous Bow Street runner, was one of the most active
among the waiters. The proceedings ended with the
singing of "God Save the King" and the drinking of the
King's health by the whole assembly.

IX.—LATER KENT.

THE new century opened with alarms, excursions, wars, and rumours of wars. In Kent the first three years were one long martial fever; men's minds were occupied with little else than preparations against invasion, and, as might be expected, in no county were the preparations more complete.

In 1803 the Secretary of War promulgated his scheme for the national defence. By this all men capable of bearing arms between the ages of 17 and 55 were to be immediately enrolled in four classes : (1) Unmarried men between 17 and 30 ; (2) unmarried men between 30 and 50 ; (3) married men, but with not more than two children, between 17 and 30 ; (4) married men between 30 and 55.

The names were to be posted upon all church doors ; each man was to receive two guineas for necessaries, and one guinea at the expiration of his period of service. Training was to take place every Sunday, and no man was to go more than three miles from his home for drill. The penalty for absence was five shillings, and not even persons serving in the Militia by substitutes were exempted.

To this national force Kent contributed 1,530 cavalry, 8,800 infantry, and 253 artillery, besides 1,026 men averaging 5 feet 2 inches in height, to the Army of Reserve. Nor was this all. A system of Coast Fencibles had been introduced in 1799 by Captain Popham, by which the seamen and fishermen were enrolled and trained to artillery work in the manning of thirty-six and forty-oared galleys armed with eighteen pounders or forty-two pound carronades. They were to be limited in their operations to their own districts, unless the enemy landed, when they would follow their commanders.

The system, however, seems to have been badly arranged, for in 1801 Nelson came down to the Kentish coast to examine the condition of the Sea Fencibles, who were exempt from impressment on the condition that they would come forward for coast defence in case of threatened invasion. At Margate in August Nelson summoned the Fencibles on board the defence ships, but out of 2,600 only 385 came forward. " They are no more willing to give up their occupations than their superiors," remarked Nelson.

This system was elaborated in 1803, and the Kentish coast divided into districts, thus :

    1.—From Dungeness to Sandgate, of which the rendezvous was New Romney.

    2.—From Sandgate to Sandown ; rendezvous, Dover.

    3.—From Sandown to the North Foreland ; rendezvous, Ramsgate.

This force numbered about 16,000 hardy, resolute, fearless fellows, who might be depended upon in any emergency. Only once had they a chance of showing of what stuff they were made, and this was when a French privateer attacked two brigs off the North Foreland, and out went forty or fifty of the Fencible galleys, beat off the Frenchman and rescued the brigs.

It was about this time that the Deal privateer *Catharine and Mary* made for herself such a name. She only cost about £1,600, and in three months she captured prizes valued at £60,000. She was at last captured, after an heroic resistance ; her sides almost blown to pieces, her rigging hanging in shreds, and half her crew dead or wounded.

Camps were formed at Coxheath, Chatham, Barham Downs, Ashford, Dover and Shorncliffe. The Military Canal was cut from Hythe to Rye, ostensibly as an

FISHER GATE
SANDWICH

obstacle to a commander accustomed to throw men by the hundred thousand over the broadest and most rapid rivers of Europe, and as a means of transporting troops and stores from point to point. The Martello towers were built, the idea of them being taken from a tower at Mortella in Corsica, which in 1794, garrisoned by only thirty-eight men, made a splendid defence against a combined sea and land attack by Lord Hood and Major-General Dundas.

The system of beacons was completed, posts being established at Canterbury, Shorncliffe, Barham, Thanet, Shottenden, Hythe, Postling Down, Westwell, Pluckley, Lyndham Hill, Coxheath, whence to Bexley and the London road, Chatham Lines, Wrotham Hill, Tenterden, Highgate near Hawkhurst, and Goudhurst, this being the order of firing according as the first fire was seen from Canterbury or Goudhurst.

A perfected system of telegraphing by day was established, by which, under favourable circumstances, a message could be sent from Deal to London, and a reply received in seven minutes and a half!

Pitt, as Colonel of the Cinque Ports Volunteers, reviewed them, 900 strong, at Sandwich. They gave him nine cheers, and he replied :

"A proud day, indeed! Now let the enemy come and I have nothing to fear. I now see I can confide in my men."

On another occasion he reviewed the Deal Sea Fencibles. Thirty-five boats, each armed with an eighteen or a twelve pounder, were paraded and went through evolutions with that perfect skill and dexterity for which Deal boatmen are famous, and, although some of the men on board must have remembered that fatal December morning nineteen years before on the same beach, they cheered with the utmost enthusiasm the "pilot who weathered the storm," especially when he, with a distinguished company, came afloat from Walmer Castle for a nearer inspection, and more especially when he repeated the visit in the afternoon.

All Kent was full of soldiers, who were billeted at Dover, Ashford, Tunbridge, Sevenoaks, Sittingbourne, Town Malling, Wrotham, Wye, Romney, Lydd and Dungeness.

There were big barracks on Brabourne Lees and at the Warren, Ashford. The roads were lively with marching regiments; the quietest towns were transformed into centres of bustle and activity; inn accommodation for the ordinary traveller was hardly to be had for love or money; children played at soldiers; old ladies talked soldiers over their twelve shilling tea; the lasses of Kent had a better time than they ever had before or ever would have again; the slouchiest rustic trimmed himself up and squared his shoulders; and every counter jumper in the county was a member of some fighting organization or other. And what a choice of corps he had! There were the Broadstairs Volunteer Artillery, (Broadstairs must have diminished wofully since the day when it could run an Artillery corps of its own!) the Canterbury Rifles, the Cinque Ports Volunteers, the Deal Volunteer Artillery, the Deal Volunteer Infantry, the Dover Volunteer Artillery, the Margate Volunteer Artillery and Infantry, the Ramsgate Independent Artillery, Volunteer Artillery and Volunteer Marksmen, the Ringwould Artillery, the Maidstone Infantry, Sandwich Artillery, Wingham Infantry, Ashford Infantry, the Royal Greenwich, the Holmesdale, the Sheppey Infantry, the Canterbury Volunteer Dispatch Corps, and a host of others.

On August 2nd, 1803, at a great meeting in Maidstone, the following address was drawn up and presented to the King:

"The humble address of the Nobility, Gentry, Clergy, Freeholders, and others of the County of Kent:

"We, your Majesty's most dutiful and loyal subjects, the Men of Kent, beg leave at this most important crisis to approach your Majesty with those sentiments with which our hearts are animated, and in conformity with which our hands are prepared to act. We acknowledge with gratitude the goodness of Divine Providence in having preserved to us our laws, our liberty, and our constitution under your Majesty's mild and paternal Government amidst the wreck and destruction of surrounding nations, and by uniting with Your Majesty in defence of these inestimable blessings we desire to prove that we are not unworthy of them. We contemplate with anxiety the formidable attack with which we are threatened, but without dismay. We are sensible that no apparent difficulties are sufficient to arrest the progress of unbounded ambition and unbounded power; and that no attempt will seem desperate to pride and revenge, intoxicated by success and irritated by resistance. In a word, we do not underrate our danger, but resolve to meet it.

"Placed as we are by nature in the situation most exposed to the assaults of the foe, and forming, as it were, the advanced guard of Your Majesty's armed subjects, we feel that more than common exertions may be expected from US, and we are prepared to make them; in humble confidence that if put to the trial, we shall justify our traditional boast, and prove to our Sovereign and to the World that Men of Kent will never be conquered."

The same month there was a great review before the Duke of York at Coxheath of Militia, Yeomanry and Maidstone Volunteers; inspections at Ashford and in Chilham Park—Mr. Wildman entertaining the troops royally at the latter place; on Barham Downs the Canterbury garrison was inspected, and there were field days at Walmer, Deal and Dover. At Maidstone at a great patriotic banquet the chorus of " Men of Kent " was sung with great enthusiasm.

It was at this time that the Prince of Wales offered his active services, saying, "I ought to be first and foremost."

To this the King replied :

" Windsor, August 7, 1803.
" My dear Son,
" Though I applaud your zeal and spirit, of which I trust

no one can suppose any of my family wanting, yet, considering the repeated declarations I have made of my determinations on your former applications to the same purpose, I had flattered myself to have heard no farther on the subject. Should the implacable enemy so far succeed to land, you will have an opportunity of shewing your zeal at the head of your regiment. It will be the duty of every man to stand forth on such an occasion, and I shall certainly think it mine to set an example in defence of everything that is dear to me and to my people."

After the Peace of 1815 came twenty years of great adversity in our country districts. The inflated war prices did not continue as had been expected, and, as there had been reckless speculation in land, etc., the great drop in prices produced forced sales and consequent misery. The Select Committee of 1833 showed that there was not one solvent tenant in the Weald of Kent and Sussex. The yeomanry were disappearing, and their places were taken by capitalists—successful merchants and so forth. In 1793 Boys had said: "The number of yeomanry of this country seems annually on the increase. There is no description of persons who can afford to give so much money for the purchase of an estate as those who buy for their own occupation. Many estates in the eastern part of this county have been sold for forty or fifty years purchase."

Hence only vigorous economy and the non-employment of labour enabled freeholders to retain lands. However, the coming of capitalist landlords relieved matters and somewhat atoned for the disappearance of the yeomanry.

In 1816 the Princess Charlotte, daughter of the Prince of Wales, was married to Prince Leopold of Coburg, and a most unpopular match it seems to have been if we may judge by the reports of public meetings held at this time.

We had been fighting the world so long that we were getting a little Chauvinistic in our patriotism : moreover, the foreign connections of our Royal families had not brought much honour and glory to the country, and so it was that the cry rang out at any rate at the Kentish meetings : " No more foreigners ! We can't afford to keep 'em. No more Hanover rats ! "

In 1820 the unhappy Queen Caroline arrived at Dover to assert the rights she considered the King had wrongfully deprived her.

She was enthusiastically received, for the people unanimously regarded her as a martyr. So great was the crowd that she was obliged to take refuge at the *York* Hotel, from the doors of which she had the guard removed in deference to the wishes of the people. The crowd took the horses out of her carriage and dragged it out of Dover : she was lighted into Canterbury by 100 men with torches, and amidst an enormous crowd drove to the *Fountain.* Her journey from Canterbury was one triumphal progress. At Sittingbourne the clergy received her. At Gravesend the people drew her to the town. From Dartford to Shooters Hill she was escorted by mounted gentlemen. Blackheath was like a fair, and here she alighted at the famous old *Green Man,* and bowed her acknowledgments to the cheering crowd, dressed in " a black twilled sarsenet gown, a fur tippet and muff, and a hat of black satin with feathers."

Smuggling continued to be extensively carried on, and it was estimated that the annual loss to the Revenue from smuggling and the cost of the Preventive Service, or the Coast Blockade as it was now called, was £1,000,000. " Guinea " smuggling especially assumed enormous dimensions during the years of the Peninsular War. Guineas were bought up at twenty-seven shillings a piece, carried over to Gravelines, Dunkirk, or Calais in ten-oared galleys, and fetched a high premium. They are said to have been largely used in payment of the French troops in Spain. Folkestone, Deal, and Dover were the chief " Guinea " ports, and the usual punishment of captured smugglers was service for a term of years in the Royal Navy. Hence a contemporary bard says :

> " They dragged us up to Dover gaol,
>   In iron bound like thieves,
>   All for to serve great George our King,
>   And force us to the seas."

Large fortunes were made in our Kentish coast towns by this traffic, in which highly respectable mercantile houses were not ashamed of dabbling, and Deal in particular attained a prosperity it never reached before or since.

In 1828 the Catholic Emancipation movement was agitating the country. Although the penalties inflicted by the severe laws against Roman Catholics in the reigns of Elizabeth and James I. had long since been repealed the disabilities remained. Many efforts had been made to remove these. At the union with Ireland in 1800 Pitt had promised that this should be done, but George III. would never consent. Three times the motion in favour of it had passed through the Commons, and as many times had been rejected by the Lords. A great county meeting was held on Penenden Heath, October 24th, 1828, at which some say were 20,000 people, some say 60,000. The High Sheriff of Kent presided; on his left were the Earl of Winchilsea and the opposition party, clergymen and dissenters, and a crowd of rough fellows in yellow smocks, armed with thick sticks, who were not there by accident. On his right were the Earl of Radnor, Lord Camden, Lord Darnley and the supporters of the Bill. The petition was proposed by Gypps and seconded by Plumptre. Violent speeches were made, and a very long one by a Mr. Shiel. What the result of the division was nobody knows to this day, so great was the disorder and so many the interruptions. The majority was said to be much in favour of the Bill, but other reports are to the contrary. Eventually the Duke of Wellington's Ministry passed the Bill by a majority of 178 in the Commons and 104 in the Lords.

The next great agitation was about Parliamentary Reform. In 1832 the Bill was finally passed, after having been repeatedly opposed by the Lords; but before this had been effected the country had gone through a period of great disorder and popular discontent. There was nothing in Kent like the terrible riot at Bristol, in which the bishop's palace, the mansion house, almost the whole of one of the principal squares, the custom house, the excise office, and the gaols were destroyed, but in all the chief towns of the county meetings were held, marked by more or less disorder, and remembered by many scores of men who had had their heads broken thereat.

By this measure no less than 54 boroughs were disenfranchised; many of these thoroughly deserved the epithet of "rotten," and all were of insufficient importance to send separate representatives. Only three of this number have since moved sufficiently with the times to have the privilege restored—East Grinsted in Sussex, Newton in Lancashire, and Appleby in Westmoreland.

As regards the County of Kent, the following changes were effected by this great Bill. Queenborough and New Romney, which had hitherto each returned two members, ceased to return any at all. Hythe, which had hitherto returned two members, was to return one only. Greenwich, a new borough, was to return two members; Chatham, also a new borough, was to return one. Sandwich, retaining its two members, was to include Deal and Walmer; whilst there were to be four Knights of the Shire in the place of two. The number of members remained the same, but the distribution was different.

Since 1832 further changes have been made in Kentish Parliamentary Representation, and for purposes of comparison I here subjoin tables of the three periods. The numbers refer to the members.

1.—*Before 1832.* The County 2, Sandwich 2, Rochester 2, Canterbury 2, Dover 2, New Romney 2, Hythe 2, Maidstone 2, and Queenborough 2.

2.—*1832.* The County 4, Canterbury 2, Dover 2, Hythe 1, Chatham 1, Greenwich 2, Maidstone 2, Rochester 2, Sandwich 2.

3.—*1898.*   *Districts:*—Ashford 1, Dartford 1, Faver-
    sham 1.
    County :—Medway 1, St. Augustine's 1,
        Sevenoaks 1, Thanet 1, Tun-
        bridge 1.
    Boroughs :—Canterbury 1, Chatham 1,
        Deptford 1, Dover 1, Graves-
        end 1, Hythe 1, Greenwich 1,
        Maidstone 1, Rochester 1,
        Woolwich 1.

Lewisham District returns 1 member, but as a Metro-
politan Constituency.

In the year 1833 the neighbourhood of the City of
Canterbury was mildly excited by the appearance there of
Sir William Percy Honeywood Courteney, Knight of
Malta, of Hales and Evington in Kent, and Powderham
in Devonshire—or rather, of an individual wearing a
purple cloak, girt with a sword, and attended by two pages
in scarlet livery, who called himself all this. At first he
was regarded merely as an eccentric ; but when he got to
haranguing the rustics about their rights and their
wrongs, and finally gave himself out to be Somebody
whom he certainly was not, more than passing attention
was paid to him.

Then he put himself up as a candidate for the Parliamentary representation of the City of Canterbury, filled the
place with posters and placards, appeared on the hustings
in Oriental dress, challenged Sir Thomas Tylden, Sir
Brook Brydges, Sir Edward Knatchbull and Sir William
Cosway to mortal combat, as "four cowards unfit to
represent the brave men of Kent," and canvassed with such
success that his rival became anxious.

Suddenly he was indicted for perjury which he had
committed in his over zeal for some Kentish smugglers ;
he was tried at Maidstone, July 25th, 1833, nnder his
real name of Thom, and sentenced to transportation, but
was found to be insane and was sent to Barming Asylum.
Here he remained four years and then was released. He

lived in the house of a Mr. Francis at Fairbrook, near
Boughton, but his wild behaviour, his violent speeches
about the new Poor Law, his exhortations and promises,
made him a nuisance as a tenant, and he changed his
quarters to Bosenden Farm.

Men gathered round him in a blind faith inexplicable in
such an age, and he paraded the villages bearing a white
flag with a blue border and stamped with a rampant lion,
his followers carrying sticks with loaves of bread stuck on
them. All about the Stour valley villages he preached his
doctrine of salvation and regeneration at the expense of
earthly powers, and to this day in cottages at Eastling,
Throwley, Selling, Badlesmere and elsewhere his portrait may be seen.

He was rapidly becoming a public nuisance, for he led
men away from their work, and at length a matter-of-fact
farmer named Curtis applied for a warrant against him.
Mears, a constable, went to Bosenden Farm early one
morning, thinking to surprise Thom. But Thom was on
the look out, asked Mears what his business was, and then
shot him dead, and wounded another man of the same
name. " The work goes well," said he, " a second Gideon
has come to slay the ungodly; and thus would perish all
who should oppose the prophet Courteney."

The alarm was now general. Thom, with his followers,
went to Bosenden Wood, the county magistrates resolved
to capture him and sent to Canterbury for soldiers of the
45th Regiment.

This was smartly done. It was 32 miles there and
back, and in $2\frac{1}{2}$ hours the answer came that the soldiers
were starting.

One hundred soldiers came, Lieutenant Bennett in
command, and were divided into two detachments to sur-
round the wood, for it was known that the madman and
his followers would make a desperate resistance. With
the soldiers went the Rev. Dr. Poore, Mr. Knatchbull,
Mr. Halford and Mr. Baldock, justices of the peace.

Bennett stepped forward and counselled Thom to surrender quietly.   Thom fired and killed him, but was
himself shot the next minute.   Thom's men rushed on
the soldiers and a desperate fight ensued, which lasted,
so it is said, from mid-day until seven at night.   The
result was that seven of Thom's men were killed and nine
wounded, whilst the soldiers had their officer and one man
killed and six wounded.

Such was the Battle of Bosenden, as it is called.

At the Maidstone Assizes of May 31st, 1838, Price and
Mears were sentenced to death, but this was commuted to
transportation for life ; six others were sentenced to one
year's imprisonment, of which one month was to be solitary
confinement.

Surely no more bitter lesson was ever read to employers
of labour upon the evil of neglecting the welfare of their
subordinates than this of these poor misguided clowns
risking their lives for the sake of a madman, almost within
sight of the Cathedral of Canterbury !

" Sir William " was a Cornishman named John Nicholas
Thom : his portrait is still to be seen on the walls of inns
and cottages in the neighbourhood, and the name of " Mad
Thom's Corner " still keeps alive the memory of what has
been fairly termed " The last English Battle," for, small as
is the list of casualties, it is longer than the killed and
wounded roll of many a conflict between great captains in
the days of heavy armour.

The list of famous Kent men during the periods embraced by these two last chapters is a goodly one.

Of Chatham and Pitt we have already spoken.   The
courtly Lord Chesterfield was a Kent man, so was General
Wolfe of Westerham, and Sir Sidney Smith the gallant
defender of St. Jean d'Acre against Bonaparte in 1799,
was, if not Kent born, educated at Tunbridge School.   The
unfortunate Admiral Byng, and Sir George Rooke, who
captured Gibraltar in 1704, belonged to our county.
George Grote, the historian of Greece, was a Kent man ;
the families of Gibbon the historian and Cowper the poet

were connected with Kent. Horace Walpole was the youngest son of Sir Robert Walpole, who married the daughter of John Shorter of Bybrook in Kennington. The Rev. John Barham, author of the *Ingoldsby Legends*, was Kentish, and if Charles Dickens was not Kentish by birth he was by latter residence, and the county is intimately associated with some of his most popular books and stories —curiously with *Pickwick* and *Edwin Drood*, his first and last books.

Lord Tennyson is associated with Kent inasmuch as his family moved to Boxley from Tunbridge Wells, whither they had gone from Lincolnshire, and the Park of Park House, Boxley, the seat of his friends the Lushingtons, is described in the Prologue to the *Princess*.

NOTE ON LATER KENT.

The disgraceful condition of the representation of the country may be exemplified by a table taken from the New Annual Register of 1813; at this time Birmingham, Leeds and Manchester were unrepresented, whilst places with twenty, and even a less number of inhabitants, returned members :—

	Members.	Electors.
City of London	4	7,000
Westminster	2	10,000
Middlesex	2	3,500
Surrey	2	4,500
Southwark	2	2,000
	12	27,000

	Members.	Electors.
Newton (Isle of Wight)	2	1
Old Sarum	2	1
Midhurst	2	1
Castle Rising (Norfolk)	2	2
Marlborough	2	2
Downton (Wilts)	2	4
	12	11

APPENDIX.

A.—ROYAL KENT.

In additional support of my contention that Kent has the best right of all Counties to the epithet Royal I subjoin a few facts in connection with some of our Kentish places. If any other County, of course excepting Middlesex, can establish a claim to closer and more constant association with the Royalty of England, Appendix A shall disappear from any future edition of this work.

1.—CANTERBURY.

After Hengist destroyed Canterbury in A.D. 460, the City lay desolate and deserted until Ethelbert re-built and re-occupied it, and throughout the duration of the Kingdom of Kent the Kings of Kent had their palace here and were buried here.

In 597 Christianity came to Canterbury, and from Canterbury was spread throughout Britain.

In 1023 Canute presented his golden crown to the Cathedral.

In 1130 Henry I. kept his Court here with David, King of Scotland, and all the bishops.

In 1174 Henry II. performed penance here for the murder of Becket, and came regularly for some years.

In 1179 Louis VII. of France came.

In 1189 Richard I. received the homage of William, King of Scotland, and came here in 1194 on his return from the Crusades.

In 1201 John and Isabella of France were crowned here, and in 1204 he kept the festival of Christmas here.

In 1220 Henry III. was here on the occasion of the translation of Becket's remains, was re-crowned here in 1236, married Eleanor of Provence here, and kept the Christmas of 1263 here.

In 1299 Edward I. was married here to Margaret of France, on which occasion he presented the Cathedral with the Royal Crown of Scotland, and in 1300 paid " chevage "—£2—for a child to be born.

In 1357 the Black Prince came here after Poictiers with his prisoner John of France ; in 1363 he married here Joan, the Fair Maid of Kent, and he was buried here.

In 1400 Emmanuel, Emperor of the East, came. Henry IV. and his Queen, Joan of Navarre, were buried here.

In 1415 Henry V. came here after Agincourt.

In 1417 Sigismund, Emperor of the West, was here.

In 1465 Edward IV. and Elizabeth Woodville were here, and presented the North Window of the Martyrdom. Henry of Richmond, afterwards Henry VII., married Elizabeth of York here, and as King often kept his Court at Canterbury.

In 1520 Henry VIII. came here, and with Charles V. of Spain was magnificently entertained. Anne of Cleves lodged in Canterbury on her way to meet Henry.

Philip of Spain was here in 1555 and Mary in 1558.

Elizabeth kept her Court here in 1573, and lodged here on the occasion of her accompanying her suitor, the Duke of Anjou, to the Coast.

Charles I. married Henrietta Maria here.

Charles II. stayed three nights here on his way to London at his Restoration.

William and Mary were here in 1689.

George I. was here in 1720; George II. in 1728; the Prince Regent in 1798.

The Prince Consort was here in 1840, and Her present Gracious Majesty in 1835 and 1842.

2.—ELTHAM.

Possibly the Anglo-Saxon Kings of Kent had a palace here.

In 1270 Henry III. kept Christmas here. This is the first record we have of Eltham after the building of it by Bec, the fighting Bishop of Durham, who presented it to Edward II., and who died here.

In 1308 Edward II. and his bride, Isabella of France, came here from Dover, and in 1316 his son, known as John of Eltham, was born here.

Edward III. held Parliaments here in 1329, in 1331—when were passed the Statutes of Eltham for the regulation of the Royal Household—and in 1375.

In 1347 Lionel, third son of Edward III., kept Christmas here during the absence of his father in France.

In 1356 John of France brought here as prisoner and was royally entertained, and 1365 he returned here voluntarily after his liberation by the Peace of Bretigny.

Richard II. lived much here, and in 1386 received here Leo of Armenia, who had been driven from his kingdom by the Turks.

Henry IV. kept the Christmas feasts of 1405, 1409 and 1412 here, and often lived here.

Henry V. kept the Christmas of 1414 here; Henry VI. was often here and kept the Christmas of 1428 here.

Edward IV. added and beautified much; he probably built the existing parts, the hall and the bridge; his fourth daughter, Bridget, was born here in 1480.

In 1482 he gave a magnificent Christmas entertainment here to two thousand guests.

Henry VII. preferred Greenwich to Eltham, but his children were brought up here, and he added a stately front to the Palace.

Henry VIII. also preferred Greenwich, but he kept the Christmas feasts of 1515 and 1526 here.

Elizabeth was frequently here as a child, but she also preferred Greenwich.

In 1612 James I. visited Eltham, hunting here with his father-in-law, Christian of Denmark, and he was the last sovereign here.

Eltham was occupied by the Earl of Essex during the Civil War, and he died here in 1646. Parliament spoiled Eltham, after the Kentish Rising of 1648, the deer were killed, the gardens and pleasure grounds wasted, and the Palace neglected. In 1650 it was sold to Major Rich, but it never recovered, although it reverted to the Crown at the Restoration. Trees were felled, the buildings knocked about, and the magnificent hall was only preserved because it made a good barn. It was valued at £2,754, and was described as having "one fair chapel, one great hall, 36 rooms and offices below stairs, with two large cellars ; above stairs 17 lodging rooms on the King's side, 12 on the Queen's and nine on the Prince's ; 78 rooms in the offices round the courtyard, which occupied one acre." The Palace was reported to be much out of repair and untenantable.

3.—GREENWICH.

Edward I. probably had a palace at Greenwich. Henry IV. in 1408 dated his will from his Manor of Greenwich, which seems to have been his favourite residence. In 1433 the King gave Duke Humphrey of Gloucester a grant of 200 acres for a park, and in 1437 leave was given him to build there a fortified mansion, and this he called *Placentia*.

Edward IV. enlarged and adorned much at Greenwich, and gave it to his Queen, Elizabeth Woodville. In 1482 the Lady Mary, Edward's daughter, died here.

Henry VII. acquired the estate by his arbitrary imprisonment of Elizabeth Woodville ; he much enlarged the Palace, frequently kept his Court here, kept the Christmas feast of 1492 here, and founded the adjoining Grey Friars' Convent. Henry VIII. was born here and baptised in the parish church. He kept Christmas, 1512, here "with great and plentiful cheer," and the same feast next year "with great solemnity, dancing, disguisings, mummeries, in a most princely manner." At the Christmas of 1515 was held the first masquerade in England.

At Greenwich the King married Katherine of Arragon, Anne Boleyn and Anne of Cleves, and his youngest sister, Princess Mary Tudor, was married to Charles Brandon, Duke of Suffolk, in Greenwich.

In 1527 a magnificent entertainment was given here in honour of the French ambassadors, who were eight persons of high quality, attended by 600 horse, in a sort of competition with that which Wolsey had just given at Hampton Court to the same grandees, but the King's excelled the minister's as much as gold excels silver, said old Stow.

Henry VIII. embellished and added to Greenwich so much that it inspired Leland to celebrate the work in Latin verse, of which Hasted gives the following translation :—

> " How bright the lofty seat appears,
>   Like Jove's great palace, pav'd with stars !
>   What roofs ! what windows charm the eye,
>   What turrets, rivals of the sky ! "

Elizabeth loved Greenwich, and kept her Court and all the great festivals, especially that of St. George, of which we modern Englishmen know and care so little, with great pomp. She entertained the Lady Ambassadress from France here, and bade farewell to all her naval heroes from here. It was off Greenwich that she was very nearly accidentally shot by a young man, Thomas Appletree by name, who fired a gun at random. "The bullet came so nere

Her Grace, within sixe foote at least." Appletree was, in the rough and ready manner of the time, condemned to death for his mishap, but Elizabeth pardoned him. It was at Greenwich, according to some authorities, at Deptford according to others, that took place the episode of Raleigh, the cloak and the puddle.

Edward VI. was born and died at Greenwich.

Mary was born here.

James I., who settled Greenwich on his wife, Anne of Denmark, was very fond of the palace and park.

Charles I. lived here much before the outbreak of the Civil War, and it was from Greenwich that he went to set up the standard of war at Nottingham in 1642. After his execution Greenwich passed out of royal hands, and was condemned to be sold. In 1652 it was given to Whitlocke, and in 1654 was appointed to be the Protector's residence. Under the Parliament the palace was much neglected and fell into such a ruinous condition that when at the Restoration it became once more royal property, Charles II. pulled it down and commenced building a new *Placentia* in magnificent style—so magnificent indeed that he could only afford to finish one wing, the Western, which still exists.

Mary, wife of William of Orange, was received at Greenwich. It was her idea to turn Charles' Wing into a Naval Hospital, but she did not live either to endow the work or to see it more than commenced; in the meanwhile Charles' Wing was kept as a reception house for foreigners of distinction.

Generally treating of the connection of royalty with the county, it may be said that if one road in all England is more Royal than any other it is that between Dover and London, along which every one of our Kings and Queens must have constantly passed, as well as every foreign sovereign or person of distinction who visited our land up to the era of railways. Sandwich and Margate were favourite ports of embarcation for our early sovereigns: the Royal list of Dover must be the longest in the world; whilst all the places on the London road—Canterbury, Sittingbourne, Rochester, Blackheath, have their associations with Royalty.

B.—THE CINQUE PORTS.

"Of what antiquity these ports and ancient towns are," says Jeake, "When enfranchised, or at what time their members were annexed to them, are things so dark and difficult to be discovered that without great labour and search (if then) little certainty can be had."

So we will at once proceed to what is *known* about them. Although the name was used soon after the Norman Conquest it first appears regularly in the reign of John.

The original Cinque Ports were: in order of precedence :— Hastings, Sandwich, Dover, Romney, and Hythe.

To these are attached the two Ancient Towns of Rye and Winchelsea.

The following is a complete table of the Cinque Ports and their "Limbs":

Hastings
{
Corporate Members : Pevensey and Seaford.
Non-corporate : Bulverhithe, Petit Iham (on the site of New Winchelsea), Hidney, Bekesbourne, and Grange (near Gillingham).
}

Sandwich {
Corporate Member : Fordwich.
Non-corporate　　: Deal, Walmer, Ramsgate, Strome, Sarre, and Bright-lingsea* in Essex.
}

*Even in 1893 Brightlingsea was reminded by the election of a deputy at Sandwich that it was still a Limb of Sandwich. This connection has existed since the reign of Henry VII. ; it paying £5 and an annual 10s. towards the Cinque Ports Navy.

Romney {
Corporate Member : Lydd.
Non-corporate　　: Old Romney, Denge Marsh, and Oswardestone, near Lydd.
}

Dover {
Corporate Members : Folkestone and Faversham.
Non-corporate　　: Margate, St. John's, Goresend, Birchington (Woodchurch), St. Peter's, Kingsdown, and Ringwould.
}

Hythe—Non-corporate Member : West Hythe.

The "Ancient Town" of Rye had a corporate Limb in Tenterden. The complete table of precedency is :

1, Hastings.　2, Sandwich.　3, Dover.　4, Romney.　5, Hythe. 6, Rye.　7, Winchelsea.　8, Seaford.　9, Pevensey.　10, Fordwich. 11, Folkestone.　12, Faversham.　13, Lydd.　14, Tenterden.

The services rendered by the Cinque Ports in return for the privileges they enjoyed, apart from the fact that for a long time their fleet constituted the Royal Navy of England, were to furnish 57 ships at their own charge every year for 15 days at the summons of the King. Each ship had 20 armed soldiers in addition to its crew, and the full complement was: 57 ships, 1,187 men, and 57 "garcions," or "gromets," or boys.

Hastings owed its recognised position as head of the Cinque Ports, perhaps either because it happened to be first named in the charters of William I. and his successors, or from a kindly feeling which he naturally held towards the port nearest the scene of the victory which gave him the dominion of England. Jeake is of opinion that Hastings really always was the most powerful, wealthy and influential port ; an opinion supported by an examination of the proportionate contributions of Hastings to the navy in early times. Thus, in the very interesting connection between the Cinque Ports and Yarmouth, whereto, during the great herring fair, which lasted from Michaelmas to Martinmas, the Ports sent their Bailiffs to represent them and were empowered to share the local Government for the time being, and allowed licence to land cargoes on the Strand, and dry nets on the Den, we find that Hastings sent two Bailiffs, whereas the other ports only sent one, and paid a double allowance to them.

These annual Yarmouth meetings were often occasions of violent strife between the Ports and the town. In 1297 a pitched battle took place at sea in which 37 Yarmouth vessels were taken or destroyed to the value of £15,000, and 171 men were killed. In 1303 Yarmouth complained that from these quarrels it had lost £20,000. So late as 1575 there was a squabble about prenomination in proclamations and the style of the Court which was temporarily settled the next year by an arrangement that the prenomination should be by alternate years. It was once proposed that Yarmouth should

be made a Cinque Port, but nothing came of it. Gradually Yarmouth discontinued the already reduced payment of £3 per annum to the Ports, and the Ports only sent two Bailiffs—one for the Eastern and one for the Western Ports.

The annual Yarmouth meeting was a grand combination of holiday and business. On the day before Michaelmas Day the Bailiffs came to Yarmouth accompanied by counsel, town clerk, two sergeants with white rods, one French horn man, one standard bearer and one gaoler. Feasting and entertainment filled up the intervals between business : The Cinque Ports Bailiffs kept open house, bringing with them eighteen hogsheads of good ale to help matters out, Yarmouth's Corporation reciprocated, and when there was no squabbling no doubt the three weeks passed all too quickly.

The privileges enjoyed by the Cinque Ports, it is said, from the days of Edward the Confessor, and since confirmed by different sovereigns from William I. to Charles II., were various. They were only taxed one-third of the amount levied upon inland towns. Even in Saxon times the freemen of the Cinque Ports ranked as nobles, for the burgesses they sent to Parliament were called Barons ; their summons and their oath of fidelity to the Crown was that they would maintain and defend to their utmost power the liberties, franchises, privileges and customs of the Cinque Ports and their members. Before the division of Parliament into two houses the names of the Peers of the Realm and of the Cinque Ports Barons were called separately from those of the knights, burgesses and citizens, and they probably ranked after the higher clergy and nobility, and before the lower clergy and other representatives. They sent 14 members to Parliament ; to-day only Hastings, Dover, and Hythe with Folkestone are represented. The Cinque Ports were independent of the Shire, the Lath and the Hundred.

In the Great Charter the privileges of the Cinque Ports and those of London are alone exclusively mentioned.

They claimed and maintained the right of supporting the canopies of the sovereigns at their coronation, the first occasion being the coronation of Henry III. and Eleanor of Provence, and only once has this custom been broken—at the coronation of James I., when the canopy was borne by eight gentlemen of the Privy Chamber.

The canopy is of purple silk, with four silvered staves, and on each staff a silver and gilt bell. Four Barons supported each stave. In the case of a double coronation the Barons of Hastings held one canopy, and after the ceremony presented it to the shrine of Saint Richard at Chichester ; the Barons of the other Ports held the second canopy and presented it to Saint Thomas Shrine at Canterbury, dividing the staves and bells among themselves.

The pulpit cloth of St. Clement's church, Hastings, is said to have been made out of the coronation canopy of George I.

An extraordinary coincidence in connection with this privilege occurred in 1820, when the late Lord Brougham, who as Henry Brougham, the Attorney-General of Queen Caroline, had arraigned King George IV. at the bar of public opinion, was, as member for Winchelsea, one of the Cinque Ports Barons to hold the canopy over the King at his coronation.

The Barons of the Cinque Ports also enjoyed the privilege of sitting at the coronation banquet at the uppermost table on the King's right hand.

At the coronation of George III. the Cinque Ports Barons complained to Lord Talbot, the Lord Steward, that no table had been set apart for them. Said he : "If you come to me as Lord Steward I tell you it is impossible; if as Lord Talbot I am a match for any of you." (Walpole's Letters).

The Cinque Ports were also free from all taxes and subsidies for the regular army.

There were of course many other privileges peculiar to different Ports. Thus, in the case of Romney, the law of the land that all waste lands belong to the Crown did not apply, for it was maintained that the Crown held no waste lands in Romney Marsh, and the first settlers might deal with any unappropriated land as they thought fit. This is still the usage of the Marsh.

Three kinds of meetings were held by the Ports—Brotherhoods, Brotherhood and Guestlings, and Guestlings.

At a Brotherhood, or a Brotherhood and Guestling, all Ports and Members had to be represented. A Guestling might be summoned by any of the Ports for business of their own, or what concerned only another Port.

The meetings were General or Special. The General Meeting was held twice a year—on the Tuesday after Easter, and on the Tuesday after St. Margaret's Day. Special Meetings were held for special occasions, and as circumstances might demand. The original meetings were held at Shepway or Shipway Cross, an open space at the junction of four roads on the top of the hills between Westenhanger and Lympne. They were first ordered to be held here by Henry III. Here the Lord Warden, whose office has been traced to that of the Ancient Count of the Saxon Shore, was elected, and here were heard cases of treason, falsifying money, services withdrawn, false judgment, and the finding of treasure.

After the Revolution of 1688 the Court of Shepway was transferred to Bredenstone Hill on the south-west of Dover. The modern Courts are held at a central Port.

At the General Guestlings the head officer of one of the Ports or of the Ancient Town presides, and is addressed as "Mr. Speaker." On each side of him are the other mayors and bailiffs, then the bailiff to Yarmouth, and below them the jurats, who were assistants to the Head Officer, and of whom each Port had twelve.

The Speakership is an annual office, and moves in rotation from Hastings. If any other town than Hastings be Speaker, Hastings always sits on the Speaker's right hand, and if Sandwich be not Speaker, Sandwich sits on his left.

The circular sent by the Speaker Town runs as follows :

"Right Worshipful Sirs : loving brethren, combarons and friends : Our right hearty affections and salutations to you presented. Whereas by Septennary Revolution (the five Ports and the two Ancient Towns) the Speakership of the Ports is now devolved upon us, we have thought meet to issue forth these our timely letters to you, whereby we pray and brotherly require your advice and subscriptions, whether, as our affairs now stand, a Brotherhood and Guestling, or either of them is necessary to be arreared this year. We for our parts considering (here the business to be transacted is detailed), are of opinion and think fit, that both a Brotherhood and a Guestling be summoned to meet at the town and port of . . . . , in the County of Kent, on the Tuesday after the Feast of St. Margaret next ensuing at the hour accustomed."

The independence of the Cinque Ports of old is exemplified in the peculiarities of their local customs and laws. Thus capital punishment varied at different Ports. At Dover criminals were thrown over Shakespeare's Cliff. At Sandwich they were buried alive on what was called Thief's Down. At Fordwich they were drowned in Thief's Well—a name still memorialised in Thew's Lane.

Scolding women were fastened by an iron collar to a post in the market place for an hour ; larceny was punished by the loss of an ear, or by a whipping, or by having a billet nailed to the ear. Immorality was punished by banishment from the town.

Sanctuary was strictly observed. The felon fled to a churchyard, and, confessing his felony, his goods and chattels were forfeited, he remained in sanctuary forty days, then was given a cross as a passport, and sent off to an assigned port, only to tarry an ebb and a flood before leaving the country.

It is notable that the Mayors of Sandwich and Fordwich carried black rods instead of white like the others ; perhaps this was for some ancient mayoral delinquency.

The *décadence* of the Cinque Ports is observable in the middle of the sixteenth century. Even Dover in 1565 is lamented over as containing but 358 inhabited houses, and owning but 20 ships. Towards the national fleet in the Armada year the Cinque Ports contributed but five ships and "one handsome pinnace." Evelyn thus describes Winchelsea in 1652 :

"I walk'd over to survey the ruines of Winchelsea, that ancient Cinque Port which, by the remaines and ruines of ancient streetes and public structures, discovers it to have been formerly a considerable and large citty. There are to be seen vast caves and vaults, walls and towers, ruines of monasteries, and of a sumptuous church, in which are handsome monuments, especially of the Templars, buried just in the manner of those in the Temple in London. This place being now all rubbish, and a few despicable hovells and cottages now standing, hath yet a mayor."

It is hardly necessary to say that the special privileges of the Cinque Ports have been much abridged, especially by the Municipal Corporations Reform Act, but the jurisdiction of the Lord Warden as Admiral of the Coast has not been touched, and this jurisdiction embraces many subjects usually confined to the Municipality. The ancient "Court of Lode Manage," at which pilots were licensed and complaints heard of misconduct or inefficiency, was only abolished in 1853, when the Trinity House took over its duties.

Fordwich (Limb of Sandwich), Seaford and Pevensey (Limbs of Hastings) were abolished by the Act of 1883.

By the courtesy of Mr. Stringer, one of the Solicitors to the Ports, I am enabled to give the address presented to Her Majesty on the occasion of Her Diamond Jubilee by the Ports as drawn up at a Court of Brotherhood and Guestling, held in the Town Hall, Dover, June 26th, 1897. Dover (speaker), Hastings, Sandwich, Romney, Rye, Deal, Ramsgate, Faversham, Folkestone, Margate, Lydd, and Tenterden sent Mayors or representatives, the former appearing in full costume, with chains, maces, and insignia ; and, after the summons, couched exactly in the language before quoted, was read out, the address was agreed to :

"May it please Your Majesty,—We, the barons and combarons, and other representatives of the Cinque Ports, two Antient Towns, and their members, assembled in Courts of Brotherhood and Guestling, especially convened for this purpose, and in accordance with ancient usage, humbly desire to assure your Majesty of our constant unabated loyalty and attachment to your Majesty's sacred person, to every member of the Royal Family, and to the Throne and Institutions of the United Kingdom, and to sincerely offer our heartfelt congratulation on the auspicious occasion of your Majesty having completed a reign of 60 years over a loyal and prosperous people, an event unparalleled in the history of our country.

"We deem it fitting to remind your Majesty that we are, in all probability, the most ancient recognised Corporate Body still in existence within your Realm. In olden times the noble deeds of our ancestors in providing and maintaining, at their own costs and charges, for your Majesty's predecessors, Kings and Queens of England, goodly fleets for the protection of our shores, were from time fully recognised and appreciated by Royal grants of various privileges and liberties, some of which are still existing. . . . . .

"Given at our Courts of Brotherhood and Guestling aforesaid, held at and in the Antient Town and Port and Borough of Dover, this 26th day of June, in the year of our Lord 1897."

"BAKER," Mayor of Dover,
Speaker of the Ports.

HENRY STRINGER,   } Ports Solicitors.
WOLLASTON KNOCKER, }

C.—TRAVELLING IN KENT.

From all accounts our county seems to have been hard and dangerous travelling ground up to a comparatively recent date, and it is much to be questioned if our Kentish Watling Street was at the end of the last century in half as good a condition as it was when the last Roman legionaries tramped along it fourteen-and-a-half centuries ago. As for cross-country journeys, even when performed by Kings and Archbishops, they must have been sore trials of patience and endurance, and we need not be surprised that the great men found it necessary to have magnificent rest houses at short intervals, and that they carried their households with them.

In the reign of Henry VIII. the roads of the Weald were so bad that in the year 1523 was passed the first known Act of Parliament for the repair and regulation of thoroughfares ; and we know that Good Queen Bess, in 1573, found in the Wild of Kent "More dangerous rocks and valleys and much worse ground than in the Peak."

In Charles II.'s time, Soubierre, the French Ambassador, preferred to travel in a waggon drawn by six horses in line to risking himself in a regular conveyance. Evelyn was obliged to have six horses to drag his carriage when he paid his visit to Scott's Hall in the same reign, during which the journey from Rye to London took two long days, and the coach from London to the Sussex coast could proceed no further than Tunbridge. In 1686 Mr. Jeake, of Rye, occupied five hours-and-a-half in performing the twenty-three miles between Rye and Lamberhurst; then he lost his way, and wound up by taking ten hours by stage coach in doing the thirty miles between Tunbridge and London.

Nor were matters much better a century later, for Hasted writing, not of by-ways, but of turnpike roads, says:

"The roads of these parts are hardly passable after any rain, being so miry that the traveller's horse frequently plunges through them up to the girths of the saddle, and the waggons sink so deep in the ruts as to slide along on the nave of the wheels and the axle of them."

In 1752 Horace Walpole travelling in Kent writes of Tunbridge:

"Now begins our chapter of woes. The inn was full of farmers and tobacco; and, the next morning, when we were bound for Penshurst, the only man in the town who had two horses would not let us have them because the roads, as he said, were so bad."

He got to Lamberhurst, and says:

"Here our woes increase. The roads grew bad beyond all badness, the night dark beyond all darkness, our guide frightened beyond all frightfulness. However, without being at all killed, we got up, or down, I forget which, it was so dark, a famous precipice called Silver Hill, and about 10 at night arrived at a wretched village called Robertsbridge. We had still six miles hither, but determined to stop, as it would be a pity to break all our necks before we had seen all we intended. But alas! there was only one bed to be had; all the rest were inhabited by smugglers, whom the people of the house called mountebanks. . . . Armed with links and lanthorns we set out again, and at two o'clock in the morning we got hither to a still worse inn, and that crammed with excise officers, one of whom had just shot a smuggler."

" Pray, whenever you travel in Kentish roads," he writes later on, " take care of keeping your driver sober."

From Sissinghurst Walpole went to " Bocton-Malherbe," " but the roads were so exceedingly bad that it was dark before we got thither . . . . I hope you will be as weary with reading our history as we have been in travelling it."

But bad roads were not the worst annoyances with which the traveller had to put up with. The great lines of communication swarmed with robbers and rascals of all sorts, from the gentleman with a crape mask who stopped passengers and eased them of their purses, to the rascally inn-keeper who charged them extortionately for the vilest of accommodation. " So are most thieves in Christendome and Kent " wrote Taylor the poet, and " a fine country inhabited by a lot of villains " is the translation of Lord Says' reply to Dick the Butcher, who asked him what he thought of Kent.

The great roads were infested with highwaymen, especially the Dover Road on Blackheath, at Shooters Hill, at Bexley Heath, Gadd's Hill and across Barham Downs, and the lines of gibbets bearing the bodies of the cowardly rascals whom so many writers exalt as romantic heroes were such familiar objects as hardly to be noticed by the traveller.

The records of the road during the seventeenth and eighteenth centuries are full of attacks and murders, and a large proportion of the criminals who provided public entertainment for the multitude on Tyburn Mondays suffered "for the highway."

In 1652 Evelyn was waylaid at Procession Oak, between Tonbridge and Bromley, three miles from the latter place, by men who eased him of his rings and money, tied him to a tree and left him. One of them was captured and "press'd to death." Hanging Wood near Woolwich was the scene of many robberies in the eighteenth century; the *Bull* Inn at the top of Shooter's Hill was a favourite rendezvous of footpads, and tradition says that Dick Turpin used to frequent it and that it was here he put the landlady on the fire to make her confess where she hid her gold. It was just beyond the *Bull* too, as we are told in the *Tale of Two Cities*, that the passengers of the Dover Mail, Mr. Jarvis Lorry, of Telson's Bank among them, were terrified by the sudden appearance of Mr. Jerry Cruncher, who however had come to deliver a message, not to have purses delivered to him.

Here too it was that Don Juan was soliloquising over the distant view of London when he was interrupted by a knife, with,

> " Damn your eyes !
> Your money or your life."

The records of Gadd's Hill alone would occupy a full chapter, and the curious in such matters cannot do better than consult Cruden's History of Gravesend. Mr. Ebsworth in his admirable notes to the ballads in the "Kentish Garland" reprints from *Mockett's Journal* the story of a Kentish ride to York, which we must quote :

" In the year 1676 a gentleman was robbed about 4 o'clock in the morning by a man Nicks, who, to prevent detection (as he afterwards confessed) proceeded to Gravesend, where he was detained nearly three hours for want of a boat to convey him across to Essex for Chelmsford ; he then proceeded to Braintree, Bockey and Wethersford (now known as Bocking and Weathersfield), over the downs to Cambridge, keeping the cross-roads to Godmanchester and Huntingdon, by Fenny Stratford, where he baited his horse and slept about half-an-hour. He then rode full speed to York (176 miles N by W of London), where he arrived in the afternoon.

" Here he changed his dress, and mixed with the company in the bowling green and soon selected out the Mayor of that city, of whom he enquired the hour of the day, who pulled out his watch and told him it wanted a quarter to eight. Some time after Mr. Nicks was prosecuted for the robbery, and the whole merit of the case turned on this single point. The person who had been robbed *swore to the man*, but Nicks produced the Mayor of York, who proved his being at the bowling green on the day in question. The jury therefore acquitted him, on the supposition that it was impossible for him to be the man and also to be in York on the same day."

As for the other Kentish road robbers, this is what Smollett wrote in 1763 about the Dover road and Dover :—" I need not tell you that this is the worst road in England with respect to the conveniences of travelling, and must certainly impress foreigners with an unfavourable opinion of the nation in general. The chambers are in general cold and comfortless, the beds paltry, the cookery execrable, the wine poison, the attendance bad, the publicans insolent, and the bills extortion ; there is not a drop of tolerable malt liquor to be had from London to Dover.

"Every landlord and every waiter harangued upon the knavery of a publican in Canterbury who had charged the French ambassador forty pounds for a supper which was not worth forty shillings. . . . . . but when they produced their own bills they appeared to be all of the same family and complexion.

"Dover is commonly termed a den of thieves, and I am afraid that it is not altogether without reason that it has acquired this appellation. The people are said to live by piracy in time of war, and by smuggling and fleecing strangers in time of peace. Without all doubt a man cannot be worse lodged or worse treated in any part of Europe ; nor will he in any other place meet with more flagrant instances of fraud, imposition and brutality. One would imagine they had formed a general conspiracy against all those who either go to or return from the Continent."

Byron's lines in Don Juan about the iniquities of Dover, although well known, are worth quoting :—

"Don Juan now saw Albion's earliest beauties,
    Thy cliffs, *dear* Dover! harbour and hotel ;
Thy custom house, with all its delicate duties,
    Thy waiters running mucks at every bell ;
Thy packets, all whose passengers are booties
    To those who upon land or water dwell ;
And last, not least, to strangers uninstructed,
    Thy long, long bills, whence nothing is deducted !"

Until 1792 the curfew bell was rung at Dartford, quite as much for the benefit of travellers over the wild, open country, who, without its guiding sound could easily have strayed to their deaths on bitter nights amongst the lone unfrequented tracks which led from the high road, as in continuance of an ancient custom.

Smollett also describes how he was robbed and insulted by the master of the vessel which was to take him to France, and later we are presented with a picture of the Cross Channel packet of the period.

" We found ourselves in a most wretched hovel, on board what is called a Folkestone cutter. The cabin was so small that a dog could hardly turn in it, and the beds put one in mind of the holes described in some catacombs, in which the bodies of the dead were deposited, being thrust in with the feet foremost. There was no getting into them but endways, and indeed they seemed so dirty that nothing but extreme necessity could have obliged one to use them. We sat up all night in a most uncomfortable position, tossed about by the sea, cramped, weary, and languishing for want of sleep."

This lasted from six one evening till three the next morning, and then, instead of stepping on shore at once, the passengers had to row three miles in a small open boat. The fare was five guineas, besides "tips" to everybody who performed the slightest service, from the captain downwards.

As a set off, however, it must be said that the travellers were even worse treated and more robbed on the French side than in Kent.

This was in time of peace. In time of war there was additional excitement in the shape of a good risk of being captured or robbed, or both; witness the following paragraph from a newspaper quoted by Mr. Clark Russell:—

"Two gentlemen, passengers from Holland, landed at Margate. They affirm they were in the evening boarded in sight of the North Foreland by a privateer cutter, whose crew in disguise confined the captain and crew of their vessel in the cabin, and then plundered it of goods to the value of £2,000, demanded the captain's money, and took what we had."

To avoid the land sharks of Kent the traveller at the beginning of this century was offered the Margate Hoy. In this dainty craft, says Mr. Clark Russell, he would be "one of a parcel of human herrings squeezed into temporary shapelessness in an interior as delicate for its aromas, as cheerful for its illumination as the rat haunted forepeak of a wooden sailing ship. Why, you will read of one of those hoys sometimes occupying a week in "turning" down the river and arriving at Margate. There was always the chance of their being blown into the Downs to strain for several days at their cable in a seaway too ugly to suffer the passengers to land!"

Charles Lamb, on the other hand, laments the old hoy, "ill-exchanged for the foppery and fresh-water niceness of the modern packet!"

The experiences of Fielding, the novelist, in 1753, when the ship in which he sailed from London to Lisbon lay off Deal, are of much the same character as Smollett's, what with the Deal dentist who pulled poor Mrs. Fielding all over the room and then gave up the job; the exorbitant charges of the Deal people for provisions and boat hire, and the miseries of an ill-found ship and a brutal captain.

In short, it was no wonder that only the very rich and those who were compelled by business travelled at all, and that no sane man dreamed of starting on a journey of more than fifty miles without seeing that his "house was in order."

D.—OLD KENT CRICKET.

To compile a History of Kent without any allusion to our Grand Old Game were to be guilty of an almost unpardonable sin of omission, for assuredly if Hampshire may claim to be the cradle of cricket Kent may fairly be called its nursery.

As briefly as may be I will deal with a large stock of material. I am indebted to Mr. Philip Norman's admirable book upon the West Kent Club for all allusions here to that Club, and to him personally for much information about Kent cricket generally; to various correspondents for communications in reply to an appeal for information which I made in the *Kentish Express;* to the standard works of Nyren, Pycroft, Felix, Box, Grace, Read and Ranjitsinhji; and to the "Gentleman's Magazine," the "Sporting Magazine," and

FULLER PILCH:

ALFRED MYNN.

the Kentish newspapers of the 18th and early 19th centuries for the rest.

The first allusion to Kentish Cricket is probably in the "Life of the Rev. Thomas Wilson," published in 1672 by George Swinnocke, who says:—"Maidstone was formerly a very prophane town, insomuch that (before 1640) I have seen morrice dancing, cudgel playing, stool ball, *crickets*, and many other sports openly and publicly on Lord's Day."

With reference to Sunday cricket playing I have more than once heard of a Kentish village, I am not sure, but I *think* it was Frittenden or Benenden, where the custom always obtained that the Parson should open the Cricket Season on Easter Sunday by bowling the first ball on the village green directly after morning service. I have also heard that he performed the ceremony in his surplice!

1705.—In the *Postman* of July 24th appears :

> "This is to give notice that a match will be plaid between 11 gentlemen of the West part of Kent and those of Chatham for eleven guineas a man, the game to take place at Maulden (Malling ?) in Kent."

1711.—Charles Box speaks of a match between Kent and All England, won by Kent, which resulted in an action of law about a bet of £25. The Court remarked, "Cricket is to be sure a manly game ; it is the ill use that is made of it by betting above £10 on it that is bad, and against the laws which ought to be construed largely, so as to prevent the mischief of excessive gambling."

1719.—We learn from *Mist's Journal* of May 26th that the Men of Kent played the Men of London in Lamb's Conduit Fields for £60 a side.

1729.—From the *London Evening Post :* " On Thursday was play'd a great cricket match on Kennington Common between the Londoners and the Dartford men for a considerable sum of money, Wagers and Betts, and the latter beat the former much."

1731.—From the *Grub Street Journal*, May 27th :

> "On Monday, 31st, will be played on Kennington Common a great cricket match between London and Sevenoaks in Kent, and at the same place the next day following will be another match between London and Chelsfield in Kent."

1734.—In the *London Evening Post*, July 2-4 :

> "On Monday next there will be a great cricket match played on Kennington Common, in the County of Surrey, between the Gentlemen of Sevenoaks and the Gentlemen of London. The ground will be roped round and all persons are desired to keep without side of the same ; the match is for a guinea a man, and the wickets are to be pitched by 1 o'clock."

From the same :

> "Last week was played at Sevenoaks in Kent a great cricket match between the Earl of Middlesex, the Lord John Sackville, and nine other gentlemen of Kent, and Sir William Gage and ten other gentlemen

of Sussex, when the Kent gentlemen beat. But the
week before when they play'd on the Downs near
Lewes the Sussex gentlemen beat considerably, so
that's thought the conqueror will be play'd in a few
days."

1735.—From the *Grub Street Journal:*
"Yesterday at the cricket match at Bromley Common between the Prince of Wales and the Earl of
Middlesex for £1,000, the Londoners got 72 the first
hands, the Kent 95. The London side went in again
and only got 9 above the Kent men, which were got
the second innings without one person being out."

1736.—"Yesterday the great cricket match was play'd on
Kennington Common between the Gentlemen of Kent
and Surrey : the Gamesters were admirably good, and
to a man performed their parts. The Kentish men
went in first and got 41 notches ; the Surrey men 71.
At the Second Hands the Kentish men got 53, and the
Surrey men had but 23 to get, which they acquir'd with
ease, and had two wickets to spare. A great deal of
money was won and lost upon the occasion ; but the
Game was so skilfully and justly play'd on each Side
that the very Losers went away satisfy'd. During the
game three Soldiers apprehended a Kentish man for
Desertion ; but the populace hearing of the matter,
join'd and rescu'd the Deserter out of their Hands, and
after a severe Discipline let them go about their
business.
"On Monday Se'night the Surrey men in their turn
are to wait upon the Kentish men at Cock's Heath
near Maidstone."

1737.—"Yesterday was played on Bromley Common the second
great cricket match between the Kentish men and
those of London and Surrey, when the former
maintain'd their honour, and beat their adversaries at
one hand. The press was so great that a woman's leg
was broken by the crowd."

In the "Gentleman's Magazine" for September, 1743, appears a
very strong letter quoted from the *British Champion* condemning
the universal popularity of cricket. I have not room for the
whole letter, but the following extracts give a notion of what
evidently was a very prevalent opinion of the day.

After saying that in Diversions as well as business what in one
man may be decent, may in another be ridiculous, the author goes
on : "I have been led into these Reflections by some odd Stories I
have heard of cricket matches, which, I own, however, to be so
strange and so incredible, that if I had not received them from Eye-
Witnesses I could never have yielded to them any Belief. Is it not
a very wild thing to be as serious in making such a Match as in the
most ordinary Occurrences in Life? Would it not be extremely odd
to see Lords and Gentlemen, Clergymen and Lawyers, associating
themselves with Butchers and Coblers in Pursuit of these
Diversions? . . . . . . Cricket is certainly a very innocent
and wholesome Exercise, yet it may be abused if either great or
little People make it their business. It is grossly abused when it is

made the Subject of publick Advertisements to draw together great Crowds of People, who ought all of them to be somewhere else. Noblemen, Gentlemen, and Clergymen, have certainly a right to divert themselves in what manner they think fit ; nor do I dispute their Privilege of making Butchers, Coblers or Tinkers their companions, provided these are qualified to keep them company. But I very much doubt whether they have any Right to invite Thousands of People to be Spectators of their Agility at the Expense of their Duty and Honesty. . . . . The Diversion of Cricket may be proper in Holiday Time, and in the Country; but upon Days when Men ought to be busy, and in the Neighbourhood of a great City, it is not only improper but mischievous in a high Degree. It draws Numbers of people from their Employment, to the Ruin of their Families. It brings together Crowds of Apprentices and Servants whose Time is not their own. It propagates a Spirit of Idleness at a Juncture when, with the utmost Industry, our Debts, Taxes, and Decay of Trade will scarce allow us to get Bread." And so forth. Upon which the only comment is the trite one about *tempora mutantur*, etc.

In 1746 Kent played All England on the Artillery Ground at Finsbury, and won by one wicket. At this match the Prince of Wales, the Duke of Cumberland, and Admiral Vernon were among the visitors. This is the first cricket match of which the score-sheet has been preserved, and it is the subject of a poem by James Dance, alias Love, alias Scriblerus Maximus, the Comedian, in 1770, beginning :

> " Hail Cricket ! Glorious, manly British game !
> First of all sports, the first alike in fame ! "

And afterwards :

> " And see where busy counties strive for fame,
> Each greatly potent at this mighty game :
> Fierce Kent, ambitious of the first applause,
> Against the world combin'd asserts her cause."

The Kent eleven on this occasion was :
Lord Sackville ; Hodswell, the tanner of Dartford, bowler ; Rumsey ; Mills, of Bromley, bowler ; "Long" Robin ; Mills ; Sawyer ; Cutbush ; Bartrum ; Kips, wicket keeper ; and Danes.

In 1751 : "A match will be play'd between the Gentlemen of the neighbourhood of Bromley and Dartford for 100 guineas."

In 1769 the famous old Vine ground at Sevenoaks was given by the Duke of Dorset to be a cricket ground for ever, although no deed of gift is discoverable. Sir Horace Mann was a great patron of Kent cricket ; he served as M.P. for Sandwich during five Parliaments—thirty-three years.

In 1771 was played at Leeds Park the Gentlemen of Bethersden against the Gentlemen of Leeds for half a guinea a man.

In 1772 Kent beat Hampshire (Hambledon) at Bishopsbourne by two wickets. This was the subject of a contemporary pœan.

In 1773 Surrey beat Kent at Bishopsbourne by 153 runs. The stake on this match was no less than £2,000, and the game was made the subject of a parody on *Chevy Chace* by John Duncombe,

entitled "Surrey Triumphant, or the Kentish Men's defeat." It
begins :

> "God prosper long our harvest work,
> Our ricks and hay carts all,
> An ill tim'd cricket match there did
> At Bishopsbourne befall."

Another verse runs :

> "From Marsh and Weald their hay-forks left,
> To Bourn the rustics hied ;
> From Romney, Cranbrook, Tenterden,
> And Darent's verdant side."

For Kent were playing : Sir Horace Mann, Hussey (Ashford),
Davis, Tom and Dick May, Simmons, Miller, Wood (Seal), Lewis,
etc.

In the "returned match" Kent had her revenge and won by six
wickets.

1774.—Kent v. Hambledon at the Vine, Kent won in 1 innings
and 35.

Kent v. Hambledon, at Hambledon, Kent won by
4 wickets.

1775.—Kent v. Hants at the Vine (Kent with 2 bowlers), Kent
won.

1776.—Kent v. Surrey at Kennington, Surrey won in 1 innings
and 65.

1779.—Mr. W. W. Read publishes in his "Cricket" an old
engraving of a match played at Sevenoaks by the
Countess of Derby and other Ladies of quality.
Verily there is nothing new under the sun!

1780.—Duke of Dorset's 11 v. Sir Horace Mann's 11 at the Vine
for 300 guineas. The latter won.

About this period there was Cricket played all over Kent, and
the newspapers are full of announcements and reports, so that one
Editor declines to publish any more on account of the space they
take up.

1786.—Kent v. Hambledon at the Vine, Kent won by 4 wickets.

1787.—Kent v. Hambledon at Coxheath, Hambledon won by
2 runs.

1788.—Kent v. England at Coxheath, England won by 1 innings
and 80.

1789.—Kent v. England at Coxheath, England won by 1 innings
and 10.

1791.—Kent v. M.C.C. (with Beldham and Fennex—the original,
no doubt of "M.C.C. and Ground")—M.C.C. won by
1 innings and 113.

"There was no mistaking the Kentish boys," says Beldham,
"when they came staring into the *Green Man*. A few of us had
grown used to London, but the Kent or Hampshire men had but to
speak and show themselves and you need not ask them which sides
they were on." This was the *Green Man and Still* in Oxford
Street, a favourite house of call for cricketers.

1792.—Gentlemen of Kent (with Beldham and Harris) v. All
England for 1,000 guineas. England won.

Gentlemen of Kent (with Beldham and Rumsey) v.
Gentlemen of Essex (with Fennex and Scott) for 500
guineas. Kent won.
Kent (with two men) v. Hants (with two men) for
1,000 guineas, on Dartford Heath. Hants won.
Kent v. Essex at Hornchurch. Kent won by 158.
Kent (with Beldham) v. Essex at Dartford. Kent
won by 81.

(From the frequent expression "with two men," in the matches
of this period, it seems as if the bowling of Gentlemen was, as it
is now, their weak point.)

1796.—Kent v. Middlesex (with Wells) at Lords. Kent won by
51.

1798.—Surrey began to rise as a cricketing county.

Missing out a number of matches we come to an extraordinary
game played in 1807 between 13 of All England and 23 of Kent on
Penenden Heath for 1,000 guineas. Kent won by 162. It was
about now that Willes started a revolutionary movement with his
"straight arm" bowling.

In 1812 the Prince's Plain Cricket Club was founded at the
Plough, Bromley Common—(once a typical old-world roadside inn
with a serving shelf in the window, now—well, suburbanised !)
This was the forerunner of the famous West Kent Cricket Club.

In 1815, on the "Knapps" at Wrotham, England beat Kent by
51.

About now was written the "Lay of the Kentish Cricketer,"
being the doings of a young Kentishman in London town :

"Now de fust thing I heerd on which made my art glad,
Was a wonnerful girt match o' cricket ;
For in Kent, ye must know, dare is many a lad
Dat is famous for bat, ball, and wicket."

He is asked to fill up a vacancy at a Lord's match, and he bowls :
"Well, I did take the ball, and a teejus good bowl I made on it,
for I broke all dere heads, arms, legs, bats an' wickets, an' pretty
soon made the game ourn ! "

The same year (1815) East Kent played West Kent on Penenden
Heath.

In 1816 wides were first scored, entered as "byes," not until 1827
were they scored separately. Prince's Plain beat M.C.C. this year by
10 wickets. In 1822 Bromley Common was enclosed, so the Prince's
Plain Club removed to the well-known ground near the *Tiger's Head*
at Chislehurst.

The "proper" cricket costume of this time was a light shirt,
hat with flattened crown (men were continually getting out by
their hats falling on the wicket), thin white cord breeches, gauze
stockings almost transparent, and silk socks turned over the
ankles. The cricket lunch was at three o'clock ; sherry was drunk
at lunch and port after, and the snuff box was always placed on
the table. At any rate this was the West Kent custom.

In 1822 the new ground at Chislehurst was inaugurated by Kent
beating M.C.C. by 149 runs.

At the Kent and England match at Lords this year, when Kent
won, Willes' "straight arm" bowling was protested against, and
in wrath he withdrew from the match.

Mynn and "Felix" both crippled themselves financially in their zeal for the county game, but, by unanimous consent, they were retained on the list of amateurs, although paid for playing.

In 1822, at Malling, Sussex beat Kent by 32. It was at this game that the first "card o' the match" was printed.

1823.—Kent v. M.C.C. Drawn in favour of Kent. In this match Alfred Mynn bowling struck *second* longstop six times running in the chest, and the man spat blood for a fortnight after-wards.

1827.—Kent v. M.C.C. Kent won by 158.
Kent v. Sussex. Sussex won by 7 wickets.

At this time arose the controversy about "fair" bowling. The *Sporting Magazine*, reporting the above match, remarks that "throwing was the order of the day," in reference to the deadly, and, according to modern notions, perfectly fair, round arm bowling of Lillywhite and Broadbridge.

In this year Sussex beat Kent at the Vine and at Brighton, no doubt thanks to Lillywhite and Broadbridge. Sussex also played three matches with All England for 1,000 guineas a side. After the second match the England players signed a protest that they would not play off the rubber unless Sussex bowled fairly.

In 1828 Mr. George Knight, of Godmersham Park, announced his proposal of a new rule to the M.C.C. Speaking strongly in favour of the new bowling on the plea that the batting was too strong for the old underhand bowling, and that matches were unduly prolonged—(nothing new, etc., again !)—he proposed that the rule should be "if any part of the bowler's hand or arm be above the shoulder at the time of delivery the umpire should call 'No Ball !'" He added that round-hand bowling had long been prevalent in Kent.

The before alluded to Willes, a Kentish yeoman, is one of the many men who are said to have had round-arm bowling suggested to them by the efforts of a little girl to throw up a cricket ball.

This same year a howl went up about the inordinate waste of time at matches. The howl has been going on ever since, yet more time than ever is wasted. But at any rate these grand old players knew nothing of the three rotting cankers of modern cricket—the individual batting average, the practice net, and the boundary system!

1832.—Kent v. M.C.C. at Chislehurst. Kent won by 3 wickets.
1833.—Gentlemen of Kent v. M.C.C. (with Pilch and Marsden). Kent won by 8 wickets.
1834.—Kent v. England. England won by 9 wickets.
This year there was a great single wicket match in which Pilch, Marsden, and Lill beat Mynn, Wenman, and Mills.

About this time Fuller Pilch, a Norfolk tailor, was brought to Town Malling under the auspices of the cricket-loving gentry of the county to develop Kentish cricket ; the result was the for-mation of the famous old Kent eleven.—The brothers Mynn ; Wenman, the wicket keeper ; W. Hillyer, a game-keeper ; Pilch ; Martingell ; Munn ; the two Dorringtons; Tom Adams ; and "Felix"—whose real name was Wanostrocht, a Surrey man by birth as was Martingell, but kept a school at Blackheath for many years.

1835.—Kent v. England at Chislehurst. Kent won in 1 innings
    and 41 runs.
1837.—Kent beat Sussex at Malling. Gentlemen wore tall white
    hats which cost 35s. each. Redgate, the fast bowler,
    wore shorts and white stockings.
1838.—Single wicket match at Malling for £100 a side between
    Mynn and Dearman of Yorkshire. Mynn made 123,
    Dearman 11.
        This year the last great match was played at
    Chislehurst—M.C.C. v. Gentlemen of Kent with
    Adams and Hillyer. Kent won by 7 wickets.
1839.—A splendid match at Malling for Pilch's benefit. Kent beat
    England by 2 runs. The Kent eleven were W. and A.
    Mynn, Hillyer, Steerman, Pilch, Wenman, Whittaker,
    Mills, Dorrington, Clifford, and Adams.
    In 1842 the Canterbury Week was started, and from now the
Cathedral City became the centre of County cricket. In a match
between the Gentlemen of Kent and the Gentlemen of England at
Lord's this year there were no less than 159 extras !
    In 1843 Kent beat England three times. In one of the matches
Mynn's bowling analysis came out thus : 24 overs and 2 balls, for
40 runs and 8 wickets.
    The Kent and Sussex match of 1846 at Brighton is the subject of
the large engraving so often to be seen in the parlours of Kent
and Sussex inns.
    In 1847 Kent won every match she played, and in this year
Willsher, of Rolvenden, came out for the county.
    From 1835 to 1853 there were thirty-five matches between Kent
and England. For the first sixteen years Kent more than held her
own.
    From 1853 to 1859—Willsher and "Farmer" Bennett's period—
Kent went to the bad. In 1859 the County Club was formed, Mr.
W. S. Norton being the first secretary.
    Sevenoaks was of old the chief cricket bat making place, and
Clout of the same town was a famous ball-maker. The great grand-
father of Duke, cricket ball maker of Penshurst, presented the
first treble-seamed ball to the Prince of Wales in 1780.
    The chief old Kent cricket grounds were at Sevenoaks, Coxheath,
Bromley Common, Chislehurst, Dandelion Fields, Thanet ; Cobham
Park, Dartford Brent, Benenden, Malling, Greenwich, Woolwich,
Penenden Heath, and Bourne Park.
    The following Advertisement appeared in "Bell's Life" and the
"Sporting Life" of 1872 :
        "The Old Kent County C.C.
    "Three old players of the above Club and natives of the celebrated
parish of Benenden, Mr. T. G. Wenman (age 71), Mr. E. G. Wenman (age 71), and Mr. R. Mills (age 77) take the liberty of giving a
public challenge to play a match of cricket with any three of
England of not less average age than 73. They will make the match
for any amount not exceeding £100."
    The challenge was not taken up.
    I would like to mention that the *doyen* of Kentish cricket, Mr.
Herbert Jenner Fust, is still alive and well although 92 years of
age. He played in the Eton Eleven at Lords so long ago as 1822,
and was President of the M.C.C. in 1833.

A verse or two from Prowse's famous poem *In Memoriam* Alfred Mynn may aptly conclude :—

" When the great old Kent Eleven, full of pluck and hope began
The grand battle with All England, single-handed, man to man,
How the hop men watched their hero, massive, muscular and tall,
As he mingled with the players, like a king amongst them all ;
Till to some old Kent enthusiasts it would seem almost a sin
E'er to doubt their county's triumph when led on by Alfred Mynn

Though Sir Frederick and the Veteran bowled straight, and sure
    and well,
Though Box behind the wicket only Lockyer can excel ;
Though Jemmy Dean as longstop would seldom grant a bye,
Though no novices at batting were George Parr and Joseph Guy ;
Said the fine old Kentish farmers, with a fine old Kentish grin,
' Why, there ain't a man among 'em as can match our Alfred Mynn !

And whatever was the issue of this frank and friendly fray,
Aye ! and often has his bowling turned the fortune of the day !
Still the Kentish men fought bravely, never losing hope or heart,
Every man of the Eleven glad and proud to play his part.
And with five such mighty cricketers 't'was but natural to win,
As Felix, Wenman, Hillyer, Fuller Pilch and Alfred Mynn !

With his tall and stately presence, with his nobly moulded form,
His broad hand was ever open, his brave heart was ever warm ;
All were proud of him, all loved him ; as the changing seasons pass
As our champion lies a sleeping underneath the Kentish grass,
Proudly, sadly, we will name him—to forget him were a sin—
Lightly lie the turf upon thee kind and manly Alfred Mynn ! "

THE END

BECKENHAM
LYCH GATE

INDEX.

Lightning Source UK Ltd.
Milton Keynes UK
UKHW02f0940240418
321511UK00001B/331/P

9 780902 664821